GRAMMAR FOR LANGUAGE LEARNING

ELEMENTS *of* SUCCESS

ANNE M. EDIGER

LINDA LEE

3A

OXFORD
UNIVERSITY PRESS

SHAPING learning TOGETHER

We would like to thank the following classes for piloting *Elements of Success*:

University of Delaware English Language Institute
Teacher: Kathleen Vodvarka
Students: Ahmad Alenzi, Bandar Manei Algahmdi, Fadi Mohammed Alhazmi, Abdel Rahman Atallah, Anna Kuzmina, Muhanna Sayer Aljuaid, Coulibaly Sita

ABC Adult School, Cerritos, CA
Teacher: Jenni Santamaria
Students: Gabriela A. Marquez Aguilar, Yijung Chen, Laura Gomez, Terry Hahn, EunKyung Lee, Subin Lee, Sunmin Lee, Jane Leelachat, Lilia Nunezuribe, Gina Olivar, Young Park, Seol Hee Seok, Kwang Mi Song

During the development of *Elements of Success*, we spoke with teachers and professionals who are passionate about teaching grammar. Their feedback led us to create *Elements of Success: Grammar for Language Learning*, a course that solves teaching challenges by presenting grammar clearly, simply, and completely. We would like to acknowledge the advice of teachers from

USA • BRAZIL • CANADA • COSTA RICA • GUATEMALA • IRAN • JAPAN • MEXICO • OMAN • RUSSIA SAUDI ARABIA • SOUTH KOREA • TUNISIA • TURKEY • UKRAINE • THE UNITED ARAB EMIRATES

Mehmet Abi, Mentese Anatolian High School, Turkey; **Anna-Marie Aldaz**, Doña Ana Community College, NM; **Diana Allen**, Oakton Community College, IL; **Marjorie Allen**, Harper College, IL; **Mark Alves**, Montgomery College, Rockville, MD; **Kelly Arce**, College of Lake County, IL; **Irma Arencibia**, Union City Adult Learning Center, NJ; **Arlys Arnold**, University of Minnesota, MN; **Marcia Arthur**, Renton Technical College, WA; **Alexander Astor**, Hostos Community College, NY; **Chris Atkins**, CHICLE Language Institute, NC; **Karin Avila-John**, University of Dayton, OH; **Ümmet Aydan**, Karabuk University, Iran; **Fabiana Azurmendi**; **John Baker**, Wayne State University, MI; **Sepehr Bamdadnia**; **Terry Barakat**, Missouri State University, MO; **Marie Bareille**, Borough of Manhattan Community College, NY; **Eileen Barlow**, SUNY Albany, NY; **Denise Barnes**, Madison English as a Second Language School, WI; **Kitty Barrera**, University of Houston, TX; **Denise Barsotti**, EID Training Solutions, FL; **Maria Bauer**, El Camino College; **Christine Bauer-Ramazani**, Saint Michael's College, VT; **Jamie Beaton**, Boston University, MA; **Gena Bennett**, Cornerstone University, NE; **Linda Berendsen**, Oakton Community College, IL; **Carol Berteotti**; **Grace Bishop**, Houston Community College, TX; **Perrin Blackman**, University of Kansas, KS; **Mara Blake-Ward**, Drexel University English Language Center, PA; **Melissa Bloom**, ELS; **Alexander Bochkov**, ELS, WA; **Marcel Bolintiam**, University of Colorado, CO; **Nancy Boyer**, Golden West College, CA; **T. Bredl**, The New School, NY; **Rosemarie Brefeld**, University of Missouri, MO; **Leticia Brereton**, Kingsborough Community College, NY; **Deborah Brooks**, Laney College, CA; **Kevin Brown**, Irvine Community College, CA; **Rachel Brown**, Center for Literacy, NY; **Tracey Brown**, Parkland College, IL; **Crystal Brunelli**, Tokyo Jogakkan Middle and High School, Japan; **Tom Burger**, Harris County Department of Education, TX; **Thom Burns**, Tokyo English Specialists College, Japan; **Caralyn Bushey**, Maryland English Institute, MD; **Gül Büyü**, Ankara University, Turkey; **Scott Callaway**, Community Family Centers, TX; **Adele Camus**, George Mason University, VA; **Nigel Caplan**, University of Delaware, DE; **Nathan Carr**, California State University, CA; **Christina Cavage**, Savannah College of Art and Design,

GA; **Neslihan Çelik**, Özdemir Sabancı Emirgan Anatolian High School, Turkey; **Shelley Cetin**, Kansas City Kansas Community College, KS; **Hoi Yuen Chan**, University of Wyoming, WY; **Esther Chase**, Berwyn Public Library, IL; **Suzidilara Çınar**, Yıldırım Beyazıt University, Turkey; **Diane Cirino**, SUNY Suffolk, NY; **Cara Codney**, Emporia State University, KS; **Catherine Coleman**, Irvine Valley College, CA; **Jenelle Collins**, Washington High School, AZ; **Greg Conner**, Orange Coast Community College, CA; **Ewelina Cope**, The Language Company, PA; **Jorge Cordon**, Colegio Montessori, Guatemala; **Kathy Cornman**, University of Michigan, MI; **Barry Costa**, Castro Valley Adult and Career Education, CA; **Cathy Costa**, Edmonds Community College, WA; **Julia Cote**, Houston Community College NE, TX; **Eileen Cotter**, Montgomery College, MD; **Winnie Cragg**, Mukogawa Fort Wright Institute, WA; **Douglas Craig**, Diplomatic Language Services, VA; **Elizabeth Craig**, Savannah College of Art and Design, GA; **Ann Telfair Cramer**, Florida State College at Jacksonville, FL; **R. M. Crocker**, Plano Independent School District, TX; **Virginia Cu**, Queens Adult Learning Center, CT; **Marc L. Cummings**, Jefferson Community and Technical College, KY; **Roberta Cummings**, Trinidad Correctional Facility, CO; **David Dahnke**, Lone Star College-North Harris, TX; **Debra Daise**, University of Denver, CO; **L. Dalgish**, Concordia College, NY; **Kristen Danek**, North Carolina State University, NC; **April Darnell**, University of Dayton, OH; **Heather Davis**, OISE Boston, MA; **Megan Davis**, Embassy English, NY; **Jeanne de Simon**, University of West Florida, FL; **Renee Delatizky**, Boston University, MA; **Sonia Delgadillo**, Sierra Community College, NY; **Gözde Burcu Demirkul**, Orkunoglu College, Turkey; **Stella L. Dennis**, Longfellow Middle School, NY; **Mary Diamond**, Auburn University, AL; **Emily Dibala**, Bucks County Community College, PA; **Cynthia Dieckmann**, West Chester East High School, PA; **Michelle DiGiorno**, Richland College, TX; **Luciana Diniz**, Portland Community College, OR; **Özgür Dirik**, Yıldız Technical University, Turkey; **Marta O. Dmytrenko-Arab**, Wayne State University, MI; **Margie Domingo**, Intergenerational Learning Community, CO; **Kellie Draheim**, Hongik University, South Korea; **Ilke Buyuk Duman**, Sehir University, Turkey; **Jennifer Eick-Magan**, Prairie State College, IL;

Juliet Emanuel, Borough of Manhattan Community College, NY; **David Emery**, Kaplan International Center, CA; **Patricia Emery**, Jefferson County Literacy Council, WI; **Eva Engelhard**, Kaplan International Center, WA; **Nancey Epperson**, Harry S. Truman College, IL; **Ken Estep**, Mentor Language Institute, CA; **Cindy Etter**, University of Washington, WA; **Rhoda Fagerland**, St. Cloud State University, MN; **Anrisa Fannin**, Diablo Valley College, CA; **Marie Farnsworth**, Union Public Schools, OK; **Jim Fenton**, Bluegrass Community Technical College, KY; **Lynn Filazzola**, Nassau BOCES Adult Learning Center, NY; **Christine Finck**, Stennis Language Lab; **Mary Fischer**, Texas Intensive English Program, TX; **Mark Fisher**, Lone Star College, TX; **Celeste Flowers**, University of Central Arkansas, AR; **Elizabeth Foss**, Washtenaw Community College, MI; **Jacqueline Fredericks**, West Contra Costa Adult Education, CA; **Patricia Gairaud**, San Jose City College, CA; **Patricia Gallo**, Delaware Technical Community College, DE; **Beverly Gandall**, Coastline Community College, CA; **Alberto Garrido**, The Community College of Baltimore County, MD; **Debbie Garza**, Park University, MO; **Karen Gelender**, Castro Valley Adult and Career Education, CA; **Ronald Gentry**, Suenos Compartidos, Mexico; **Kathie Madden Gerecke**, North Shore Community College, MA; **Jeanne Gibson**, Colorado State University, CO; **A. Elizabeth Gilfillan**, Houston Community College, TX; **Melanie Gobert**, The Higher Colleges of Technology, UAE; **Ellen Goldman**, West Valley College, CA; **Jo Golub**, Houston Community College, TX; **Maria Renata Gonzalez**, Colegio Montessori, Guatemala; **Elisabeth Goodwin**, Pima Community College, AZ; **John Graney**, Santa Fe College, FL; **Karina Greene**, CUNY in the Heights, NY; **Katherine Gregorio**, CASA de Maryland, MD; **Claudia Gronsbell**, La Escuelita, NY; **Yvonne Groseil**, Hunter College, NY; **Alejandra Gutierrez**, Hartnell College, CA; **Eugene Guza**, North Orange County Community College District, CA; **Mary Beth Haan**, El Paso Community College, TX; **Elizabeth Haga**, State College of Florida, FL; **Saeede Haghi**, Ozyegin University, Turkey; **Laura Halvorson**, Lorain County Community College, OH; **Nancy Hamadou**, Pima Community College, AZ; **Kerri Hamberg**, Brookline Community and Adult Education, MA;

Katia Hameg, L'Envol Des Langues, Québec, Canada; **Sunsook Han**, King Abdulaziz University, Saudi Arabia; **Aniko Harrier**, Valencia College, FL; **James M. Harris**, University of Texas-Pan American, TX; **Susan Haskins-Doloff**, Pratt Institute, NY; **Olcay Havalan**, Bursa Anadolu Erkek Lisesi, Turkey; **Marla Heath**, Sacred Heart University, CT; **Jean Hendrickson**, SUNY Stony Brook, NY; **Tracy Henninger-Willey**, Lane Community College, OR; **Emily Herrick**, University of Nebraska, NE; **Jan Hinson**, Carson Newman University, TN; **Lisa Hockstein**, SUNY Westchester, NY; **Sarah Hodge**, Defense Language Institute, TX; **Kristie Hofelich**, Brown Mackie College, KY; **Harry Holden**, North Lake Community College, TX; **Elke Holtz**, Escuela Sierra Nevada, Mexico; **Hirofumi Hosokawa**, Fukuoka Jo Gakuin University, Japan; **Elisa Hunt**, North Dakota State University, ND; **Lutfi Hussein**, Mesa Community College, AZ; **Curt Hutchison**, Leeward Community College, HI; **Elizabeth Iannotti**, LaGuardia Community College, NY; **Barbara Inerfeld**, Rutgers University, NJ; **Julie Ingber**, Columbia University, NY; **Debbie Janysek**, Victoria College, TX; **Joan Jarrett**, Feather River College, CA; **Shawn Jarvis**, St. Cloud State University, MN; **Justin Jernigan**, Georgia Gwinnett College, GA; **Melanie Jipping**, Tokyo International University of America, OR; **Catherine Jones**, Excellent Interpreting, CO; **Jackie Jones**, Wayne State University, MI; **Irene Juzkiw**, University of Missouri, MO; **Aysegul Liman Kaban**, Gedik University, Turkey; **Vivian Kahn**, Long Island University, NY; **Eleanor Kamataris**, Harris Middle School, TX; **Gursharan Kandola**, University of Houston, TX; **Emily Kaney**, Northern Michigan University, MI; **Krystal Kaplan**, Pace University, NY; **Linda Karlen**, Oakton Community College, IL; **Katherine Katsenis**, Lyceum Tutorial Services, LLC, CA; **Martha Kehl**, Ohlone College, CA; **Scott Keller**, Literacy Volunteers of Leon County, FL; **Robert Kelso**, Miami Dade College, FL; **Alicia N. Kenter**, City College of San Francisco, CA; **Paul Kern**, Green River Community College, WA; **Mignon Kery**, H-B Woodlawn Secondary Program, VA; **Candace Khanna**, Laney College, CA; **Joy Kidstry**, University of Phoenix, AZ; **Cynthia Kilpatrick**, The University of Texas at Arlington, TX; **Doe-Hyung Kim**, Georgia Gwinnett College, GA; **Kindra Kinyon**, Los Angeles Trade-Technical College, CA; **James Kirchner**, Macomb Community College, MI; **Renee La Rue**, Lone Star College-Montgomery, TX; **Marjorie Labe**, Montgomery County Community College, PA; **Peter LaFontaine**, Alexandria Adult Learning Center, VA; **Katie Land**, St. Giles International, Canada; **Renee Lane**, Oxnard Adult School, CA; **Alan Lanes**, The Higher Colleges of Technology, UAE; **Stephanie Lange**, Cuyamaca College, CA; **T. Jonathan Lathers**, Macomb Community College, MI; **Margaret Vera Layton**, University of Nevada, NV; **Susan Leckart**, Middlesex County College, NJ; **Suzanne Leduc**, The New America College, CO; **Judy Lee**, Central Connecticut State University, CT; **Joy Leventhal**, Cuyahoga Community College, OH; **Helen Lin**, University of Florida, FL; **Amy Lindstrom**, University of New Mexico, NM; **Gytis Liulevicius**, Wellstone International High School, MN; **Robyn Lockwood**, Stanford University, CA; **Victoria Loeb**, Houston Community College, TX; **Janet Long**, University of Missouri, MO; **Roland Lopez**, Santa Monica College, CA; **Alexandra Lowe**, Westchester Community College (SUNY), NY; **Mary Lozano**, Pierce College, CA; **Gail Lugo**, Trine University, IN; **Joanna Luper**, Liberty University, VA; **Jaime Lyon**, University of Northern Iowa, IA; **Doris Macdonald**, Northern Illinois University, IL; **Bridgette MacFarlane**, Brewster Technical Center, FL; **Kevin Mackie**, Austin Community College, TX; **Mercedes Martinez**, Global Language Institute, MN; **Tetiana Maslova**, Kyiv Polytechnic Institute, Ukraine; **Terry Masters**, American School for Women and Children, OH; **Maryann Matheny**, Campbellsville University, KY; **Jennifer Maxwell**, Daytona State College, FL; **Halina Mazurak**, Cleveland State University, OH; **Susan McAlister**, University of Houston, TX; **Luke McCarthy**, Norwalk Community College, CT; **Marlo McClurg**, Cosumnes River College, CA; **Deb McCormick**, Doña Ana Community College, NM; **Chris McDaniel**, Yale University, CT; **Bridget McDonald**, Independent Learning Services, MA; **Deborah McGraw**, Syracuse University, NY; **Lisa McHenry**, GEOS Languages Plus, CA; **Deirdre McMurtry**, University of Nebraska at Omaha, NE; **Aziah McNamara**, Kansas State University, KS; **Ellen Measday**, Middlesex County College, NJ; **Nancy Megarity**, Collin College, TX; **Diane Mehegan**, Harvard University, MA; **Michelle Merritt**, Harmony School of Innovation, TX; **Nila Middleton**, Lone Star College-Cypress, TX; **Brandon Mills**, ELS Language Center, ND; **Malgorzata Moll**, St. Louis Community College, MO; **Kathleen Molzan**, Cuyahoga Community College, OH; **Adrienne Monaco**, Erie 1 BOCES, NY; **Beth Montag**, University of Nebraska at Kearney, NE; **Elisabete Montero**, Val Hala escola de idiomas, Brazil; **Do Sik Moon**, Hanyang Cyber University, South Korea; **Diane Mora**, Johnson County Community College, KS; **Micheline Morena**, College of the Desert, CA; **Gloria Munson**, University of Texas, TX; **Gino Muzzatti**, Santa Rosa Junior College, CA; **Myo Myint**, Mission College, CA; **Kathy Najafi**, Houston Community College, TX; **Patricia Nation**, Miami Dade College, FL; **Elizabeth Neblett**, Union County College, NJ; **Karen Nelson**, Pittsburgh State University, PA; **Marley Nelson**, English Center USA, IL; **Anastasia Nizamova**, New York University, NY; **Sharon Nunn**, Englishdom; **Karla Odenwald**, Boston University, MA; **Tina O'Donnell**, Language Center International, MI; **Ann O'Driscoll**, Southern Oregon University, OR; **Donna Ogle**, Arkansas Tech University, AR; **Nastaran Ohadi**, Ganjineh Danesh, Iran; **Iris Oriaro**, Arkansas State University, AR; **Fernanda Ortiz**, University of Arizona, AZ; **Susan Osuch**, Englishworks, Inc., TX; **Kris Oswald**, Kansas State University, KS; **Stephanie Owens**, ELS, CT; **Gorkem Oztur**, Özel Manavgat Bahcesehir Anadolu Lisesi, Turkey; **Ümit Öztürk**, İzmir-Torbalı Anatolian Teacher Training High School, Turkey; **Murat Ozudogru**, Maltepe University, Turkey; **Marilyn Padgett**, Calhoun Middle School, NY; **Bilsev Pastakkaya**, Yalova University, Turkey; **Angela Pastore-Nikitenko**, Embassy English, CA; **Wendy Patriquin**, Parkland College, IL; **Irina Patten**, Lone Star College, TX; **Jennifer Paz**, Auburn University, AL; **Mary Peacock**, Richland College, TX; **Randi Lynn Peerlman**, Texas A&M University, TX; **Jeanne Peine**, University of Houston, TX; **Nuran Peker**, Nazilli High School, Turkey; **Susan Pelley**, Doña Ana Community College, NM; **Jorge Perez**, Southwestern College, CA; **Kim Perkins**, Boston University, MA; **William Phelps**, Southern Illinois University, IL; **Tom Pierce**, Central New Mexico Community College, NM; **Jennifer Piotrowski**, Language Center International, MI; **Carole Poppleton-Schrading**, Johns Hopkins University, MD; **Valentina Portnov**, Kingsborough Community College, NY; **Nancy Price**, University of Missouri, MO; **Catherine Ramberg**, Albany Adult School, CA; **Brian Ramey**, Sehir University, Turkey; **Steven Rashba**, University of Bridgeport, CT; **Victoria Reis**, Language Studies International, NY; **Amy Renehan**, University of Washington, WA; **Elizabeth Reyes**, Elgin Community College, IL; **Kathleen Reynolds**, Harper College, IL; **Tom Riedmiller**, University of Northern Iowa, IA; **Dzidra Rodins**, DePaul University, IL; **Ana Rodriguez**, Elliston School of Languages, CA; **Ann Roemer**, Utah State University, UT; **Margot Rose**, Pierce College, WA; **David Ross**, Houston Community College, TX; **Robert Ruddy**, Northeastern University, MA; **Peter Ruggiero**, Boston University, MA; **Phil Ruggiero**, The University of Missouri, MO; **Anne Sadberry**, The Language Company, OK; **Jessica Saigh**, University of Missouri-St. Louis, MO; **Irene Sakk**, Northwestern University, IL; **Kamila Salimova**, TGT, Russia; **Chari Sanchinelli**, Colegio Valle Verde, Guatemala; **Christen Savage**, University of Houston, TX; **Boutheina Sayadi**, Virtual University of Tunis, Tunisia; **Rosemary Schmid**, University of North Carolina, NC; **Diana Schoolman**, St. John's University, NY; **Myrna Schwarz**, La Roche College, PA; **Karen Schwenke**, Biola University, CA; **Dilek Batur Secer**, Toros University, Turkey; **Diana Sefchik**, Raritan Valley Community College, NJ; **Ertan Selimoglu**, Yildiz Technical University, Turkey; **Rene Serrano**, Universidad Nacional Autónoma de México, Mexico; **Gul Shamim**; **Amir Sharifi**, California State University, CA; **Caroline Sharp**, University of Maryland, MD; **Shixian Sheng**, Boston Chinatown Neighborhood Center, MA; **Oksana Shevchenko**, Horlivka Language School, Ukraine; **A. Shipley**, Academy of Art University, CA; **D. H. Shreve**, University of North Texas, TX; **Meire Silva**, Celebration Language Institute, FL; **Fiore Sireci**, Hunter College, NY; **Anita Teresa Smith**, Majan College, Oman; **Jacqueline Smith**, The New School, NY; **Jeff Smith**, Ohio Northern University, OH; **Lorraine Smith**, Queens College, NY; **Barbara Smith-Palinkas**, Hillsborough Community College, FL; **Kimberly Spallinger**, Bowling Green State University, OH; **James Stakenburg**, Rennert International, NY; **Katrina Tamura**, Palomar College, CA; **Dan Tannacito**, Indiana University of Pennsylvania, PA; **Jamie Tanzman**, Northern Kentucky University, KY; **Tara Tarpey**, New York University, NY; **Amy Tate**, Houston Community College, TX; **Rose Tauscher**, Skyline High School, TX; **Tamara Taylor**, University of North Texas-IELI, TX; **Cihan Tekin**, İMKB 24 Kasım Anadolu Lisesi, Turkey; **Kelly Tennison**, Roseville Area High School, MN; **Abby Thomas**, Northern Essex Community College, MA; **Brett Thomas**, Sacramento City College, CA; **Linda Thomas**, Lone Star College-Montgomery, TX; **Edith Thompson**, Purdy R-II School District, MO; **Sylwia Thorne**, Kent State University, OH; **Donna Tooker**, Miramar College, CA; **Beth Topping**, Auburn University, AL; **Carolyn Trachtova**, Webster University, MO; **William Trudeau**, Ohio Northern University, OH; **Kathy Truman**, Haverford High School, PA; **Karen Tucker**, Georgia Institute of Technology, GA; **Gretchen Twohig**, ASC English, MA; **Blanca Ugraskan**, Del Mar Community College, TX; **Serkan Ülgü**, Air Force Academy, Turkey; **Mecit Uzun**, Gaziosmanpaşa, Turkey; **Cynthia Valdez**, Palisade High, CO; **Kanako Valencia Suda**, De Anza College, CA; **Michelle Van de Sande**, Arapahoe Community College, CO; **Sharon Van Houte**, Lorain County Community College, OH; **Sara Vandenberg**, University of Colorado, CO; **Lillian Vargas**, University of Florida, FL; **Tara Vassallo**, Pace University, NY; **Stephanie Viol**, Palm House; **Kathleen Vodvarka**, University of Delaware, DE; **Kerry Vrabel**, GateWay Community College, AZ; **Carol Wachana**, ELS Language School; **Christine Waddail**, Johns Hopkins University, MD; **Christina Wade**, Liberty University, VA; **Wendy Walsh**, College of Marin, CA; **Colin Ward**, Lone Star College-North Harris, TX; **Mary Kay Wedum**, Colorado State University, CO; **Linda Wesley**, Pennsylvania State University, PA; **Lynne Wilkins**, The English Center, CA; **Betty Williams**; **Jeff Wilson**, Irvine Community College, CA; **Lori Wilson-Patterson**, Ivy Tech Community College, IN; **Kirsten Windahl**, Cuyahoga Community College, OH; **Aleasha Winters**, Lingo TEFL Language Institute, Costa Rica; **Jing Zhou**, Defense Language Institute, CA; **Yelena Zimon**, Fremont Adult School, CA; **Koraljka Zunic**, Grossmont College, CA

Contents

6|Adverb Clauses

1 Present, Past, and Future Forms

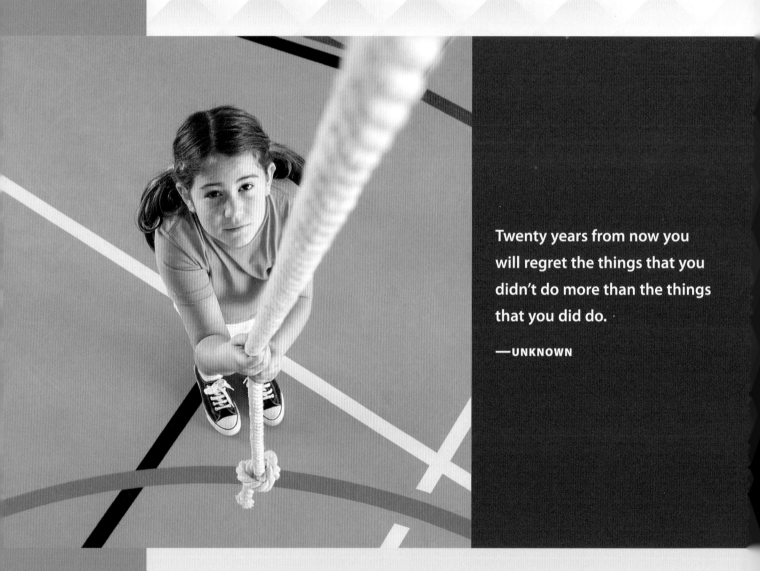

Twenty years from now you will regret the things that you didn't do more than the things that you did do.

—UNKNOWN

Talk about It Do you agree or disagree with the quotation above? Why?

WARM-UP

A | Read these statements and check (✓) *Fact* or *Opinion*. Then compare answers with your classmates. Do you agree or disagree with the opinions below? Why?

Television: Fact or Opinion?

	FACT	OPINION
1. TV programs **were** much better ten years ago.	☐	☐
2. Most young children **spend** too much time in front of a television.	☐	☐
3. When Neil Armstrong **stepped** onto the surface of the moon in 1969, about 500 million people **were watching** him on TV.	☐	☐
4. Fewer young people **are watching** television, according to a report by media analysts at Ofcom.	☐	☐
5. Television in the future **is going to be** totally different.	☐	☐
6. Sixty-six percent of Americans regularly **watch** television while they **are eating** dinner.	☐	☐
7. The first television sets **were** huge but they **had** very small screens.	☐	☐
8. TV **makes** children less intelligent.	☐	☐
9. In the future, you **won't need** a screen to watch television.	☐	☐

B | Answer these questions about the statements above.

1. The words in **green** above are verbs. Which verb forms do you see? Write the number of the sentence next to each verb form below.

   simple present _____

   present progressive _____

   simple past _____

   past progressive _____

   future with *will* _____

   future with *be going to* _____

2. Which of the statements above give general information that might be true anytime? How do you know?

3. Which statements describe a specific time? How do you know?

C | Look back at the quotation on page 2. Identify any present, past, or future verb forms.

1.1 Useful Things to Remember about Verbs

A

```
                    VERBS
        ┌─────────────┴─────────────┐
   HELPING VERBS              MAIN VERBS
be, do, have, can, will, etc.  learn, change, disappear, etc.
```

1 Children **learn** languages easily.

2 Languages **are** always **changing**.

3 Many languages **have disappeared**.

4 How **can** I **improve** my language abilities?

The English language has **main verbs** and **helping verbs**. We describe states, actions, and events with main verbs, as in **1**. Helping verbs primarily give grammatical information. We use helping verbs together with main verbs, as in **2 – 4**.

For a list of irregular verbs, see the Resources, page R-3.

B

COMPARE MAIN VERBS AND HELPING VERBS

5a No one **is** here.
5b No one **is coming** here.

6a Somebody **did** all the work.
6b **Did** you **do** anything yesterday?

7a We **have** plenty of time.
7b I **haven't seen** them all day.

We can use the verbs *be*, *do*, and *have* as either a main verb, as in **5a – 7a**, or a helping verb, as in **5b – 7b**.

GRAMMAR TERM: Helping verbs are also called **auxiliary verbs**. Main verbs are also called **lexical verbs**.

C

8 I **need** a new computer. (1 clause)

9 I **need** a new computer, but I **can't afford** it. (2 clauses)

10 When you **study**, you **should turn off** the TV. (2 clauses)

11 I **don't know** what she **wants**, but I'm **going to find out**.
(3 clauses)

A clause is a group of words with a subject and a main verb. A sentence can have one or more clauses, but each clause needs a main verb, as in **8 – 11**.

D

12 How far **can** you **run**? (run = go quickly on foot)

13 He **runs** a restaurant. (run = manage)

14 This road **runs** south to Dover. (run = extend; reach)

Many main verbs have more than one meaning, as in **12 – 14**.

1 | Identifying Main Verbs and Helping Verbs Is each **bold** word a main verb or a helping verb? Underline the main verbs and circle the helping verbs in this essay. **1.1 A**

The Worst Advice I Have Ever Received

The worst advice I have ever received <u>was</u> from a friend. She **told** me not to take an overseas trip I **was planning** because it **would be** too expensive. I **ignored** her advice and **took** the trip anyway. I **had** the most thrilling time of my life. I **am** a classical pianist, and I **was** already **planning** a trip to St. Petersburg, Russia to play in a piano competition there. At the time, I **was living** in Los Angeles, California, so it **was** quite a long journey to Russia. I **thought** to myself, as long as I **would be** 6,000 miles away from home, I **might** as well **stay** longer than just the two-day competition. I **would visit** some other places near St. Petersburg, too.

Because I **am** a classical musician, I **wanted** to visit the homes of some great composers. I **went** to Finland and **saw** the small house where Jean Sibelius **had composed** most of his symphonies. In St. Petersburg, I **took** a tour of the home of Nikolai Rimsky-Korsakov. He **was** a composer and teacher. His most famous student **was** Igor Stravinsky—I actually **played** on Stravinsky's piano. For a pianist like me, it **was** a great thrill.

After three fantastic weeks in Finland and Russia, it **was** time to go home. My friend **was** right—the trip **wasn't** cheap. But I'm **glad** that I **ignored** her advice and **went** on the trip. Now I **have** memories that **will stay** with me for the rest of my life.

2 | *Be, Do,* and *Have*: Main Verb or Helping Verb? Is the **bold** verb in each sentence a main verb or a helping verb? Check (✓) your answer. 1.1 B

	MAIN VERB	HELPING VERB
POPULATION FACTS		
1. There **are** about 7 billion people in the world today.	✓	☐
2. The number of people in the world **is** increasing.	☐	☐
3. Populations **have** doubled in many countries over the last 20–30 years.	☐	☐
4. The fastest-growing country **is** Uganda.	☐	☐
5. In some countries, the population **is** decreasing.	☐	☐
6. The U.S. population **has** grown by nearly 18 million since 2000.	☐	☐
7. Many countries **do** a census every 5 or 10 years. That's when the government counts the number of people in the country.	☐	☐
8. Today roughly¹ 301 million people **are** living in the U.S.	☐	☐
9. Some experts believe that in 50 years, the world will **have** 9 billion people.	☐	☐
10. New York City's population **has** passed 8.25 million.	☐	☐
11. "We **have** an enormous population here," said the mayor of New York.	☐	☐
12. Human population **is** a key² factor in the health of the planet.	☐	☐
13. Population **has** always been a controversial topic³.	☐	☐
14. Some countries **don't** have a population problem.	☐	☐
15. During the period from 1877 to 1913, the U.S. population **was** growing at a staggering⁴ rate.	☐	☐

3 | Identifying Main Verbs Underline the main verb in each highlighted clause. 1.1 C

ACADEMIC DEGREES

1. Some students <u>pursue</u> master's degrees, while others <u>study</u> to receive doctorates.
2. For example, business students get an MBA, which means "Master of Business Administration."
3. A doctorate is the highest degree that a student can earn.
4. Most medical doctors train for an MD, which comes from the Latin *medicinae doctor.*
5. Someone with a PhD is a doctor of philosophy.
6. Many students earn a PhD, but not many study the field of philosophy specifically.
7. In 2010, almost 50,000 students received a PhD.
8. Most of the degrees were in science and engineering.
9. Some students complete a master's program before they start a PhD program.
10. A PhD usually requires three years of full-time study, and then students must pass special exams.
11. PhD students also carry out⁵ original⁶ research.
12. Students present their findings by writing a long research report or dissertation, which can take years to complete.
13. Doctoral students may experience a lot of stress.

Talk about It What other academic degrees do you know about? Tell a partner.

---

¹ **roughly:** about
² **key:** important; essential
³ **controversial topic:** something people disagree about

⁴ **staggering:** shocking; amazing
⁵ **carry out:** to do
⁶ **original:** new

4 | Learning Grammar from a Dictionary Read the entry and answer the questions below. `1.1D`

> **see** /si/ *verb* (**saw**, **seen**, **see·ing**)
>
> ***verb (used with an object)***
> **1.** to perceive with the eye: *I see something in the distance.*
> **2.** find out: *See who is on the phone.*
> **3.** to imagine; believe possible: *I see her as a famous writer someday.*
> **4.** to attend; view: *We saw a great movie.*
> **5.** to visit/meet: *They've been seeing a lot of each other lately.*
> **6.** to understand: *I don't see the point.*
>
> ***verb (used without an object)***
> **7.** to have the power of sight: *I can't see without glasses.*
> **8.** to think; consider: *Let's see, what do you want to do next?*

QUESTIONS

1. What is the simple past form of the verb *see*? _____

2. What is the past participle? _____

3. What is the meaning of the verb *see* in each sentence below?
   Match the **bold** verbs with the dictionary definitions.

_2_ a. Please **see** if anyone is here yet.

____ b. I'm beginning to **see** the advantages of living in a city.

____ c. I **see** us living in the country in 20 years.

____ d. You can **see** that bus from two miles away.

____ e. You should **see** a doctor right away.

____ f. You must **see** the exhibit before it closes!

____ g. My grandfather doesn't **see** very well.

Write about It Write sentences using three of the definitions above. Then share ideas with a partner.

1.2 The Simple Present

A

1 Most people **need** about eight hours of sleep a night.
2 Adults **have** 206 bones. Babies **have** 270 to 300.
3 An apple a day **keeps** the doctor away.

4 I never **get** to bed before midnight.
5 The class **meets** from 10:00 to 12:00.

6 I **don't want** to go.
7 My arm **hurts**.

We use the **simple present** to describe:

• general statements or timeless truths, as in **1 – 3**
• habits or routines, as in **4 – 5**
• present states, as in **6 – 7**

For a list of spelling rules for the *-s/-es* form of verbs, see the Resources, page R-4.

B

8 My mother and father **like** it here.

9 The difference between us **is** hard to explain.

10 The programs on television **aren't** very good.

11 Everyone **is** here.

12 **Does** anything exciting ever **happen** here?

Sometimes it is difficult to determine correct subject-verb agreement in a sentence. For example:

• when two subjects are connected with *and*, as in **8**
• when there is a prepositional phrase after the subject, as in **9 – 10**
• when the subject is an indefinite pronoun, as in **11 – 12**

C

CORRECT THE COMMON ERRORS (See page R-10.)

13 ✗ Everyone have the duty to vote.

14 ✗ My brother always get what he wants.

15 ✗ I very proud to be a part of this group.

16 ✗ People in a big city has more trouble sleeping at night.

5 | Exploring Uses of the Simple Present What kind of information does each sentence give? Write the letter of the correct type from the box. `1.2 A`

> a. general statement or timeless truth   b. habit or routine   c. present state

1. Most people don't get enough sleep. _a_
2. Silence is golden. ____
3. It snows here a lot in the winter. ____
4. I'm a little hungry now. ____
5. I have dark brown hair and brown eyes. ____
6. I don't need anything right now. ____
7. Some scientists say musical training seems to improve communication skills. ____
8. It takes two or three years to get a master's degree. ____
9. I don't always have breakfast. ____
10. You need a license to practice medicine. ____
11. The General Assembly of the United Nations meets for several months every year. ____

> **F Y I**
>
> Important! Much of the time, the simple present form does not describe something that is happening right now.

Think about It Do any of the sentences above describe what is happening now?

6 | Spelling Analysis How do you spell the simple present of third-person singular verbs? Study the irregular spellings and answer the questions below. Then compare ideas with a partner. `1.2 A`

Base form	Third-person singular	Base form	Third-person singular
buy	buys	finish	finishes
destroy	destroys	publish	publishes
pay	pays	wish	wishes
carry	carries	catch	catches
copy	copies	touch	touches
cry	cries	watch	watches
fly	flies	discuss	discusses
identify	identifies	pass	passes
reply	replies	quiz	quizzes
try	tries	fix	fixes
worry	worries	tax	taxes

QUESTIONS

1. When the base form of a verb ends in -y, we sometimes change the -y to -i and add -es. Other times we just add -s. What is the difference between these verbs?

2. For most simple present verbs, we add -s to the base form to make the third-person singular. When do we add -es instead of -s?

3. Write the third-person singular form of each verb below.

a. deny   _denies_   f. miss _____   k. fax _____

b. match _____   g. fry _____   l. reach _____

c. suggest _____   h. sleep _____   m. push _____

d. relax _____   i. express _____   n. dress _____

e. supply _____   j. modify _____   o. play _____

7 | Subject-Verb Agreement Complete the paragraphs with the simple present form of the verbs.

1.2 B

EXCERPTS FROM RESEARCH REPORTS

1. The caffeine in three cups of coffee _____*seems*_____ to have a positive

   (seem)

   effect on women but not men. According to one study, female coffee

   drinkers over the age of 60 _____ less likely to experience a

   (be)

   decline in verbal skills.

2. Experts _____ that most people _____ about 8

   (say)   (need)

   hours of sleep a night. Unfortunately, not everyone _____ it.

   (get)

   According to the National Sleep Foundation's annual survey, the average

   adult _____ just 6.9 hours of sleep a night. New research _____

   (get)   (suggest)

   that a decline in sleep time _____ a decline in your health.

   (mean)

3. Tobacco smoke _____ over 4,000 chemicals. Researchers _____

   (contain)   (claim)

   that tobacco smoke _____ as many as 60 substances[7] that may cause cancer.

   (have)

4. Many people today _____ jobs frequently. As a matter of fact[8], some

   (change)

   studies say that the average person _____ at least 7 jobs before he or she

   (hold)

   _____ age 30. What may be more surprising, though, is that many people

   (reach)

   _____ several careers in their lifetime.

   (have)

   People _____ many reasons for making career changes. Some

   (have)

   _____ to the end of their career plan. Others _____ that their

   (come)   (find)

   career plan _____ no longer right for them. Many people _____

   (be)   (want)

   to pursue personal interests or _____ a business of their own.

   (run)

5. Vitamin C in large doses[9] _____ to do little harm. But recent studies also

   (appear)

   _____ that it is largely ineffective.

   (show)

Think about It Why did these writers use the simple present form of verbs?

---

[7]**substances:** materials
[8]**as a matter of fact:** in reality; actually

[9]**doses:** portions of a vitamin or medicine

8 | Error Correction Correct any errors in these paragraphs. (Some sentences may not have any errors.)

1. I really admire my father. He is a mechanic, and he know a lot about cars, stoves, and other machines. My father is self-employed, and he travel to people's houses to fix things. Whenever I'm home, I go with him on his jobs so that I can watch him. In my opinion, anybody who know how to fix things is a genius. I guess that make my father a genius.

2. My grandfather take very good care of himself. He is get up early in the morning so he can do tai chi in the park near his house. He try to get his wife, my grandmother, to join him, but she doesn't like to exercise, so he always go by himself.

3. My mother is the most hard-working person I know. She don't have a paying job like my father; she has a job that don't pay. My mother takes care of our house. She take care of everyone and everything in our house. She keep the house clean, and she cook the best food you will ever have. Beyond all this, I think my mother is the only person who understand me.

4. I am from Costa Rica, but my roommate is from the U.S. Needless to say, her English is a lot better than mine. The thing I especially like about her is that she help me with my English. Whenever I say something incorrectly, she just says it correctly for me.

Write about It Write three to four sentences about someone you admire. Explain what you like about this person.

1.3 The Present Progressive

A	**THE PRESENT PROGRESSIVE** We use the **present progressive** when we think of an action as temporary or in progress now, as in **1a – 5a**. **1a** I'm **living** with my aunt until I get my own place. **2a** What **are** you **talking** about? **3a** I'm sorry. I'm **not explaining** this very well. **4a** She'll be here soon. She's just **checking** her email. **5a** I see that you **are reading** *The New Yorker*. For a list of spelling rules for the *-ing* form of verbs, see the Resources, page R-4.	**THE SIMPLE PRESENT** In contrast, we use the **simple present** to signal that a state or activity is generally true or habitual, as in **1b – 5b**. **1b** My aunt **lives** near the university. **2b** What **do** you and your friends **talk** about? **3b** Professor Sutton **explains** things very well. **4b** She **checks** her email every hour. **5b** I always **read** *The New Yorker* from cover to cover.
B	**6** It's **becoming** harder and harder to find a job. **7** It's only five, and it's already **getting** dark.	We often use the present progressive with verbs such as *become* and *get* to describe changing states or situations, as in **6 – 7**.
C	**8** He **is forever** taking my things. **9** You **are always eating**! **10** They **are constantly** arguing.	When we use the present progressive to comment on habitual behavior, it can signal our disapproval, as in **8 – 10**. We often use the adverbs *forever*, *always*, or *constantly* in these situations.

9 | Simple Present or Present Progressive? Complete the conversations with the appropriate verb form in parentheses. Then practice with a partner. [1.3 A]

1. A: Nice piano. Who _____*plays*_____ it? (plays/is playing)

   B: Nobody anymore.

2. A: That's my favorite piano piece. Who _____

   it? (plays/is playing)

   B: That's Uchida.

3. A: David tells us you _____ furniture.

   (move/are moving)

   B: That's right. It's a family business.

4. A: Why _____ the furniture? (do you move/

   are you moving)

   B: Because I need to clean the floor.

5. A: I don't know how to say this.

   B: Say what?

   A: Well, um, I just . . . I just . . .

   B: What _____ to say, James? (do you try/are you trying)

   A: I, um, I lost my job.

6. A: I can't move this thing.

   B: Yes, you can. You just _____ hard enough. (don't try/aren't trying)

7. A: What _____ to? (do you listen/are you listening)

   B: It's a group called the Bald Eagles. Do you like it?

   A: Not especially. Could you turn it down?

8. A: Do you want to choose some music for the trip?

   B: Sure. What kind of music _____ to? (do you listen/are you listening)

   A: Usually jazz, but anything's OK.

9. A: What _____ up so late? (do you do/are you doing)

   B: I have jet lag.[10]

10. A: That's a steep[11] driveway. What _____ when it snows? (do you do/are you doing)

    B: I stay home.

11. A: Why _____ a coat? (do you wear/are you wearing)

    B: Because it's cold in here.

12. A: _____ a school uniform? (do you wear/are you wearing)

    B: Yes, it's brown and white. I'll show it to you someday.

Think about It Why did each speaker choose the present progressive or the simple present? Choose a reason from the box.

Reasons for using the present progressive	Reasons for using the simple present
The speaker is talking or asking about something: • temporary • in progress now	The speaker is talking or asking about something: • generally true • habitual

[10]**jet lag:** the feeling of being tired or awake due to traveling across time zones   [11]**steep:** almost straight up and down

10 | Habitual or Temporary? Does each situation describe habitual behavior (H) or a temporary event in progress now (T)? Circle your answer and the form of the verb that expresses that meaning. (More than one answer may be possible.) `1.3 A`

H | (T)
1. **Amanda sees John at his computer.**

   Amanda: Why (do you talk / (are you talking)) to the computer?

   John: I (try / am trying) to follow every step correctly to set up this program!

H | T
2. **Emma and her husband, Matt, share the housecleaning. This week it is Matt's turn to clean the house.**

   Matt: Emma, can you pick up your clothes? You (leave / are leaving) them on the floor all the time!

   Emma: But I (pick up / am picking up) my clothes when I clean the house!

H | T
3. **Kate sees her husband emptying boxes on the floor of the living room.**

   Kate: What (do you do / are you doing)?

   Husband: I (look for / am looking for) my cell phone.

   Kate: But you (make / are making) a big mess of everything! I just packed those boxes!

H | T
4. **Mika and Isabel like to do gardening.**

   Mika: When (do roses bloom / are roses blooming) in this part of the country?

   Isabel: I think they (bloom / are blooming) in late June.

H | T
5. **Sarah has decided to change some things in her life because she wants a healthier lifestyle. Rob notices the change.**

   Rob: (Do you exercise / Are you exercising) every day now?

   Sarah: Yes, and I (don't eat / am not eating) meat anymore. I (eat / am eating) more vegetables and fruits instead.

H | T
6. **Mary is taking her daughter to school in the morning. Mary sees her daughter behind her and calls out to her.**

   Mary: Hurry up! Why (do you walk / are you walking) so slowly?

Think about It How do we form statements and questions with present progressive verbs? Work with several classmates to explain the rules.

11 | Present Verb Forms in Essay Responses Complete the paragraph with the simple present or the present progressive form of the verb in parentheses. `1.3 A–B`

> Essay Prompt: Is the traditional role of fathers changing? Discuss.
>
> I think that the traditional role of fathers _____*is changing*_____. The most obvious way
> (1. change)
> it _____ is in work and career. In the past, fathers had a career and
> (2. change)
> went to work each day, while mothers stayed at home to take care of the children. But today it
> _____ common for mothers to work and have a career just like fathers. Many times
> (3. be)
> when this _____ the case, the children _____ to daycare.
> (4. be)   (5. go)

But another option _____ available. Some fathers _____
  (6. become)   (7. choose)
to stay at home and take care of their children while their wives _____
                                                                        (8. go)
to work. It _____ not yet a common thing, but more and more fathers
              (9. be)
_____ their careers to take care of their children.
      (10. leave)

12 | Describing Changes with the Present Progressive Choose six topics from the box. Write one sentence for each topic describing how it is changing. Use the verb *get* or *become* in each sentence. [1.3 B]

TOPICS

air travel	computer power	technology	the news
cars	family life	telephones	the world
children	men	television	women

Air travel is getting less comfortable.   OR   *Air travel is becoming safer.*

Common verbs used with the present progressive include:

buy, cry, do, feel, hope, listen, look, rain, say, shop, speak, stare, study, talk, tell, think, watch, wonder

CORPL

Write about It Choose one of your sentences from above and write a paragraph. Give reasons and/or examples to explain your idea.

Air travel is getting less comfortable. Nowadays, the airlines want to save money on fuel, so they are crowding more passengers onto fewer airplanes. To make more money, some airlines are also charging for each suitcase you check. As a result, many passengers are carrying extra luggage onto the airplane. This makes the airplane feel crowded. . . .

13 | Commenting on Habitual Behavior Think of someone you know who fits each general statement below. Write two or more sentences about the person. Include a sentence in the present progressive with *forever, always,* or *constantly.* [1.3 C]

GENERAL STATEMENTS

1. Some people can't stop shopping. They feel a need to spend money. _____

   _____

   Example: My friend Sam is one of those people. He is always buying things he doesn't really need.

2. Some people work all the time. They seem unhappy when they are not working. _____

   _____

3. Some people talk on the phone all the time. _____

   _____

4. Some people think it's OK to borrow things without asking permission. _____

   _____

5. Some people gossip a lot. They love to talk about other people. _____

   _____

1.4 Non-Action Verbs

A

ACTION VERBS

1 He's **leaving** now.

2 Most people **don't get** enough exercise.

NON-ACTION VERBS

3 He **appears** to understand the problem.

4 She's sick.

5 I **know** him well. (NOT: I am knowing him well.)

6 I **own** this car now. (NOT: I am owning this car.)

Many verbs describe actions and activities, as in **1 – 2**. We call these verbs **action verbs**. Other verbs describe states or situations, as in **3 – 6**. We call these verbs **non-action verbs**.

With some non-action verbs, we rarely use the progressive form, as in **5 – 6**. Examples of these verbs include:

agree	belong	consist of	know	possess
believe	concern	exist	own	prefer

GRAMMAR TERM: Non-action verbs are also called **stative verbs**. For a list of non-action verbs, see the Resources, page R-2.

B

NON-ACTIVE MEANING

7a He **has** a new computer. (has = owns)

8a She **looks** great. (looks = appears)

9a I **see** something in the distance. (see = view)

ACTIVE MEANING

7b I'm **having** trouble with my computer.
(having = experiencing)

8b Why are you **looking** at me? (looking = gazing)

9b My brother is **seeing** a new play tomorrow.
(seeing = viewing)

Some verbs have both an active meaning and a non-active meaning, as in **7a – 9b**. We sometimes use the progressive form with the active meaning of these verbs, as in **7b – 9b**.

Common verbs with both active and non-active meanings include:

appear	doubt	have	love	see	taste
be	feel	look	mind	smell	think

14 | Distinguishing Action and Non-Action Verbs Circle the subjects and underline the verbs in these quotations. Then write *A* (action verb) or *N* (non-action verb) over each verb. 1.4 A

Quotations from Famous People

1. *A*
   (Everybody) is talking today about the economy. *(Joschka Fischer, politician)*

2. Men and women belong to different species[12], and communication between them is still in its infancy[13].
   (Bill Cosby, comedian)

3. The Internet is becoming the town square for the global village of tomorrow. *(Bill Gates, businessman)*

4. Whenever people agree with me, I always feel I must be wrong. *(Oscar Wilde, writer)*

5. A man possesses talent; genius possesses the man. *(Isaac Stern, musician)*

6. I buy expensive suits. They just look cheap on me. *(Warren Buffett, businessman)*

7. I know that I am intelligent because I know that I know nothing. *(Socrates, philosopher)*

8. The more I see, the less I know for sure. *(John Lennon, musician)*

9. I don't care what anybody says about me as long as it isn't true. *(Truman Capote, writer)*

10. We hire people who want to make the best things in the world. *(Steve Jobs, businessman)*

Think about It Look at the sentences above. What verb form(s) do we use with active meanings? What verb form(s) do we use with non-active meanings?

[12] **species:** biological categories   [13] **infancy:** the time when one is a baby

15 | Choosing the Correct Meaning Match the **bold** verbs with the correct definitions. (You may not use all the definitions.) `1.4 B`

_b_ 1. A: We're **having** some friends over tonight. Can you come?

B: Sure. I'd love to.

____ 2. A: Do you want to go out to dinner?

B: No, I don't **have** any money.

____ 3. A: Are you **having** fun?

B: Sure. Why do you ask?

____ 4. A: So what changes when you **have** a baby?

B: What changes? You mean what _doesn't_ change!

HAVE
a. to possess
b. to give; to host
c. to experience
d. to give birth to

____ 5. A: Are you going anywhere during the break?

B: I **doubt** it.

____ 6. A: Are you sure you didn't see my ring?

B: Are you **doubting** me?

A: No, of course not.

DOUBT
a. to be uncertain about
b. to disbelieve; to distrust

____ 7. A: What are you doing tonight?

B: I'm meeting Paul for dinner.

A: When are you **seeing** him?

B: Right after work.

____ 8. A: Do you **see** anyone out there?

B: No, there's nobody there.

____ 9. A: There's no reason to do this again.

B: I **see** what you mean.

SEE
a. to view
b. to meet; to go out with
c. to understand
d. to spend time with
e. to imagine

____ 10. Clive Ellington is **appearing** for the first time at the Everett Theater on Monday, July 13, at 7:30.

____ 11. A new study, which **appears** in the July issue of the _American Journal of Public Health,_ suggests that strong social ties can delay memory problems.

____ 12. The president and his wife **appear** to be excellent parents.

____ 13. When I click _Save,_ an error box **appears** on the screen.

APPEAR
a. to become visible
b. to seem; to have the appearance of being
c. to perform in public
d. to be published

____ 14. A: What do you **think** of the new library?

B: It's beautiful.

____ 15. A: Are you really **thinking** about cutting your hair?

B: Yes, it's much too long.

____ 16. A: What are you **thinking** about?

B: Nothing special.

THINK
a. to have an opinion
b. to use your mind; to wonder
c. to consider

Think about It Do each of the definitions above have an active or non-active meaning? Share ideas with your classmates.

"For the verb have, _definitions b, c, and d have an active meaning. Definition a has a non-active meaning."_

Write about It Write two sentences or conversations using the verbs above. Read them to your classmates. Ask them which definitions you used.

16 | Usage Note: Present Progressive with _Be_ Read the note. Then do Activity 17.

> We sometimes use the progressive form of the verb _be_ + an adjective to show that a state is temporary or changing.
>
> | **Active meaning** | **Non-active meaning** |
> |---|---|
> | You **are being** silly. | You **are** silly. |
> | (= You are acting in a silly manner right now.) | (= In general, you are a silly person.) |
> | | |
> | Why **is** he **being** so rude? | Why **is** he so rude? |
> | (= His rudeness is temporary. He's not usually rude.) | (= In general, he is a rude person.) |

17 | Simple Present or Present Progressive? Complete these conversations with the simple present or present progressive form of the verb in parentheses. (More than one answer may be possible.) Then practice with a partner. `1.4 B`

1. A: What are you doing in Los Angeles?

   B: Oh, we _____ _are seeing_ _____ some old friends from college. (see)

2. A: Why are you worrying so much about Matt?

   B: Because I _____ how he's going to find a job.
   He's not even trying. (not/see)

3. A: Do you like to travel?

   B: Yes, I _____ to. (love)

4. A: How's your vacation going?

   B: We _____ every minute of it. (love)

5. A: What do you think of your new boss?

   B: She _____ a really nice person. (be)

6. A: Are the children behaving themselves?

   B: No, they _____ unusually naughty today. (be)

7. A: Can I use your phone?

   B: Sorry, but I _____ one. (not/have)

8. A: This is my friend Carlos. He _____ dinner here, too. (have)

   B: Nice to meet you.

9. A: I think we need to talk.

   B: What about?

   A: I _____ that you aren't doing your share of the work. (feel)

   B: Why do you think that?

   A: Well, for one thing, you're never here when I need you.

10. A: I'm really angry about last night.

    B: I'm sorry you _____ that way. (feel)

11. A: Do you know what you are going to do?

    B: Yeah. I _____ of taking some time off to relax. (think)

12. A: What _____ you _____ of the food here? (think)

    B: It's not bad.

18 | Error Correction   Correct any errors in these conversations. (Some conversations may not have any errors.)

1. A: Is this your car?

   B: No, I don't own a car.

2. A: The chess club is meeting tonight. Are you going?

   B: No, I'm not belonging to that club.

3. A: Are you preferring to stay home tonight?

   B: I don't care. What do you want to do?

4. A: What's that noise?

   B: I'm not hearing anything.

5. A: Why do you look at me like that?

   B: Like what?

   A: Angry. You look angry.

6. A: What are you thinking of this TV? Do you like it better than the other one?

   B: Well, this one's bigger, but the other one's cheaper.

7. A: What are you looking at?

   B: There's something on the street over there.

   A: What is it?

   B: I'm not sure. It looks like a box.

8. A: Is this wood or plastic? I can't tell.

   B: It's feeling like plastic.

9. A: Are you looking for something?

   B: Yes, I'm needing something to write with.

1.5   The Simple Past

A

1 The modern Olympics **started** in 1896 and **became** an international event in 1924.

2 In 1998, Tara Lipinski **won** an Olympic gold medal. She **was** just 15 years old at the time.

3 We **didn't get** to see the Games.

COMPARE SIMPLE PAST AND SIMPLE PRESENT

4a **Did** you still **want** to read my novel?
4b **Do** you still **want** to read my novel?

5a I just **wanted** to say one thing.
5b I just **want** to say one thing.

We use the **simple past** to talk about something that is distant from us in some way. For example, the simple past may signal that:

- an action, event, or state was completed at a definite time in the past (distant in time), as in **1 – 3**. This is the most common use of the simple past.
- the speaker wants to show social or psychological distance, as in **4a** and **5a**. Generally, signaling more distance between people shows more formality or indirectness. Sentences **4a** and **5a** sound more polite and formal than sentences **4b** and **5b**.

For a list of spelling rules for the -ed form of verbs, see the Resources, page R-5. For a list of irregular verbs, see the Resources, page R-3.

B

6 In 2002, we **moved** to New York. We **lived** there **for two years**, and **then** we **moved** to India.

7 Mozart **composed** music **throughout his short life**.

8 **During the 1800s**, many people **moved** across the country.

We often use a time expression in a sentence with the simple past, as in **6 – 8**. These expressions describe a specific time in the recent or distant past.

9 **When we moved** to India, we **didn't have** much money.

10 **When I was younger**, I **had** a lot of big plans.

11 He **stopped** playing football **after he hurt** his knee **during a game**.

When we use a time clause to identify a time in the past, it's important to use the simple past in both parts of the sentence, as in **9 – 11**.

For more information on time clauses, see Unit 6, page 176.

C

CORRECT THE COMMON ERRORS (See page R-10.)

12 ✗ Later I remember that I was not well prepared to take the test.

13 ✗ We didn't want to leave home because we want to take care of our grandparents.

14 ✗ Although she looked nice when she wear that suit, she didn't feel comfortable in it.

15 ✗ When I got there, I sat and think for a while.

19 | **Distinguishing Regular and Irregular Verbs** Underline the simple past verb forms in this text. Then write each verb under the correct group in the chart below and give the base form. `1.5 A`

Counting Heads

After the American War of Independence, the new government <u>ordered</u> a census—a count of the number of people in each state. Work on the census started in August 1790, about a year after George Washington became president. The law required that census takers visit every family. These workers walked or rode on horseback to gather their data. In all, they counted 3.9 million people.

The first census asked for little more than a person's name and address. Over the years, the government added more questions to the census. By 1820, there were questions about a person's job. Later, questions about crime, education, and wages[14] appeared on the census form.

As the country's population grew and the quantity of data increased, new technology helped census workers. In 1890, clerks began to use a keypunch device to add the numbers. In 1950, the census used its first computer to process data.

Today most people receive a census form in the mail. If they don't fill it out and return it by mail, they still get a visit from a census taker.

REGULAR VERBS		IRREGULAR VERBS	
Base form	Simple past form	Base form	Simple past form
order	*ordered*		

20 | **Using the Simple Past** Complete this text with the simple past form of the verbs in parentheses. `1.5 A`

WHO WAS LEONARDO DA VINCI?

Leonardo da Vinci (1452–1519) _____*grew up*_____ in a small town near
                    (1. grow up)
Florence, Italy. As the son of a wealthy man, he _____ the best
                             (2. receive)
education that Florence could offer. Leonardo _____ known
                             (3. become)
for his ability to create sculptures and paintings that _____
                             (4. look)
almost lifelike. Much of his success in this area _____ from his
                             (5. come)

[14] **wages:** salary; money received for work

interest in nature. He also _____ human anatomy and _____ this knowledge
(6. study)   (7. use)
to make his figures realistic.

As a child, Leonardo was fascinated with machines and _____ to draw his own
(8. begin)
inventions. He _____ flying machines, armored tanks[15], and aircraft landing gear. He
(9. draw)
even _____ a diver's suit with tubes and air chambers[16] to allow a swimmer to stay
(10. design)
underwater for long periods of time.

Much of what we know about Leonardo comes from the thousands of pages of notes and

sketches he _____ in his notebooks. He _____ mirror, or reverse, writing,
(11. keep)   (12. use)
starting at the right side of the page and moving across to the left. No one is sure why Leonardo

_____ this way. Some think he _____ to keep people from[17] reading and
(13. write)   (14. want)
stealing his ideas.

Talk about It Write three questions about Leonardo da Vinci. Look for answers to your questions in
books or online and present the answers to your classmates. Pay special attention to your use of simple
past verbs.

21 | Exploring Uses of the Simple Past Write answers to these questions. Then compare ideas with
your classmates. **1.5 A**

1. Think of a famous person. What did this person do to become famous?

_____

_____

2. What was one important event in the news last year?

_____

_____

3. What was the best thing that happened to you last year?

_____

_____

4. How could you make these sentences more formal and less direct?

a. Do you want something? _____

b. I want to ask you a favor. _____

c. How do you want to pay for this? _____

d. What is your name again? _____

e. Do you need to speak to me? _____

> **F Y I**
>
> Most simple past verbs
> end in -ed. Only about
> 200 verbs are irregular.
>
> For a list of irregular
> verbs, see the Resources,
> page R-3.

Think about It How many simple past verbs did you and your classmates use in your answers above?
Which ones are regular verbs? Which are irregular verbs?

[15] **armored tanks:** vehicles for fighting in wars   [17] **keep people from:** to stop people from
[16] **air chambers:** containers filled with air

22 | Using Time Expressions and Clauses Complete each pair of sentences with information about yourself. Make one sentence in each pair false. `1.5 B`

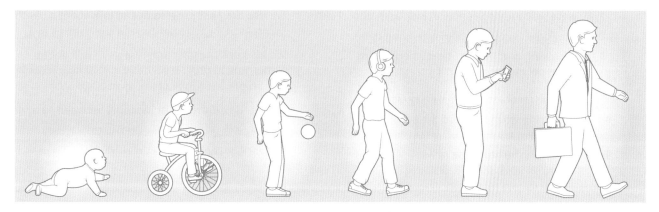

DESCRIBING PAST EXPERIENCES

1. a. I _____ five years ago.

   b. I _____ a year ago.

2. a. I _____ throughout the '90s.

   b. I _____ in 2010.

3. a. During the 2000s, I _____.

   b. Between 2005 and 2010, I _____.

4. a. When I was 5 years old, I _____.

   b. When I was 10 years old, I _____.

5. a. I _____ when I was 15 years old.

   b. I _____ after I graduated from high school.

6. a. _____ before I started school.

   b. _____ when I was a child.

Talk about It Read each pair of sentences you wrote above to a partner. See if your partner can identify the false statement.

23 | Error Correction Correct any errors in these sentences. (Some sentences may not have any errors.)

1. In the past, a woman's place was in the home. Women take care of their families and the house. Men earned the money that supports the family.

2. In high school, we had a lot of clubs. My best friend and I join the chess club even though we weren't really interested in chess.

3. Today I am going to talk about dangerous sports. This topic interested me because I play a dangerous sport.

4. When I was 18, I went hiking in the mountains with my friends. The only thing I take with me was my father's expensive camera because I want to take some pictures from the top of the mountain. I carry that camera very carefully all the way to the top of the mountain, but when I get there, the camera don't work.

5. Jaime is one of my best friends now. I meet him last year when this class began. I think we get along because we like many of the same things.

6. My father's illness affect me a lot because I thought he was a young and healthy person. Everything happen so fast.

1.6 The Past Progressive

A

1 We **were** still **studying** at nine o'clock last night.

2 I **got** my driver's license while I **was living** there.

3 I **was walking** down Water Street when I **heard** footsteps behind me.

COMPARE PAST PROGRESSIVE AND SIMPLE PAST

4a He **was crying** when he **heard** the news.
(= He was crying, and then he heard the news.)

4b He **cried** when he **heard** the news.
(= He heard the news, and then he started to cry.)

We use the **past progressive** to talk about something in progress at a particular time in the past, as in **1**.

We also use the past progressive to talk about something in progress when another action (usually in the simple past) took place, as in **2 – 3**.

Notice the difference in meaning between **4a** and **4b**.

Remember: For the past progressive, we use a past form of the helping verb *be* (*was / were*) + the *-ing* form of the main verb.

B

COMPARE PRESENT AND PAST PROGRESSIVE

5a **Are** you **looking** for me?
5b **Were** you **looking** for me?

6a **Do** you **need** some help?
6b I **was wondering** if you **needed** some help.

7a **Do** you **want** to go out tonight?
7b I **was wondering** if you **wanted** to go out tonight.

We sometimes use the past progressive to sound less direct and more polite, as in **5b**.

We sometimes use the past progressive of the verb *wonder* + *if* + a past form to make questions, offers, and invitations more polite, as in **6b** and **7b**.

 GO ONLINE

24 | Noticing Past Progressive Verbs Underline the past progressive verbs in this text. `1.6 A`

WHAT WERE YOU DOING WHEN . . . ?
by Thomas Thurman

I remember exactly what I <u>was doing</u> when I first heard the news on September 11, 2001. I'd gone to the kitchen at work to get coffee, and I was walking back past co-workers' desks to the other end of the office. As I passed, I caught people's voices: ". . . a plane . . . the North Tower . . . ," and I realized something was up. I got back to my desk, sat down, and looked up BBC News. I got no further work done that day. I was 26.

I remember exactly what I was doing when I heard that Princess Diana had died. I woke up to the news on the radio. I was 22.

I remember exactly what I was doing when I heard that Margaret Thatcher had resigned[18]. I walked, slightly[19] late, into a math class. Ben Anderson, a classmate, looked up and said, "She's resigned." I asked, "Who?" I was almost 16.

I remember what I was doing when my mum told us we were going to have another baby in the family. We were home from school for lunch. I cried with the shock. I was 10.

Think about It The writer uses both the past progressive and the simple past in some of the sentences above. Why?

---

[18] **resign:** to give up a job

[19] **slightly:** a little

25 | Describing Events in the Past Use the pictures to complete each person's answer to the question. (More than one answer may be possible.) `1.6 A`

WHAT WERE YOU DOING AT MIDNIGHT ON DECEMBER 31?

1. "I live in the south of France, so when it was midnight here, it was only 6:00 in New York. Anyway, at that hour a friend and I _____ *were watching TV* _____."

2. "At midnight, as the photo indicates[20], I was out with friends and we _____."

3. "I _____ in a crowded subway car in New York City, somewhere near Times Square."

4. "We _____, and all of a sudden my friend asked, 'What time is it?' I looked at the clock, and it was midnight."

5. "At midnight we _____ the fireworks outside. That went on for about ten minutes!"

6. "To be honest, I _____ at midnight. I had to get up early the next day, so I couldn't stay up until midnight."

7. "I _____ on an airplane. The flight attendant announced that it was midnight, and everyone started cheering."

8. "I had a paper I needed to finish, so _____ in the library until 2:00 a.m. I didn't even notice when it was midnight."

Talk about It What were you doing at midnight on December 31? Tell a partner.

[20]**indicate:** to show

26 | Remembering a Frightening Event Complete these paragraphs with the past progressive or simple past form of the verbs in parentheses. (More than one answer may be possible.) `1.6 A`

The scariest experience I remember was an airplane flight I took many

years ago. I _____ from Istanbul to Prague and I
      (1. travel)

_____ two flights. First, I _____
      (2. have)   (3. fly)

to Zurich, and then I _____ planes to fly to Prague.
                          (4. change)

The first flight was fine, but by the time I _____ in
                                                  (5. land)

Zurich, it _____ heavily.
              (6. snow)

   The snowstorm _____ worse and worse by
                      (7. get)

the minute, but we still _____. As the plane
                              (8. take off)

_____, the turbulence _____.
      (9. climb)   (10. start)

The plane _____ back and forth and up and down.
              (11. shake)

I _____ the armrest as hard as I could. Some of
    (12. squeeze)

the other passengers _____, and one woman
                          (13. cry)

_____ when the plane _____
      (14. scream)   (15. hit)

a big bump.

   When we _____ the final altitude, the
              (16. reach)

turbulence suddenly _____. The passengers
                          (17. stop)

_____ for the pilot and most people
      (18. clap)

_____. But I _____ my seat belt
      (19. relax)   (20. keep)

on for the rest of the flight!

Write about It Think of a frightening event that took place in your life. Write a paragraph about it.

27 | Making Polite Requests Use *I was wondering if* + the simple past to make these requests more indirect. (NOTE: The past form of *can* is *could*.) `1.6 B`

1. Can you help me?

   I was wondering if you could help me.

2. Do you need some help?
3. Can you send me an application form?
4. Can I make an appointment to talk with you?
5. Are you ready to eat?
6. Can you come over and help me for a minute?
7. Do you have a few minutes to talk?
8. Are you doing anything tomorrow night?
9. Can you explain that to me again?

1.7 Talking about the Future with *Be Going To* and *Will*

A

PLANS OR INTENTIONS

1 Don't forget. I**'m going to call** you later.
(= I plan to call you later.)

2 I'm ready to go. I**'ll meet** you out front.
(= I plan to meet you out front.)

PREDICTIONS OR EXPECTATIONS

3 Put that down. Someone**'s going to get** hurt.
(= I predict that someone is going to get hurt.)

4 Millions of people **will be watching** the program.
(= I expect that millions of people will be watching.)

In English, we use several different verb forms to talk about the future. Two common forms are **be going to** and **will**. We use both *be going to* and *will* to:

- express future plans or intentions, as in **1 – 2**
- make predictions or express expectations about the future, as in **3 – 4**

Remember: We use *will* + the base form of the main verb or *will* + *be* + the *-ing* form to describe future events.

We use a present form of the helping verb *be* (*am / is / are*) + *going to* + the base form of the main verb to describe future events.

B

PLANS OR INTENTIONS

5 We made a plan for this last week. Let me explain what we**'re going to do.**

6 We have a busy schedule for you today. First we**'re going to show** you around the office.

7 Oh, I have an idea. Here's what we**'ll do.**

8 Wait here. I**'ll be** right back.

9 I**'ll give** you a ride home from school.

10 Will you **excuse** us, please?

11 I**'ll call** you as soon as I get home.

We use both *be going to* and *will* to express future intentions or plans, but we use them in different ways.

We often use *be going to* when we:

- talk about a future event that has already been planned or scheduled, as in **5 – 6**

We often use *will* to:

- express a decision made at the moment of speaking, as in **7 – 8**
- offer help or make a request, as in **9 – 10**
- make a promise, as in **11**

Notice: When a decision is made at the moment of speaking, we usually use the contraction *'ll*.

C

PREDICTIONS OR EXPECTATIONS

12 In the future, we**'re going to get** most of our food from the ocean.

13 In the future, we **will get** most of our food from the ocean.

14 Look at those dark clouds. It**'s going to rain.**
(NOT: Look at those dark clouds. It will rain.)

15 The average child in the U.S. **will eat** approximately 1,500 peanut butter sandwiches by high school.

We can usually use either *be going to* or *will* to make predictions or express expectations, as in **12 – 13**. However, sometimes the choice of *be going to* or *will* depends on the context:

- When we have clear physical evidence that something is going to happen, we usually use *be going to*, as in **14**.
- When we are stating a general belief or an absolute certainty, we often use *will*, as in **15**.

GO ONLINE

28 | Prediction or Future Plan?   Underline the future verb forms in these quotations. Is the person stating a prediction/expectation or expressing a future plan? Check (✓) your answer. **1.7 A**

QUOTATIONS	PREDICTION/ EXPECTATION	FUTURE PLAN
1. I <u>am going to produce</u> a movie of my own. *(Kabir Bedi, actor)*	☐	☑
2. Choose a job you love, and you will never have to work a day in your life. *(Confucius, philosopher)*	☐	☐
3. It's going to be a season with lots of accidents. *(Ayrton Senna, race car driver)*	☐	☐

	PREDICTION/ EXPECTATION	FUTURE PLAN
4. I am not young, but I feel young. The day I feel old, I will go to bed and stay there. (*Coco Chanel, fashion designer*)	☐	☐
5. Look deep into nature, and then you will understand everything better. (*Albert Einstein, scientist*)	☐	☐
6. I'm not going to change the way I look or the way I feel to conform to anything. (*John Lennon, musician*)	☐	☐
7. A quick temper will make a fool of you soon enough. (*Bruce Lee, martial artist*)	☐	☐
8. Give me six hours to chop down a tree, and I will spend the first four sharpening the axe. (*Abraham Lincoln, U.S. president*)	☐	☐
9. I am going to spend my time today just thanking the people that played a role in my career. (*Nolan Ryan, athlete*)	☐	☐
10. America is the most grandiose[21] experiment the world has seen, but, I am afraid, it is not going to be a success. (*Sigmund Freud, psychologist*)	☐	☐
11. In the next 50 to 75 years, people will be living to be 130 or 140. They'll be working until they're 100. (*Willard Scott, entertainer*)	☐	☐
12. At an Olympic Game, you want to enjoy it—especially if you know it's going to be your last one. (*Shannon Miller, Olympic gymnast*)	☐	☐

Think about It In sentence 11 above, it is possible to say either *will be living* or *will live*. Why do you think the speaker chose *will be living*?

Think about It Do an online search for other quotations about future predictions or plans and share them with your classmates.

29 | Expressing Future Plans Complete these conversations with *be going to* or *will* + the verb in parentheses. (Use a contraction where possible.) `1.7 B`

1. A: I'm really tired.

   B: Come on, then. I ___'ll take_____ you home. (take)

2. A: We need to do something about the car.

   B: Don't worry about it. I _____ it. (take care of)

3. A: Have you heard the news about Lisa and Tim?

   B: No, what news?

   A: They _____ in the fall. (get married)

4. A: Come on. Hurry up. Let's do something.

   B: _____ you _____, please? (relax)

5. A: Did you talk to Bob about the presentation?

   B: No, I forgot. Sorry about that. I _____ him tomorrow. (call)

6. A: Are you ready to order?

   B: Yes, I _____ the fish special and a salad. (have)

RESEARCH SAYS...

In general, *will* is more formal than *be going to*.

Sorry. **I'm going to be** late tonight. (less formal)

I'm very sorry, but **I'll be** late tonight. (more formal)

---

[21] **grandiose:** more complicated than necessary; extravagant

7. A: The food looks delicious.

   B: I hope everything is OK. _____ you _____ one of
   the sandwiches and tell me if it tastes good? (try)

8. A: Can you help me next week?

   B: Oh, I didn't tell you?

   A: Tell me what?

   B: We _____ in California all next week. (be)

9. A: Can I get you anything else?

   B: Yes, I think I _____ another cup of coffee. (have)

Think about It Why did you choose *will* or *be going to* in the conversations in Activity 29? Compare ideas with your classmates.

Reason for using *be going to*	Reasons for using *will*
• For a future event that has already been planned or scheduled	• For a decision made at the moment of speaking • For a promise • For a request or offer of help

I chose will *for number one because the person offered to help.*

30 | Analyzing Predictions Underline the uses of *will* in this article. Circle the uses of *be going to*. Why do you think the writer uses each future form? **1.7 C**

Growing Demand for Coal

The demand for coal is growing steadily. Coal accounted for 26 percent of energy consumed in 2004 worldwide, according to the U.S. Energy Information Agency, and will grow to 28 percent by 2030. Total energy consumption, however, will be going up a few percentage points a year, so in the same period of time, coal consumption will rise 74 percent.

India and China will account for 72 percent of the increase, but coal consumption is expected to also rise in Russia, South Africa, and the U.S. In the U.S., the growth could decline, but coal will still be a big part of the energy profile[22].

"Ninety percent of the fossil fuel reserves in the U.S., India, and China are in coal, and China and India are not going to move from this fuel in the future," said Jeremy Carl of Stanford University. "They are not going to turn off the lights."

Think about It Could the writer use either *be going to* or *will* in any of the sentences above? Why?

---

[22] **profile:** a set of data that gives the most important features of something

31 | Making Predictions with *Will* Complete each prediction with *will* and a verb from the box. `1.7 C`

be	be	be able to	become	have	have	make	work

PREDICTIONS FOR LIFE 100 YEARS FROM NOW

1. We _____ control the weather.

2. Most people _____ from their homes.

3. There _____ one kind of money for the whole world.

4. Everyone _____ computers wired to their brains.

5. Space elevators _____ space travel cheap.

6. Deserts _____ tropical forests.

7. We _____ the ability to communicate through thought transmission[23].

8. There _____ only three languages in the world—English, Spanish, and Chinese.

> **F Y I**
>
> We can use *will* with phrasal modals like *be able to*.
>
> You **will be able to** see Mars clearly in October.

Talk about It Choose one of the predictions above. How likely is it to come true in the next 100 years? Choose a number from 10 (very likely) to 0 (not likely at all) and give reasons for your answer.

32 | Using *Be Going To* for Predictions Complete the predictions with *be going to*. Then match the evidence with the predictions. `1.7 C`

EVIDENCE

1. The sun is rising, and there are no clouds in the sky. You think to yourself: _g_

2. It's half an hour after class usually starts, and your teacher still hasn't arrived. One of your classmates says: ____

3. You get to the bus stop in the morning just as the bus is leaving. You say to yourself: ____

4. A friend sees you using a tool incorrectly. He says to you: ____

5. You see a family member eating a second big bowl of ice cream. You say: ____

6. Your friend is cooking fish for dinner, but he bakes it too long, and it burns completely. You say: ____

7. You expected 50 people to come to the lecture, but already there are more than 50 people in the room. You say to your assistant: ____

8. You and your friends are planning to drive to the beach. You try to start the car, but nothing happens. One of your friends says: ____

PREDICTIONS

a. I guess we _____ class today. (not/have)

b. Be careful. You _____ hurt. (get)

c. You _____ yourself sick. (make)

d. I guess we _____ anywhere today. (not/go)

e. We _____ more chairs. (need)

f. Now I _____ late for work. (be)

g. It ___*is going to be*___ a nice day. (be)

h. I guess we _____ fish for dinner. (not/have)

---

[23] **thought transmission:** the ability to send thoughts from mind to mind

1.8 Using Present Forms to Talk about the Future

A

1 School **starts** on September 3rd this year.

2 The plane **leaves** in an hour.

3 The library **closes** at noon today.

4 When **are** we **meeting** this week?

5 Most stores **are closing** early tonight.

6 I'm **leaving** for London tomorrow night.

In addition to the more common uses of the **simple present** and **present progressive**, we can also use these verb forms to talk about scheduled events and arrangements in the future, as in **1 – 6**.

Notice: We almost always use a time expression (such as *in an hour*, *this week*, or *tonight*) to show that we are referring to the future, not the present, as in **1 – 6**.

B

SIMPLE PRESENT VS. PRESENT PROGRESSIVE

7 We **meet** at 10 on Tuesday. Don't forget to bring your laptop. (= We meet regularly at 10 on Tuesday.)

8 Saturday's game **begins** at noon.

9 Don't forget. We're **meeting** at 9 instead of 10 on Tuesday. (= We're meeting at 9 this Tuesday.)

10 Why **is** the game **starting** late tonight?

When we talk about a scheduled event that takes place regularly, we usually use the simple present, as in **7 – 8**.

When a scheduled event is temporary or changing, we often use the present progressive, as in **9 – 10**.

C

PRESENT PROGRESSIVE VS. *BE GOING TO*

11 We're **leaving** next month.

12 We're **going to leave** next month.

13 It's **going to rain** tomorrow. (NOT: ~~It's raining tomorrow.~~)

When we talk about personal plans and arrangements, we sometimes use the present progressive instead of *be going to*, as in **11 – 12**.

WARNING! Unlike *be going to*, we do not use the present progressive to make predictions, as in **13**.

D

14 I **am to meet** the president at 10:00. (= I am required to meet the president at 10:00.)

15 The company **is to announce** its quarterly earnings in December. (= The company is obligated to do this.)

In formal contexts, we sometimes use *am / is / are* + **to- infinitive** to refer to the future, as in **14 – 15**. Using this form suggests that the future event is an obligation or requirement.

 GO ONLINE

🔊 33 | Talking about the Future with Present Forms Listen to these conversations and write the missing words. Then practice with a partner. **1.8 A**

1. A: When _____ *is* _____ your flight tomorrow?

   B: I think it _____ at 6, but I'm not sure.

   A: Nonstop flight?

   B: No, I _____ in London.

   A: _____ you _____ a long layover[24]?

   B: No, only two hours.

   A: Oh, that's not bad.

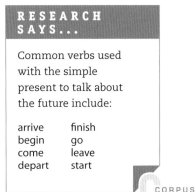

RESEARCH SAYS...

Common verbs used with the simple present to talk about the future include:

arrive	finish
begin	go
come	leave
depart	start

CORPUS

---

[24] **layover:** a stop between flights

2. A: _____ you _____
   to the meeting next week?

   B: Yes, I plan to.

   A: What time _____ it _____?

   B: At 7.

3. A: _____ you _____
   anything special this weekend?

   B: Um, I already _____ plans for Saturday,

   but _____ free on Sunday.

   A: Great. _____ a concert in the afternoon. Interested?

   B: Sure.

   A: It _____ at 3, so I'll come by at 2.

   B: OK.

4. A: _____ the last day of school?

   B: June 15.

   A: _____ that a Friday?

   B: No, _____ a Wednesday.

5. A: _____ you _____
   to the concert tonight?

   B: Yeah. What time _____ it _____?

   A: Let me check.

Think about It What time expressions do the speakers use in the conversations in Activity 33? Circle them.

Talk about It Tell your classmates about an event scheduled for later this week.

34 | Present or Future? Listen to ten short conversations. Are the speakers talking about an action in progress now or an event in the future? Check (✓) your answer. **1.8 A**

	Now	In the future
1.	☐	✓
2.	☐	☐
3.	☐	☐
4.	☐	☐
5.	☐	☐

	Now	In the future
6.	☐	☐
7.	☐	☐
8.	☐	☐
9.	☐	☐
10.	☐	☐

Think about It Listen to the conversations again. In the future sentences, what time expressions do the speakers use to show that they are talking about the future? Write at least six.

_____   _____

_____   _____

_____   _____

35 | Simple Present or Present Progressive? Complete these conversations with the simple present or present progressive form of the verb in parentheses. (More than one answer may be possible.) `1.8 B`

1. A: When _____ the first train _____ tomorrow morning? (leave)

   B: At seven.

2. A: Where's the train?

   B: You didn't hear the announcement?

   A: No. What did it say?

   B: The seven o'clock train _____ an hour late this morning. (leave)

3. A: Hurry up. We're going to be late.

   B: What time _____ the movie _____? (start)

   A: In 15 minutes.

4. A: Do you want to go for lunch tomorrow?

   B: Um, I _____ tomorrow. I have a doctor's appointment. (not/work)

5. A: Who _____ to the meeting tonight? (come)

   B: I'm not sure.

6. A: I have some good news.

   B: What is it?

   A: They _____ the elevators tomorrow, so the office

   _____ until 11 in the morning. (fix) (not/open)

Think about It In which of the conversations above is a scheduled event temporary or changing?

36 | Present Progressive or *Be Going To*? Complete these quotations. Where possible, use the present progressive to talk about the future. Where you can't, use *be going to*. `1.8 C`

QUOTATIONS FROM FAMOUS PEOPLE

1. I don't know where I _____ from here, but I promise it won't be boring. (go)

   —*David Bowie, musician*

2. If you can't read, it _____ hard to realize dreams. (be)

   —*Booker T. Washington, educator*

3. I _____ to college. I don't care if it ruins my career. I'd rather be smart than a movie

   star. (go) —*Natalie Portman, actor*

4. The desktop market has entered the dark ages, and it _____ in the dark ages for the

   next ten years. (be) —*Steve Jobs, businessman*

5. I know this _____ bad, but I'm going to pretend it _____ good.

   (end/end) —*Johnny Knoxville, actor*

6. It _____ easy to change things. (not/be) —*Daniel Berrigan, activist*

7. Things _____ a lot worse before they get worse. (get) —*Lily Tomlin, actor*

8. Sooner or later I _____, but I'm not going to retire. (die) —*Margaret Mead, scientist*

Think about It In which of the quotations in Activity 36 did you use *be going to* instead of the present progressive? Why?

37 | Talking about Future Requirements Circle the expressions in these sentences that suggest an obligation or requirement. Then rewrite the sentences using *am/is/are* + *to-* infinitive. `1.8 D`

1. Class begins at 9, and you (need to be) here on time.

   Class begins at 9, and you are to be here on time.

2. The school field trip will be on June 15. Your child should bring a lunch and something to drink.

3. The bus is going to leave at 7:15, so everyone should be at the parking lot by 7.

4. Your appointment with the mayor is at noon. You need to arrive at the reception desk by 11:45.

5. I need to go out for a few minutes, but no one should leave the room while I am away. Is that clear?

6. You will have 30 minutes to answer the exam question. When I say stop, you should put down your pencil.

7. Your doctor's appointment is at 10 a.m. Please don't eat or drink anything in the morning.

8. We have important visitors next Monday. Everyone should dress up a bit.

1.9 Using Present Forms in Speaking

A	**USING CONTRACTIONS** **1** Your books're here. **2** The flowers're dying. **3** They're here. **4** What're you doing? **5** Who're they talking to? **6** How're you doing?	In conversation, we usually contract the *am / is / are* after nouns, pronouns, and question words, as in **1 – 6**. By not using contractions, we may sound more formal or insistent than we intend. We sometimes use the full form for special emphasis or in formal speaking situations such as speeches.
B	**NON-ACTION VERBS IN CONVERSATION** **7** I think so. **8** I doubt it. **9** I suppose so. **10** I don't know. **11** It doesn't matter. **12** I don't mind. **13** I don't care. **14** I don't want to.	In conversation, the **simple present** is much more common than the simple past. This is partly because a few verbs are used frequently. Many of these are non-action verbs showing how the speaker feels or thinks about something, as in **7 – 14**.
C	**USING THE PRESENT TO TELL A STORY** **15** So I'm leaving the store, and this woman stops me and asks to use my phone. I don't know what to say to her, I mean, I don't know her. . . .	We sometimes use the **simple present** and **present progressive** to tell a story that took place in the past, as in **15**. Using present verb forms makes the story seem more vivid.

38 | Using Contractions Match the questions with the responses. Listen and check your answers. Then practice with a partner. `1.9 A`

QUESTIONS

1. What are you doing? __e__
2. What is the matter? ____
3. When is she leaving? ____
4. How far is your house from here? ____
5. When is the next exam? ____
6. Where are my shoes? ____
7. How far is Tokyo from here? ____
8. Who are you calling? ____
9. Why are you always yelling at me? ____
10. How long are they going to be there? ____

RESPONSES

a. Not long. I think they are coming back in a week.
b. Because you are always misbehaving.
c. It is on the fifth. That is a Friday.
d. Tomorrow. She is taking the noon train tomorrow.
e. Nothing special. I am just taking a break.
f. My brother. He is in Toronto this week.
g. I think I am going to lose my job.
h. I am not sure, but it is closer than Beijing.
i. They are in the closet.
j. It is just around the corner.

Talk about It Ask a partner four of the questions above again. Give your own answers.

39 | Common Verbs in the Simple Present Work with a partner. Take turns saying a sentence from Column A. Your partner responds with a sentence from Column B. (Many responses are possible.) `1.9 B`

COLUMN A

1. Where do you want to go for lunch?
2. Are you coming to class tomorrow?
3. We have a test tomorrow.
4. It's late.
5. It's time to go.
6. You aren't being funny.
7. Does this computer work?
8. Do you know what I mean?
9. What's the matter with you?
10. Why aren't you coming to the concert?
11. Is it cold outside?
12. Somebody's using your computer.
13. I don't have any money.
14. Is it going to rain tomorrow?

COLUMN B

I suppose so.
I doubt it.
I don't care.
I don't mind.
It doesn't matter.
I don't want to.
I know.
I don't know.
I think so.
I don't think so.

Talk about It Work with a partner. Write three more short conversations using verbs in the box below. Then present your conversations to the class.

COMMON VERBS IN THE SIMPLE PRESENT

| care | doubt | know | matter | mind | suppose | think | want |

40 | Telling a Story Make up a story using these pictures. Use present verb forms to make your story vivid. Tell your story to a partner. Listen to your partner's story. **1.9 C**

Talk about It Tell a partner a story that happened to you. Use present verb forms.

A	**SUMMARIES AND ABSTRACTS** **1** This paper **examines** the relationship between exercise and mood. Evidence from a number of studies **suggests** that regular exercise **leads** to an improvement in mood. Possible signs of depression **decrease** over the course of a 10-week regular exercise program. The paper also **discusses** other emotional benefits of regular exercise.	We often use the **simple present** in summaries and abstracts of academic papers, as in **1**. Using the simple present signals that the writer views the statement as a fact or general truth.
B	**ADDING DETAILS TO GENERAL STATEMENTS** **2** Lying **is** usually unacceptable behavior, but there **are** rare times when it **is** better to tell a lie than to tell the truth. I **learned** this the hard way. When I **was** 15, . . .	Writers often use the **simple present** to make a general statement, as in **2**. They then explain or support the general statement with specific details and examples using the **simple past**.
C	**WRITING ABOUT RESEARCH** **3** Researchers from University College **studied** brain scans of 105 people—80 of whom were bilingual. The researchers **found** that learning other languages changed the gray matter in the left part of the brain. This research **demonstrates** how learning languages **develops** the brain.	In academic writing, writers often use the **simple past** to describe the steps in a study or experiment, as in **3**. They then evaluate the results of the study using the **simple present**. The simple present signals that the writer believes the information is scientific fact.

41 | Using the Simple Present in Summaries Underline the simple present verbs in these summaries. Then answer the questions on page 34. `1.10 A`

Abstracts of Articles

1. **TITLE:** Real Men Don't Need Work-Life Balance
   AUTHOR: Tanvi Gautam
   SOURCE: *Forbes* magazine
   SUMMARY: This article <u>focuses</u> on the issue of work-life balance for men. Many firms assume that men do not need career flexibility or work-life integration. However, these assumptions are generally not accurate. The author argues that firms need to consider men when they design policies to promote flexibility.

> **FYI**
>
> An abstract is a short summary of a longer piece of writing. Abstracts are used by researchers to understand the main ideas of an article quickly.

2. **TITLE:** Margaret C. Anderson's *Little Review*
   AUTHORS: Sophia Estante; Lorrie Moore
   SOURCE: The Writing Center at the University of Wisconsin–Madison
   SUMMARY: This research looks at the work of Margaret C. Anderson, the editor of the *Little Review*. The research draws upon mostly primary sources including memoirs, published letters, and a complete collection of the *Little Review*. Most prior research on Anderson focuses on her connection to the famous writers and personalities that she published and associated with. This focus undermines[25] her role as the dominant[26] creative force behind one of the most influential little magazines published in the twentieth century. This case example shows how little magazine publishing is arguably a literary art.

---

[25] **undermine:** to injure; to weaken   [26] **dominant:** superior; leading

3. **TITLE:** The Connection between Hypertension[27] and Stress
   AUTHORS: Michael Anderson; Karina Gomez; Peizhu Liu
   SOURCE: *Medical Monthly*. 2014; 58: 556-570.
   SUMMARY: It has been established that stressful situations cause temporary spikes[28] in blood pressure, but researchers are unsure of the relationship between stress and long-term hypertension. The purpose of this study is to understand this relationship and to find out if short-term spikes in blood pressure due to stress can add up and cause high blood pressure in the long term. The data for this study comes from a series of tests conducted on forty participants of various backgrounds in the San Francisco Bay Area over a period of twenty years. The researchers also looked at statistical[29] data from the California Board of Health over the past twenty years. Even though the researchers found mixed test results, the study shows that daily exercise and focused stress management lowers the risk of hypertension over time. However, medical researchers must conduct more studies in order to determine the link between the frequency of short term spikes in stress and long-term hypertension.

QUESTIONS

1. Besides the simple present, what other verb forms do the writers use in the summaries above?
2. What kinds of information do these writers include in the summaries?
3. What kinds of information do these writers leave out of the summaries?
4. What is the purpose of an abstract or summary?

42 | Evaluate Read these paragraphs and underline the verbs. Then answer the questions below. `1.10 B`

A	B
Self-discipline is the most important ingredient for success. When you set a goal for yourself, you have to work to reach it. You need to study, earn money, or do whatever is necessary for your particular[30] goal. You need to make a plan and follow it, even when you feel discouraged[31]. Without self-discipline, it is easy to lose sight of your goal. There is no value in having a goal if you do not have self-discipline.	Self-discipline is the most important ingredient for success. My brother is a good example of the connection between self-discipline and success. When he was only 15, he decided that he wanted to be a doctor. From that point, he stopped playing sports and doing things with his friends so that he would have time to study. Every summer he gave up his vacation so that he could work in a hospital. Because he was self-disciplined, my brother is now a successful family doctor in my hometown.

QUESTIONS

1. What differences in the verbs do you notice between the two paragraphs above? Why?
2. Which paragraph is more interesting to you? Why?
3. Which paragraph provides specific details and examples?

[27] **hypertension:** high blood pressure
[28] **spike:** a sudden increase in something
[29] **statistical:** mathematical; numeric

[30] **particular:** specific
[31] **discouraged:** without confidence; hopeless

43 | Using the Simple Past to Give Specific Examples Read these general statements and check (✓) *Agree* or *Disagree*. Then write a short paragraph giving a specific example to explain why you agree or disagree with each statement. `1.10 B`

	AGREE	DISAGREE
1. Athletic competition is not good for very young children.	☐	☐
2. Anger is sometimes beneficial[32].	☐	☐
3. In spite of advances in scientific knowledge, people are still superstitious[33].	☐	☐
4. Learning a second language is not good for young children.	☐	☐

1. Agree: Athletic competition is not good for very young children. When my brother was very young, he played on a children's soccer team. His best friend wanted to play on the team too, but he wasn't a very good player. The other children on the team didn't want my brother's friend to be on the team because they wanted to win. Soccer was a competition for them, not a game, and so at the age of seven, my brother's friend quit playing soccer.

44 | Exploring Verb Forms in Research Reports Complete each research report with the correct form of the verbs in parentheses. `1.10 C`

1. In one report on how intelligence develops in young children, American researchers _____studied_____ (study) nearly 500 boys and girls born in New Jersey hospitals between 1984 and 1987. When they were born, each child _____ (weigh) less than 2,000 grams, and they were approximately 16 years old when they _____ (participate) in the study. The children _____ (take) intelligence and motor skill tests at home. (Motor skills are skills that require living things to effectively use their muscles.)

   The test results were then compared with test results of other children of the same age. The study _____ (report) that the children with low birth weight often have more problems with motor skills than the other children. This _____ (suggest) that babies with low birth weight may be more likely than other children to have physical and mental problems as they develop.

2. A major study from the University of North Carolina _____ (compare) two groups of children. One group of children _____ (attend) an all-day childcare center from when they _____ (be) a few weeks old until the age of 5. This high-quality program _____ (offer) some social, health, and educational programs, and it _____ (provide) healthy food for the children. The other group of children _____ (not / go) to a childcare center at any time. Both groups _____ (attend) public schools after the age of 5.

   The two groups of children _____ (be) similar when they _____ (be) babies, but different after the age of about 18 months. As babies, both groups _____ (have) similar results in tests for mental and physical skills. However, the children in the childcare program _____ (score) much higher in tests after the age of 18 months. The children _____ (take) tests again at the ages of 12 and 15 years. Again, the children from the childcare center _____ (show) better test scores.

---

[32]**beneficial:** helpful

[33]**superstitious:** believing in something you can't explain

The study _____ that education during the first months and years of life _____
(suggest)   (be)

important for development later in life. The researchers say that with early education, poorer

children could become more successful and do better in school. They _____ their study
(believe)

_____ a need for the government to spend money on public education at an early age. They
(show)

_____ these kinds of programs _____ better success overall in American schools.
(claim)   (create)

WRAP-UP Demonstrate Your Knowledge

A | WRITE Write three paragraphs with information about yourself ten years ago, now, and ten years from now.

Ten years ago	Now	Ten years from now
I was living in Mexico with my parents. It was a happy time for my family because everyone was healthy....	*I am living here with my wife....*	*I will probably be living here. Hopefully I will have a good job....*

B | SURVEY Choose a topic related to habits. Think of five to ten questions to use in a survey. Ask your classmates the questions and record their answers. What conclusions can you draw? Are there similarities in the answers? Did males and females answer differently?

Topic: Study Habits
How many hours per week do you usually study outside of class?
Did you usually do your homework in high school?

C | PRESENTATION Choose a topic—a person, place, or thing—that interests you. Look for ten interesting facts about this topic and present the facts to your class.

D | WEB SEARCH What happened on the month and day you were born? Do an online search of your date of birth. Choose five interesting things that happened that day and report them to the class.

1.11 Summary of Present, Past, and Future Forms

SIMPLE PRESENT

I You We They	know. do not know. don't know.
He She It	knows. does not know. doesn't know.

USES

We use the simple present to describe:
- current habitual behavior
- timeless truths
- general truths
- the state of something now
- regular scheduled events in the future

SIMPLE PAST

I You We They He She It	knew. did not know. didn't know. arrived. did not arrive. didn't arrive.

USES

We use the simple past to:
- signal an action, event, or state was completed at a definite time in the past
- indicate social or psychological distance

PRESENT PROGRESSIVE

I	am listening. 'm listening. am not listening. 'm not listening.
He She It	is listening. 's listening. is not listening. 's not listening. isn't listening.
You We They	are listening. 're listening. are not listening. 're not listening. aren't listening.

USES

We use the present progressive to:
- signal that a state or activity is temporary or in progress now
- talk about planned events in the future

PAST PROGRESSIVE

I He She It	was listening. was not listening. wasn't listening.
You We They	were listening. were not listening. weren't listening.

USES

We use the past progressive to:
- talk about something in progress at a particular time in the past
- describe a developing or changing situation in the past
- show social or psychological distance

FUTURE WITH *BE GOING TO*

I	am going to help. 'm going to help. am not going to help. 'm not going to help.
He She It	is going to help. 's going to help. is not going to help. 's not going to help. isn't going to help.
You We They	are going to help. 're going to help. are not going to help. 're not going to help. aren't going to help.

USES

We often use *be going to* to:
- talk about planned future events
- make predictions

FUTURE WITH *WILL*

I He She It You We They	will do it. 'll do it. will not do it. won't do it.

USES

We often use *will* to:
- make promises
- offer help and make requests
- talk about spontaneous plans
- make predictions

2 Perfect Forms

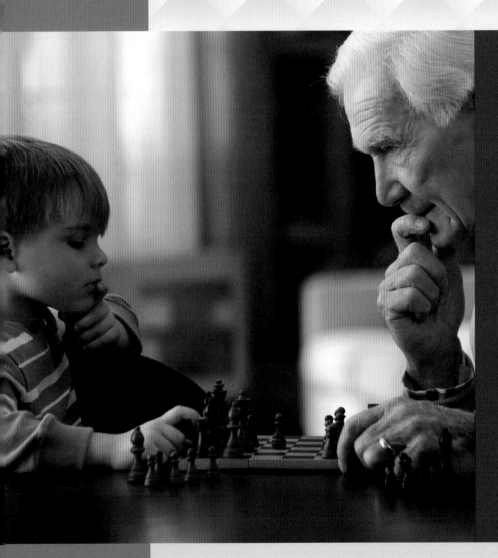

Children have never been very good at listening to their elders[1], but they have never failed to imitate them.

—JAMES BALDWIN, WRITER

(1924–1987)

Talk about It What does the quotation above mean? Do you agree or disagree?

[1] **elders:** people who are older than you

WARM-UP

A | Study the graph on the right. Then read the statements and write *T* (true) or *F* (false). Do you find any of this information surprising? Tell your classmates.

World Population Growth

___ 1. The population of the world **has been increasing** since 1750.

___ 2. Over the past 50 years, the populations of developing and industrial regions **have gone up** at the same rate.

___ 3. In 1800, there were about 1 billion people in the world. By 1900, the population **had** almost **reached** 2 billion.

___ 4. The population of developing regions started to grow more rapidly around 1950. The population of industrial regions **has risen** much less in comparison.

___ 5. By 2050, the population of the world **will have reached** 9 billion people.

World Population Growth

10 billion
8
6
4
2

1750   1850   1950   2050

◑ **Developing regions** parts of the world with fewer factories and businesses

● **Industrial regions** parts of the world with many factories and businesses

Sources: United Nations Population Division and Population Reference Bureau, 1993.

B | Answer these questions about the statements above.

1. The words in green are perfect forms of verbs. How many different perfect forms do you see in the statements?

2. What time words are used with the perfect verb forms?

3. When do you think we use perfect forms of verbs?

C | Look back at the quotation on page 38. Identify any perfect verb forms.

2.1 Overview of the Present Perfect

A

1 Life expectancy **has increased** since 1900. It's not uncommon for people to live into their eighties now.

2 Technology **has helped** people in many ways, but too much technology isn't healthy.

3 **I've watched** that movie too many times. I think I know it by heart.

4 Many roads here **have become** crowded, and this causes frequent traffic jams.

5 A: I need to talk to Barbara for a minute. Is she here?
B: No, she**'s gone** to the library.
(= She went to the library. She isn't here now.)

6 A: Are you hungry?
B: No, I**'ve already eaten**.
(= I ate something earlier so now I'm not hungry.)

When we want to show that a past action, event, or state is *connected to now* (the moment of speaking), we use the **present perfect** form of a verb, as in **1 – 6**. The past action, event, or state might be something that:

- started in the past and continues to the present, as in **1 – 2**
- happened repeatedly in the past and has an effect on something in the present, as in **3 – 4**
- started and ended in the past but has an effect on something in the present, as in **5 – 6**

Remember: We form the present perfect with *have / has* (+ *not*) + the past participle (*-ed/-en* form) of the main verb. For a list of past participles of irregular verbs, see the Resources, page R-3.

B

7 A: How's the movie?
B: It**'s been** great **so far**.

8 A: Is Uncle Bill here?
B: No, he **hasn't come** in **yet**.

9 We**'ve spoken** several times **in the past month**, and I think we are now ready to make a decision.

10 You**'ve always been** unhappy with your job. I think it's time to do something about it.

11 I**'ve just finished** my paper.

12 A: Sorry I'm late. How long **have** you **been** here?
B: Don't worry about it. I**'ve only been** here **for ten minutes**.

13 I **haven't worked since** last December. I really need to find a job soon.

We often use **adverbs** and **time expressions** with the present perfect, as in **7 – 13**. Some examples include:

already	just	never	yet
always	lately	so far	

in	+	the past few days / the last ten minutes
over	+	the past month / the last two years
for	+	a week / a year / the last two years
since	+	1980 / last year / January / then / my birthday

Notice: We can use some adverbs (such as *already, always, just,* and *never*) between *have / has* and the past participle, as in **10 – 11**.

We use *for* + a period of time, as in **12**. We use *since* + a specific time, as in **13**.

 GO ONLINE

1 | Connecting Past Actions to Now What does each **bold** verb in the conversations below describe? Read the meanings in the box. Then write *a, b,* or *c*. (More than one answer may be possible.) `2.1 A`

The verb describes something that:
a. started in the past and continues to the present
b. happened repeatedly in the past and has an effect on something in the present
c. started and ended in the past but has an effect on something in the present

MEANING

_c_ 1. A: Are you OK?

B: No, I**'ve twisted** my ankle.

A: Does it hurt?

B: Of course it hurts. Can you get me a chair?

____ 2. A: Ms. James is your academic advisor, isn't she?

       B: Yes, but we **haven't had** many meetings.

____ 3. A: Do you know Isabel Martinez?

       B: Yeah, I**'ve known** her for years. Why do you ask?

       A: She's my new boss.

____ 4. A: Do you know Los Angeles very well?

       B: Sure. I**'ve been** there several times. What do you want to know?

       A: What's the public transportation like?

       B: It's not so great. You really need a car.

____ 5. A: Does your brother still live in Santa Fe?

       B: No, he**'s moved** to El Paso, but he still has lots of friends in Santa Fe.

____ 6. A: Do you want to go to the game tonight?

       B: Sorry, I can't. I**'ve made** other plans.

____ 7. A: **Have** you **seen** my wallet?

       B: Yes, it's on the bureau.

____ 8. A: Ever since the summer, you**'ve been** different.

       B: What do you mean?

       A: I don't know. You're just more distracted now.

> **FYI**
>
> When we use the present perfect, the connection to now is not always stated directly.
>
> The exhibit was in California, but now it **has moved on** to New York.
>
> (= now it's in New York)

Think about It What other verb forms do the speakers use in the conversations in Activity 1? What does this say about how we often use the present perfect?

Think about It Think about each situation in Activity 1. For each present perfect verb, what connection(s) to *now* do you think the speaker is making? Write your ideas in this chart. (Many answers are possible.)

Present perfect action, event, or state	Connection(s) to now
1. I've twisted my ankle.	*My ankle hurts.*
2. I haven't had many meetings with Ms. James.	*I don't know Ms. James very well.*
3. I've known Isabel Martinez for years.	
4. I've been to Los Angeles several times.	
5. My brother has moved to El Paso.	
6. I've made other plans for tonight.	
7. I have seen your wallet.	
8. You've been different since the summer.	

2 | Using the Present Perfect Read this essay response and complete it with the present perfect form of the verbs in parentheses. `2.1 A–B`

> **Essay Prompt: In general, people are living longer now. Discuss the causes of this. Use specific reasons and details to develop your essay.**
>
> It's true. People are living longer now. Today it is not uncommon for men and women to live into their eighties or even their nineties. The average life expectancy _____ greatly since 1900. At
> (1. increase)
> that time, the average life expectancy in this country was 47 years. Today the average life expectancy is 78 years. A few specific things _____ to increase life expectancy. These include vaccinations[2],
> (2. help)
> a decrease in smoking, and workplace safety rules.
>
> The use of vaccinations _____ greatly to the increase in life expectancy. The law says that
> (3. contribute[3])
> schoolchildren must be vaccinated against certain deadly diseases. And they must receive these vaccinations before they can start school. This _____ a number of deadly diseases. In addition, the
> (4. eliminate[4])
> reduction in the number of people smoking cigarettes _____ millions of smoking-related
> (5. prevent)
> deaths. This change _____ the life expectancy of both former smokers and the people who
> (6. raise)
> had to breathe secondhand smoke[5].
>
> Another reason for the increase in life expectancy is that workplaces _____ safer. In the
> (7. become)
> past, it was not uncommon to be injured or even killed on the job. However, in the middle of the twentieth century, the government passed workplace safety laws. As a result, there was a 40 percent decrease in on-the-job deaths in places such as factories and construction sites.
>
> These are three important reasons why people are living longer today. All of these behaviors and others will continue to allow people to live longer and healthier lives.

Think about It Why does the writer use the present perfect in each sentence above? Choose reasons from this box.

> The writer uses the present perfect to describe:
> 1. something started in the past and continues to the present.
> 2. something happened repeatedly in the past and has an effect on something in the present.
> 3. something started and ended in the past but has an effect on something in the present.

In #1 the writer uses the present perfect to describe something that started in the past and continues to the present.

Think about It Circle any uses of time expressions with the present perfect above. Are there many uses or only a few? What does this say about how we often use time expressions with the present perfect?

Talk about It Can you think of some other reasons why people are living longer today? Work with a partner to write at least three reasons. Try to use the present perfect in your sentences.

---

[2] **vaccinations:** shots to prevent disease
[3] **contribute:** to help make something happen

[4] **eliminate:** to get rid of; to remove
[5] **secondhand smoke:** smoke from another person's cigarette

3 | Using the Present Perfect Complete these sentences with the present perfect. `2.1 A–B`

1. The United Nations Children's Fund (UNICEF) _____*has been*_____ very active in vaccinating⁶ children around the world. (be)

2. I'm still feeling a pain in my right leg, so I _____ to the gym this week. (not/go)

3. I _____ discouraged before—just like everyone else. (be)

4. I _____ a vacation in years, so I'm really looking forward to this trip. (not/take)

5. My sister _____ more in five years than most people do in a lifetime. (do)

6. It is my hard work that _____ me a success. (make)

7. Thank you for the interest you _____ in my work. (show)

8. My boss is very serious about the project. She _____ about it a lot. (talk)

9. I walk everywhere and I play basketball. I do that three times a week, and I _____ 30 pounds so far. I feel so much better. (lose)

10. It _____ much for the past few years, and a number of ski resorts are closing. (not/snow)

11. Improvements in technology _____ us to determine that Pluto is not a planet. (allow)

12. Scientists are just now discovering some of the strange living things that _____ to life in the deep ocean. (adapt)

13. The basic design of a bicycle _____ pretty much the same since the 1800s. Most bikes still use a foot-powered system that powers the back wheel. (remain)

14. Modern technology _____ it easier for businesspeople to succeed. However, they still have problems getting money to start businesses. (make)

15. China _____ the world's dominant producer of solar panels⁷ in the last two years. It was responsible for half the world's production last year. (become)

RESEARCH SAYS...

Common verbs used with the present perfect include:

be	give	say
become	go	see
call	have	show
come	lose	take
do	make	think
get	put	win

CORPUS

Think about It Underline the time expressions in the sentences above. (Some of the sentences don't have a time expression.) Then write each time expression under the correct group in this chart.

Time expressions with the simple present	Time expressions with the present progressive	Time expressions with the present perfect	Time expressions with the simple past
	still		

Think about It Which of the time expressions above can be used with more than one verb form?

---

⁶**vaccinating:** giving a shot to prevent disease   ⁷**solar panels:** devices used to gather energy from the sun

4 | Using Time Expressions with the Present Perfect Complete the sentences below with a time expression from the box. (More than one answer may be possible.) **2.1 B**

| already | for | since | so far | yet |

SCIENCE AND RESEARCH

1. Thousands of people visited the King Tutankhamun exhibit when it was in Chicago. _____*Since*_____ then, the exhibit has moved to Philadelphia, and it is going to move to London in November.

2. Children learn new words at a very fast rate. Scientists have wondered _____ a long time how this is possible.

3. According to the *World Book Encyclopedia*, scientists have named more than 1½ million animals _____. Over half of these are types of insects.

4. Someone with a PhD is a doctor of philosophy. Many people earn PhDs, but they aren't all philosophers. The name has survived _____ the Middle Ages when many areas of study were called philosophy.

5. _____ scientists have not found a way to determine the exact age of the Earth.

6. Antarctica may help us solve some of the most difficult problems of the past and future of our planet. For example, scientists have _____ found that Antarctica is the largest storehouse of fresh water on the planet.

7. _____ ancient times, people have used parts of the willow tree to reduce pain.

8. Researchers have _____ found cures for many deadly diseases, but they haven't found a cure for skin cancer _____.

9. Researchers haven't _____ discovered how to cure the illness, but there are ways to treat the symptoms.

10. Scientists have discovered other stars with orbiting planets, but _____ they have only discovered one place that supports complex life forms: Earth.

mask of
King Tutankhamun

FYI

Time expressions with the present perfect help to show "time up to now."

I **haven't worked** since last December. (= last December up to now)

I **haven't finished** it yet, but I will soon. (= not finished in the past up to now)

5 | Error Correction Correct any errors in these sentences. (Some sentences may not have any errors.)

1. My parents been here for only three years, but they like it very much.

   My parents have been here for only three years, but they like it very much.

2. I has only been here for a month, so I still get lost a lot.
3. My sister doesn't live with me anymore. She gone to live in another state.
4. My mother is very smart even though she was never been to college.
5. I've try to make a lot of new friends here, but it isn't easy.
6. My father has always give me help when I needed it.
7. I admire my professor because she have taught me to express my ideas better.

8. My parents have always give me good advice. I know I can go to them when I have a problem.

9. I want to go someplace I never been to before.

10. I miss my brother a lot. I haven't seen him for more than a year because he is been in Asia.

11. My brother doesn't know I have a new job because I not told him.

12. Computers are changed our lives in many different ways. For example, in the past, it took days or weeks to communicate with someone on the other side of the world.

2.2 The Simple Past vs. the Present Perfect

A

SIMPLE PAST

The **simple past** is a past form. We usually use it to describe an action, event, or state that was completed in the past. It is *separate from now* (the moment of speaking), as in **1 – 2**.

1 A 2009 study **showed** that a diet high in fruit and vegetables **decreased** the risk of heart failure by 37 percent.

2 In 1652, the first samples of tea **reached** England. By then, tea drinking **was** already popular in France.

PRESENT PERFECT

The **present perfect** is a present form. We usually use it to describe an action, event, or state that happened or started in the past and is *connected to now*. We are thinking of how the past affects the **present**, as in **3 – 4**.

3 Research in the last several years **has shown** that people with some diseases often **have** low levels of vitamin D. More doctors **are now having** their patients tested for their vitamin D levels.

4 He's **been** a teacher here for ten years, and the students **love** him. He definitely **deserves** a raise.

B

SIMPLE PAST

We usually use the simple past with **time expressions** that indicate a finished time period, as in **5**.

SIMPLE PAST OR PRESENT PERFECT

Some **time expressions** can be used with either the simple past or the present perfect, as in **6**.

PRESENT PERFECT

We use the present perfect with **time expressions** that indicate a time period "up until now," as in **7**.

5
- **in** 1990 / 2010 • **yesterday**
- **last** night / week / month / year
- a week / several days / a year **ago**
- **from** 1850 **to** 1860 / 7:00 **to** 10:00
- **when** I was a child / he was ten

6
- **already** • **before** • **recently**
- **always** • **ever** • **never**
- **today** • **this** week / month
- **for** two years / a long time

7
- **lately** • **so far** • **yet**
- **before now** • **until now**
- **in the past** month / few years
- **over the past** few days / year
- **(ever) since** I was a child / he was ten

With the time expressions in **6**, the choice of verb form depends on how we interpret the event and when it happened, as in **8 – 9**.

SIMPLE PAST

8a I **didn't see** him **today**.
(I didn't see him at any time today.)

9a I **didn't see** him **for ten years**.
(I didn't see him from 1990 to 2000.)

PRESENT PERFECT

8b I **haven't seen** him **today**.
(I haven't seen him at any time from this morning until now.)

9b I **haven't seen** him **for ten years**.
(I haven't seen him from ten years ago until now.)

C

CORRECT THE COMMON ERRORS (See page R-11.)

10 ✗ I have seen many things when I was a child.

11 ✗ I have been here since three weeks.

12 ✗ I lived in Toronto for three years. I really love it here.

13 ✗ He is the most optimistic person I ever know.

6 | Pronunciation Note: Simple Past or Present Perfect? Listen to the note. Then do Activity 7.

In conversation, it is sometimes difficult to distinguish **simple past** and **present perfect** verbs. Compare:

1 I **lost** my keys.   I**'ve lost** my keys.   **3** She **left**.   She**'s left**.

2 He **hurt** his leg.   He**'s hurt** his leg.   **4** They **called**.   They**'ve called**.

The other words in a conversation can help you understand a speaker's meaning.

PAST CONTEXT

5 A: Why didn't you drive home?
   B: Because I **lost** my keys.

PRESENT CONTEXT

6 A: Where are your keys?
   B: I don't know. I think I**'ve lost** them.

7 | Simple Past or Present Perfect? Listen and write the missing verbs. Use contractions. 2.2 A

1. He _'s lost_ a lot of weight.
2. They _____ to go.
3. We _____ about it.
4. I _____ that house.
5. The game _____ .
6. I _____ several movies.
7. We _____ not to go.

8. He _____ a lot of new friends there.
9. She _____ her phone number.
10. We _____ an hour for them.
11. I _____ to go there.
12. She _____ him.
13. He _____ a lot of money.
14. They _____ their house.

Talk about It Work with a partner. Choose one of the sentences above and use it to create a short conversation. Present your conversation to the class.

8 | Finished Time or Time Up Until Now? Check (✓) the time period that the **bold** expressions describe. Then complete the sentences with the correct verb form. 2.2 B

TEN FACTS ABOUT U.S. HISTORY	FINISHED TIME PERIOD	TIME PERIOD UP UNTIL NOW
1. Washington, D.C., _has been_ the U.S. capital **since 1800**. (was / has been)	☐	✓
2. **From 1790 to 1800**, Philadelphia, Pennsylvania _____ (was / has been) the capital.	☐	☐
3. The U.S. Constitution was written in 1789, but it _____ (changed / has changed) **over the years**.	☐	☐
4. **From 1800 to 1900**, the U.S. _____ (experienced / has experienced) tremendous growth.	☐	☐
5. The U.S. _____ (had / has had) one civil war **since it became a nation**.	☐	☐
6. The U.S. Civil War _____ (took place / has taken place) **in the mid-1800s**.	☐	☐

		FINISHED TIME PERIOD	TIME PERIOD UP UNTIL NOW
7.	**Ever since the Civil War began in 1861**, people _____ (argued / have argued) over what caused the war.	☐	☐
8.	**In the past 200 years**, Supreme Court decisions and laws _____ the duties of the U.S. president. (increased / have increased)	☐	☐
9.	**In the past few years**, the government _____ the (used / has used) Supreme Court for new purposes, such as determining the outcome of an election.	☐	☐
10.	**In 2005**, the president _____ a new chief justice (appointed / has appointed) of the Supreme Court, John Roberts.	☐	☐

9 | Simple Past or Present Perfect? Complete these sentences with the simple past or present perfect form of the verb. Use contractions where possible. Then check (✓) if each sentence is *True* or *False* for you. `2.2 A–B`

PERSONAL FACTS	TRUE	FALSE
1. I *'ve lived* _____ here for the past five years. (live)	☐	☐
2. I _____ to Egypt yet, but I hope to go someday. (not/go)	☐	☐
3. I _____ in junior high school from 2009 to 2012. (be)	☐	☐
4. When I was a child, I sometimes _____ trouble. (get into)	☐	☐
5. I _____ a lot of new words since I started school here. (learn)	☐	☐
6. I _____ to study English when I was 15 years old. (begin)	☐	☐
7. So far I _____ to eight different countries. (be)	☐	☐
8. Last year _____ a great year for me. (be)	☐	☐
9. I _____ anything since I had dinner last night. (not/eat)	☐	☐
10. I _____ my phone at all yesterday. (not/use)	☐	☐
11. I _____ very much over the past three years. (not/travel)	☐	☐
12. I _____ any homework since we took the test a week ago. (not/do)	☐	☐

Write about It Change the information in the false statements above to make them true for you.

I haven't lived here for the past five years.   OR   *I have lived here for the past two years.*

Write about It Write three true statements and one false statement using the time expressions in the box. Read your sentences to the class, and ask your classmates to identify the false statement.

a year ago	in 2010	over the past few years	since I was a child

10 | Simple Past and Present Perfect in Context Read this essay response. Circle the simple past verbs. Underline the present perfect verbs. Then answer the questions below. 2.2 A–B

Essay Prompt: The twentieth century saw great change. In your opinion, what was one of the biggest changes that took place in the twentieth century? Use specific reasons and details to explain your choice.

The development of new and more advanced technology (increased) rapidly in the twentieth century. In the beginning of the 1900s, people relied on horses to get around. Letters took days or weeks to arrive, and traveling to other countries wasn't easy. However, by the end of the century, people had cars, subways, and buses to get where they wanted to go. They communicated instantly by email. Travel from one country to another took hours, not months. Because of these things, I think that the growth in technology was one of the most important changes in the twentieth century.

Advances in technology have done more than make travel and communication quicker and more convenient; they have saved lives. People live much longer now than they did just 100 years ago. Some diseases that were once deadly have now been cured or can at least be treated with medications. Doctors have learned to keep individuals alive longer using new technologies.

Although technology has been very positive for the health of people, in some ways it has had a negative effect on the planet. The technological advances of the nineteenth and twentieth centuries have caused great damage to the earth's atmosphere[8]. There is also a shortage of natural resources caused by the rapid growth of the human population. Today scientists are working on ways to solve these problems. Hopefully, the twenty-first century will see the development of new technologies that can solve the problems created by the old.

QUESTIONS

1. Why does the writer use a lot of simple past verbs in the first paragraph?
2. Why does the writer use a lot of present perfect verbs in the second and third paragraphs?
3. What time expressions do you see in the sentences with the simple past or the present perfect? Write them under the correct group in this chart.

Time expressions with the simple past	Time expressions with the present perfect
in the twentieth century	

4. Is a time expression always necessary with the present perfect? Why do you think this?
5. According to the writer, how have advances in technology changed the way we live?

11 | Simple Past or Present Perfect? Complete these paragraphs with the words in parentheses. Use the simple past or present perfect form of the verb. 2.2 A–B

1. Hayao Miyazaki _____*began*_____ his career as an animator in 1963.
(begin)
He _____ his first feature anime[9] film 16 years later. Then
(direct)
he _____ a movie company of his own in 1985. In 2001,
(start)
his movie *Spirited Away* _____ Best Film at the Japanese
(win)
Academy Awards.

a scene from *Spirited Away*

[8] **atmosphere:** the mixture of gases that surrounds a planet   [9] **anime:** Japanese style of cartoons or animation

2. I _____ collecting comic books when I was young. My grandfather often took me to
   (start)
   comic book stores, and I _____ a fan ever since. I know it's not the deepest reading in the
   (be)
   world, but that's why comic books are a great stress reliever.

3. History tells us a lot about ourselves. We can see how people _____ things a hundred
   (do)
   years ago and figure out what we want to keep and what we want to change. Look at how different
   everything is today from what it was a hundred years ago. We _____ some things like
   (keep)
   schools and family but changed many other things.

4. My grandparents were born in Poland and later immigrated to the U.S. They _____ their
   (leave)
   families behind to start a new family here. I have many cousins in Poland but I _____
   (never / meet)
   them. I think it would be fun to meet them and see how they live. I would also like to see where my
   grandparents _____ in Poland and learn about what life was like for them when they
   (live)
   were growing up.

5. Bicycles _____ a great form of transportation. They're safe, fun, and economical.
   (always / be)
   Today they're also more convenient than ever. Bicycle designers _____ a way to
   (come up with)
   fold them so that now you can ride your bike to work, fold it up, and take it in with you.

6. Water shortages are a serious problem. Many areas _____ droughts[10] because of
   (experience)
   climate change. Other places have access to water, but the water is polluted.

12 | Asking Questions Read this information. What *else* do you want to know about the person? Write six
questions to ask for more information. Use the present perfect and the simple past. `2.2 A–B`

FACT FILE

Name: Edwidge Danticat
Date of Birth: 1/19/1969
Birthplace: Port-au-Prince, Haiti

Academic degrees: Received a bachelor of arts degree in French
literature from Barnard College and a master of fine arts degree from
Brown University.

Awards: Finalist for a National Book Award for novel *Krik? Krak!* and
memoir *Brother, I'm Dying*; 1995 Pushcart Short Story Prize; 1998 Oprah's
Book Club selection for novel *Breath, Eyes, Memory*.

Other: Moved to the U.S. ten years after her parents moved to the U.S.
Employment: Taught at New York University and the University of Miami.

Examples: When did you get your bachelor of arts?   *How long have you lived in the U.S.?*

Talk about It Look online for answers to the questions you wrote above. Tell your classmates what
you learned.

¹⁰ **droughts:** periods of extremely dry weather

13 | Using Different Verb Forms Complete these common job interview questions. Use the simple present, simple past, or present perfect form of the verb. Then answer the questions below. `2.2 A–B`

FREQUENTLY ASKED JOB INTERVIEW QUESTIONS

1. What goals ___*have*___ you ___*set*___ for your career? (set)

2. What _____ you _____ best about your previous job? (like)

3. What _____ your major strengths? Your major weaknesses? (be)

4. How _____ you _____ your last job? (get)

5. What _____ you _____ with your free time? (do)

6. What _____ your biggest professional achievement[11]? (be)

7. Describe the best boss you _____ in your professional career. (have)

8. _____ you ever _____ for a difficult person? (work)

9. How will the academic program and course work you _____ benefit your career? (take)

10. Where _____ you _____ to be professionally in five years? (hope)

QUESTIONS

a. Which verb form is a person most likely to use to answer each of the questions above? Is the verb form used in the answer the same as or different from the form in the question?

b. In a job interview, the interviewer often asks questions with present perfect verbs. Why is this?

Talk about It Using some of the questions above, role-play a job interview with a classmate.

14 | Error Correction Correct any errors in these sentences. (Some sentences may not have any errors.)

1. I arrived in the U.S. in 2002. Since I came here, I had trouble communicating with people because I don't speak English very well.

2. One of my favorite movies is the film *Australia*. I can't tell you how many times I saw the movie, but every time I see it, I like it better.

3. While computers have made life easier, they also made it more stressful.

4. My mother has always encouraged me to do big things. I wanted to get a job when I finished high school, but my mother told me to continue my education. She said I could do more with my life with a university education. She also encourage me to get a scholarship to pay for my education.

5. Since I came here, I have made a lot of friends, but one person in particular has helped me a lot. I have met Jennifer at the Learning Center at the beginning of the semester. She was looking for a Spanish tutor, and I needed help with my English. Since then, we got together several times a week just to talk.

6. One person who has had a great effect on my life is my father. He owns a clothing store, and I have worked with him at his store every time I have a holiday. From this experience I learn a lot about the business world.

---

[11] **achievement:** something that someone has done after trying hard

7. My parents have always encourage me to do what I want to do. When I have needed help, they support me. When I have decided to become an engineer, they helped pay for my education.

8. The Internet made communication faster and cheaper. Today you can use programs such as email or Skype to get an immediate response from someone, and they are much cheaper than a telephone call.

2.3 The Present Perfect Progressive vs. the Present Perfect

A

We form the **present perfect progressive** with **have / has** (**+ not**) **+ been +** the **-ing form of the main verb**, as in **1 – 2**.

		have (+ not)	been	verb + -ing	
1	I	**have**	**been**	**working**	all week.
	You	**'ve**			
	We / Bill and I	**have not**			
	They / My friends*	**haven't**			

		has (+ not)	been	verb + -ing	
2	He / My brother	**has**	**been**	**working**	all week.
	She / His wife	**'s**			
	It / The car	**has not**			
		hasn't			

*In writing, we don't contract nouns like *My friends* with *have*.

B

COMPARE

3a I've **been writing** for this magazine for 14 years, and I still don't have my own office.

3b I've **written** for this magazine for 14 years. I can't imagine working anywhere else.

With most verbs, we can use either the **present perfect** or the **present perfect progressive** to talk about an activity that started in the past and continues to the present, as in **3a – 3b**. However, the progressive form emphasizes that the action is ongoing.

4 I've **known** him for several years, but we don't get together very often. (NOT: I've been knowing him . . .)

5 I've **finished** three books so far, but I have four more to read. (NOT: I've been finishing . . .)

We don't normally use the present perfect progressive:
- with verbs that have a non-active meaning, as in **4**
- with verbs that describe a single point in time (such as *leave, start, stop, finish,* etc.), as in **5**

For a list of non-action verbs, see the Resources, page R-2.

C

COMPARE

6a I've **tried** to call Jack all day.

6b I've **been trying** to call Jack all day.

6c I've **tried** to call Jack **several times** today.
(NOT: I've been trying to call Jack several times . . .)

We can often use either form to describe an activity that happened repeatedly in the past and has an effect on the present, as in **6a – 6b**. However, with frequency words such as *once, twice,* or *several times,* we use the present perfect, as in **6c**.

7a Someone **has used** my name to apply for a credit card. I don't know what to do. (= started and ended in the past)

7b Someone **has been using** that credit card I lost. I don't know what to do. (= continues up to now)

We can use the present perfect to show that something started and ended in the past (but affects the present), as in **7a**. Using the present perfect progressive shows that the activity was repeated or ongoing up to now, as in **7b**.

15 | Forming the Present Perfect Progressive Complete these conversations with the present perfect progressive. Use contractions where possible. Then practice with a partner. `2.3 A`

1. A: When do you want dinner?

   B: Not for a while. I ___'ve been eating___ all day. (eat)

2. A: What _____ you _____ all day? (do)

   B: Not much. What about you?

3. A: Somebody _____ my computer. (use)

   B: How do you know?

   A: It was off when I left this morning but now it's on.

4. A: Want something to drink?

   B: I'd love a cup of coffee.

   A: I thought you didn't drink coffee.

   B: Oh, come on. I _____ coffee for years. (drink)

5. A: Have you ever heard of the movie director Sam Giorgio?

   B: Sure. He _____ films for years. (make)

6. A: I'm worried about David.

   B: Why?

   A: Well, I _____ to reach him for three days, and he hasn't called me back. (try)

   B: Hmm. That's strange.

7. A: How long _____ the children _____ television? (watch)

   B: Only for half an hour.

8. A: Have you found a new apartment yet?

   B: No, but we _____ only _____ for a few days. (look)

9. A: How's your back?

   B: It _____ better but it's still bothering me. (get)

10. A: Do your parents know where they are going on vacation?

    B: They _____ about going to visit my brother, but they haven't decided yet. (talk)

Think about It Did the speakers use any time expressions in the conversations above? Underline them.

16 | Using the Present Perfect or Present Perfect Progressive Complete these conversations with the present perfect or present perfect progressive. Use contractions where possible. (In some sentences, either form may be possible.) Then practice with a partner. `2.3 B`

1. A: Where _____have_____ you _____been_____? (be)

   B: What do you mean?

   A: I _____ all over the place for you. (look)

   B: Sorry. I just went out for a minute.

2. A: Where have you been?

   B: At the gym. Why?

   A: I _____ to reach you for the last 20 minutes. (try)

   B: Sorry, I turned my phone off.

Where have you been?

3. A: Who's Amanda talking to?

   B: Her friend in Japan.

   A: Japan! That's going to be expensive.

   B: Yeah, I know. And she _____ to him for an hour. (talk)

4. A: Is the soup ready to eat?

   B: Almost. It _____ for about 30 minutes. (cook)

5. A: Do you know Sam Bradford?

   B: Of course. I _____ him for years. How do you know him? (know)

   A: I met him last week at a conference.

6. A: _____ you _____ the remote? I can't find it anywhere. (see)

   B: I think it's on the floor next to the couch.

7. A: Are you having a good time?

   B: Absolutely. I _____ so much fun in years. (not/have)

8. A: Are you going out with us this weekend?

   B: Of course. I _____ it all week. (look forward to)

9. A: What do you think of this music?

   B: I don't know. It's OK, I guess. I _____ just never _____ jazz. (like)

10. A: Aren't you finished yet?

    B: Be patient. I _____ on it for an hour. (only/work)

11. A: Did you know that your doorbell isn't working?

    B: Oh, right. I _____ to fix it. (mean)

12. A: How long have you been studying here?

    B: Not long. My class just started a week ago. What about you?

    A: My class _____ yet. (not/start)

13. A: I hear you won your last three races.

    B: Yeah, I _____ on a lucky streak lately. (be)

14. A: Have you decided what you are going to do next year?

    B: Yeah. My parents _____ finally _____ to let me study overseas. (agree)

Think about It For which verbs in Activity 16 did you **not** use the progressive form? Why not?

Think about It Is the speaker annoyed or complaining in any of the conversations in Activity 16? Which ones?

> **F Y I**
>
> As with other progressive forms, the present perfect progressive can indicate that the speaker is annoyed or complaining.
>
> Hurry up. I**'ve been waiting** for you all afternoon, and now we're going to be late.

17 | Present Perfect or Present Perfect Progressive? Complete one sentence in each pair with the present perfect form of the verb in the box. Complete the other sentence with the present perfect progressive. Use contractions where possible. 2.3 C

1. a. I _'ve drunk_____ four cups of coffee since I got up this morning, so I shouldn't drink any more.

   b. I _____ coffee since I got up this morning. Maybe that's why I can't sit still.

   > drink

2. a. I _____ *The Call of the Wild* for a few days. I just can't put it down.

   b. I _____ *The Call of the Wild* twice. I highly recommend it.

   > read

3. a. We _____ to the gym several times this week, so we're going to take tomorrow off.

   b. We _____ to the gym since January, and we already feel a lot better.

   > go

4. a. She _____ already _____ at them twice today for making too much noise. I hope they behave now.

   b. She _____ at them all day. It's really irritating.

   > yell

5. a. I _____ to Toshi several times this week, but he still doesn't want to come.

   b. I _____ to friends about taking a trip to Istanbul this summer.

   > talk

6. a. I hope Hassan's OK. He _____ sick several times this winter.

   b. I can tell winter is coming. The nights _____ colder and colder.

   > get

7. a. My brother thinks that I _____ his phone all week, but it's not true.

   b. If you need help with your new phone, I think Carlos _____ one a few times.

   > use

8. a. I _____ you to clean your room three times this week. I'm not going to ask you again.

   b. I _____ you to clean your room all week. Could you please just do it?

   > ask

9. a. You don't need to cook anything. I _____ dinner already.

   b. I _____ phone calls all day, so now I have a bad headache.

   > make

10. a. I _____ several time to fix this computer, but it still won't work.

    b. Why didn't you answer your phone. I _____ to call you all morning.

    > try

2.4 The Past Perfect and the Past Perfect Progressive

A

We use the **past perfect** to make the order of two past events clear. The past perfect signals the earlier event. The later event is often in the **simple past**, as in **1 – 2**. We can also use the past perfect in a sentence with a time phrase, as in **3**.

earlier event	later event
1 Somebody **had left** a newspaper on a chair,	so I **took** it and **sat** down.

later event	earlier event
2 By the time Thomas **arrived** in Phoenix,	his parents **had** already **left**.

later time	earlier event
3 By the 1960s,	the population of the world **had reached** 3 billion.

4 By the time we got there, they **had eaten** all the sandwiches and **drunk** all the juice.

> Remember: We form the past perfect with *had* (+ *not*) + the past participle (-*ed* /-*en* form) of the main verb.
>
> When we use two past perfect verbs together, it's not necessary to repeat the helping verb *had*, as in **4**.

B

5 She **was** angry **because** he **had forgotten** to call.

6 He **looked as though** he'd hardly **slept** at all.

7 **When** I **met** him, he **hadn't graduated** from college yet.

8 I **met** him **before** he **graduated** from college.

9 I **met** him **after** he **graduated** from college.

COMPARE

10a We **left** when he **got** there. (He got there and then we left.)

10b We'**d left** when he **got** there. (We left and then he got there.)

We often use the past perfect in sentences with *because*, *as though*, or *when*. The past perfect signals which past event happened first, as in **5 – 7**.

The words *before* and *after* make the order of events clear. We can use the simple past after these words, as in **8 – 9**. The past perfect is not necessary.

Notice the difference in meaning when we use the simple past compared to the past perfect, as in **10a – 10b**.

C

COMPARE

11a He was sure that someone **had used** his computer.
(Someone had used his computer at least one time.)

11b He was sure that someone **had been using** his computer.
(Someone had been using his computer repeatedly or for an ongoing period of time.)

We can use the **past perfect progressive** instead of the past perfect to emphasize that an earlier activity was ongoing or repeated, as in **11b**.

> We form the past perfect progressive with *had* (+ *not*) + *been* + the -*ing* form of the main verb.

18 | Using the Past Perfect
Underline the verbs in these quotations. Then write the number *1* above the event in each sentence that took place first. **2.4 A**

QUOTATIONS ABOUT FAMILIES AND GROWING UP

1. We <u>were</u> a family who <u>had</u> ¹<u>come</u> from nothing, and now we <u>had</u> respect from French people of all sorts¹². *(Zinedine Zidane, soccer player)*

2. My grandmother had wanted to be a music teacher herself, and so she steered¹³ my mother into that profession. *(Renée Fleming, singer)*

3. My mother had meant to be an opera star or even a movie star . . . but the [birth] of a baby put an end to that. *(Renée Fleming, singer)*

4. By the time I was 15, my mother had turned me into a real clotheshorse¹⁴. *(Gloria Swanson, movie star)*

Zinedine Zidane

¹² **sorts:** different kinds
¹³ **steer:** to guide

¹⁴ **clotheshorse:** someone who loves clothes

5. My mother had been a country and western singer, but when she moved out to Hollywood she found it very difficult to get work, so when I was born they put me into dance classes and singing classes as soon as I could walk, actually. *(Morgan Brittany, actor)*

6. My mother had always taught me to write about my feelings instead of sharing really personal things with others, so I spent many evenings writing in my diary, eating everything in the kitchen and waiting for Mr. Wrong to call. *(Cathy Guisewite, cartoonist)*

7. I had traveled 10 states and played over 50 cities by the time I was 4. *(Sammy Davis, Jr., entertainer)*

8. Interestingly enough, I met and had classes from several professors that my father had had many years before. *(Daniel J. Evans, politician)*

9. My mother was a very literate person who had educated herself. *(Lynn Johnston, cartoonist)*

10. Music was around in my family in two ways. My mother would occasionally sing to me, but I was mostly stimulated[15] by the classical music my father had left behind. *(Tom Glazer, musician)*

RESEARCH SAYS...

Common verbs used with the past perfect include:

be	have
come	leave
do	make
go	take

CORP

Think about It What is similar about the form of the verbs you labeled "1" in Activity 18?

Write about It Think of a way to complete these sentences with information about yourself. Then share your sentences with your classmates.

By the time I was 15, _____ .

I _____ by the time I was 4.

19 | Using the Past Perfect with *Because* and *As Though* Match the beginnings of these sentences with their endings. `2.4 B`

REASONS AND CONTRASTS

1. His clothes were wet because he __*h*__   a. had run there.

2. She quit her job because her boss ____   b. had run over him.

3. He didn't call me because he ____   c. had been empty for years.

4. I felt sick last night because I ____   d. had criticized her.

5. He was ashamed because he ____   e. had insulted him.

6. He was angry because she ____   f. had eaten too much at dinner.

7. His back hurt so much he felt as though a car ____   g. had been rude to his parents.

8. The house looked as though it ____   h. had fallen in the river.

9. She was breathless as though she ____   i. had hurt herself.

10. The child cried out as though she ____   j. had lost my phone number.

Talk about It Work with a partner. Think of another way to complete each sentence above.

"His clothes were wet because he had forgotten to bring an umbrella."

[15] **stimulate:** to energize

20 | Sentences with _When_ Write the number *1* above the event that happened first in each sentence. Then rewrite the sentence using *when* and the past perfect. `2.4 B`

1. She called me after I left the house. (with "1" above "left")

   When she called me, I had already left the house.

2. After 20 minutes went by, we finally got a table at the restaurant.

3. The sun came up before we did all our work.

4. I still have the watch my father gave me before I left home.

5. After the smoke cleared, we saw the house in the distance.

6. After my cousin got her PhD, she got a job in the high-tech industry.

7. Everyone got out of the bus before it burst into flames.

8. After the last person left, we went inside and had lunch.

9. After the plane landed, the person next to me suddenly started laughing.

FYI

When we give a series of past events in chronological order, we can usually just use the simple past because the order of events is clear.

Tamae Watanabe **was** 63 years old when she **climbed** Mount Everest for the first time. Then, when she **was** 73 years old, she **climbed** it again.

21 | Simple Past or Past Perfect? Complete this article. Use the simple past or the past perfect form of the verb. `2.4 A–B`

PATSY CLINE: 1932–1963

FANS[16] LOVED THIS YOUNG COUNTRY MUSIC STAR

Patsy Cline, born Virginia Patterson Hensley, _____recorded_____ her first
(1. record)

big hit[17] in 1957. It was called "Walkin' After Midnight" and it became No. 2

on the list of country music hit recordings and No. 16 on the list of most

popular music.

   Patsy _____ for many years to make that first successful record.
(2. work)

She _____ singing when she was a young girl in her hometown of
(3. begin)

Winchester, Virginia. Patsy sang anywhere she could. If there was a stage, she

tried to sing there. She sang at weddings, dances, restaurants, and other public

places. She earned $8 a night. Her friends and family said she worked hard to

improve her singing and make a successful record.

   In 1947, she _____ if she could perform on a local radio show.
(4. ask)

People loved her performance, and the radio station soon _____ her
(5. invite)

back to perform again. Patsy continued to perform and in 1954 she _____
(6. win)

a country music competition near her home. She _____ 22 years old. She
(7. be)

was then invited to sing on a country music TV show in Washington, D.C. She also

performed on radio shows in Virginia and recorded some records.

---

[16]**fans:** people who like someone or something very much   [17]**hit:** very successful

Patsy Cline _____ (8. appear) on a national television show in New York City. It was on this show in 1957 that millions of people first _____ (9. hear) her sing. She sang a song she _____ (10. recently / record) called "Walkin' After Midnight." This performance helped make her career a major success. Patsy continued to record more songs, and soon made another major hit called "I Fall to Pieces." By this time, her voice _____ (11. already / become) something special. Patsy _____ (12. learn) to control not only the sound of her voice, but also the feelings expressed in her songs. People especially loved her slow, sad love songs like "I Fall to Pieces." "I Fall to Pieces" became Patsy's first No. 1 hit, and she was now a major star. She also _____ (13. begin) performing at the Grand Ole Opry, a famous country music theater in Nashville, Tennessee.

The people who knew her after she _____ (14. become) a star say Patsy Cline was a great friend. Many young musicians _____ (15. become) important stars with her help. At the age of 30, Patsy Cline was killed in a plane crash on March 5, 1963. Earlier, she _____ (16. take part) in a special show in Kansas City to raise money for the family of a country music performer who recently _____ (17. die), and she was flying home to Nashville. Thousands of people _____ (18. come) to her funeral near her hometown. Ten years after her death, she became the first female musician elected to the Country Music Hall of Fame.

Think about It Answer these questions about the article in Activity 21.

1. Which event in each pair of sentences took place first? Check (✓) the sentence.
   a. ☐ She recorded her first big hit.
      ☐ She worked hard for many years to make a successful record.
   b. ☐ She appeared on a national television show.
      ☐ She recorded the song "Walkin' After Midnight."
   c. ☐ She recorded the song "I Fall to Pieces."
      ☐ She learned to control the sound and feelings in her songs.
2. What had Cline accomplished by the time she was 30 years old?

Write about It Use these time expressions to write four sentences about Patsy Cline. Make three sentences true and one false. Read your sentences to a partner, and let your partner identify the false statement.

1. (by 1957) _____

   _____

2. (in 1957) _____

   _____

3. (by 1963) _____

   _____

4. (in 1963) _____

   _____

22 | Using the Past Perfect Progressive Underline the past perfect progressive verbs in these sentences. Then decide if the action was ongoing or repeated. Check (✓) your answers. **2.4 C**

	ONGOING	REPEATED
1. After I <u>had been working</u> at the bank for a few years, I decided I wanted a more interesting job.	✓	☐
2. Before I moved to Australia, I had been teaching myself English.	☐	☐
3. I had been drawing pictures the whole time I was in Italy, so when I returned home, my parents were very pleased.	☐	☐
4. I had been feeling a little ill, but I didn't think it was anything serious.	☐	☐
5. I had been thinking for a while how much I missed my family.	☐	☐
6. When she joined the band, the other members had been playing together for years.	☐	☐
7. When I got home in the morning, I discovered that my parents had been waiting up all night.	☐	☐
8. The car that hit the tree had been going too fast.	☐	☐
9. We had been going there every Saturday for the past six months.	☐	☐
10. According to the police, the driver had been texting just before he went off the road.	☐	☐

Think about It Look at the past perfect progressive verbs you underlined above. Which part of each verb shows the "perfect" meaning? Which part shows the "progressive" meaning?

23 | Error Correction Correct any errors in these sentences. (Some sentences may not have any errors.)

1. My father grown up in the U.S., but his mother always speaks to him in Spanish when he was a baby.

   My father grew up in the U.S., but his mother had always spoken to him in Spanish when he was a baby.

2. In the story, the main character lose a lot of money.
3. My parents have never gone abroad, but they wanted their children to see the world.
4. By the 1900s, traveling became easier because there were better roads.
5. I have been studying English for many years before I came here.
6. I liked to sing when we got together.
7. By the time I was born, my parents got married for three years.
8. I didn't pass my first exams even though I been studying every night for weeks.
9. My cousin was living in this country for five years when his father died.
10. I was very lonely when I arrived here because I left all my friends.

A

FUTURE PERFECT

	will (+ not)	have	past participle	
I You He She It We They	will 'll will not won't	have	finished	by the end of the day.

1

We form the **future perfect** with **will** (+ **not**) + **have** + the **past participle of the main verb**, as in **1**.

2 By next October, we **will have lived** here for ten years. It's hard to believe.

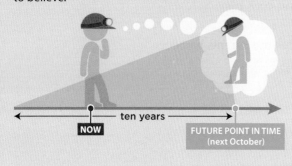

ten years

NOW

FUTURE POINT IN TIME (next October)

3 By the time they finish building the new school, the town **will have spent** $10 million.

4 I'm sure I **will have talked** to her **by the end of the week**.

We use the future perfect when we imagine ourselves at a future point in time. From this future viewpoint, we describe an event that will be completed by or before that time, as in **2 – 4**.

Notice that we often describe the future point in time using *by*. We may use:

• a time clause with *by*, as in **3**
• *by* + a time word or phrase, as in **4**

WARNING! We use a present form in the time clause even though we are talking about a future time, as in **3**.

FUTURE PERFECT PROGRESSIVE

5 By 5 o'clock, I **will have been driving** for three hours. I think I'll be ready for a stop.

6 By 6, we **will have been waiting** for an hour.

The **future perfect progressive** is very rare. It emphasizes that an activity will be ongoing up to a future point in time (and may continue after that time), as in **5 – 6**.

We form the future perfect progressive with *will* (+ *not*) + *have* + *been* + the *-ing* form of the main verb.

24 | Noticing Future Perfect Forms Underline the future perfect forms in these predictions. Then decide how likely each prediction is. Check (✓) *Very Likely, Somewhat Likely,* or *Not Likely.* **2.5 A**

FUTURE PREDICTIONS	VERY LIKELY	SOMEWHAT LIKELY	NOT LIKELY
By the year 2050,			
1. the population of the world <u>will have reached</u> 10 billion.	☐	☐	☐
2. the world will have become paperless[18].	☐	☐	☐
3. we will have found a cure for all cancers.	☐	☐	☐
4. we will have stopped using coal, oil, and gas for energy.	☐	☐	☐
5. we will have had another world war.	☐	☐	☐
6. the number of fish in the oceans will have decreased by a large amount.	☐	☐	☐
7. people will have lived on Mars for many years.	☐	☐	☐
8. the world will have become a better place.	☐	☐	☐

[18] **paperless:** using computers instead of paper

Talk about It What else will have happened by the year 2050? Share ideas like the ones in Activity 24 with your classmates.

Think about It Look back at the diagram of the future perfect in Chart 2.5 on page 60. Can you draw similar diagrams to show the meaning of sentences 1, 3 and 4? How would they be different from the diagram for sentence 2?

25 | Using Future Perfect Forms Complete these sentences with the future perfect form of the verb in parentheses. `2.5 A`

The Average Person

1. By 18 months of age, most children _____*will have learned*_____ 5 to 20 words—mostly nouns. By 24 months, the vocabulary of most children _____ to between 150 and 300 words. (learn/expand)

2. In a 65-year lifespan, the average person _____ 9 years watching television. (spend)

3. By the age of 20, most people _____ video games for 10,000 hours. (play)

4. The average person _____ to 10,500 hours of music by the end of his or her teen years. (listen)

5. The average person _____ for 91,250 hours by the end of his or her life. (work)

6. By the time you stop working, you _____ ten different jobs. (have)

7. By the time you retire, you _____ careers three to five times. (change)

8. By the age of 65, the average person _____ 2 million television commercials. (see)

9. By age 70, the average person _____ a distance equal to four times around the world. (walk)

10. By the end of his or her life, the average person _____ 7,163 baths. (take)

Talk about It What kind of "average person" are the statements above about? Do you think all of these statements describe your life?

Write about It What are some other things that the average person will have done by the time he or she is 65? What are some things he or she won't have done? Write four to six sentences.

The average person will probably have eaten a lot of junk food by age 65.
The average person probably won't have traveled into space.

Talk about It What will you have accomplished in 10 years? In 20 years? Tell your classmates.

"In 10 years, I will have finished college and found a job."

2.6 Using Perfect Forms in Speaking

A

STARTING A CONVERSATION

1 What **have** you **been** up to?

2 **Haven't** we **met** before?

3 **Haven't** I **seen** you somewhere before?

ENDING A CONVERSATION

4 **It's been** good to talk to you.

5 **I've enjoyed** talking with you.

6 **It's been** great seeing you again.

We often use the **present perfect** when we ask general questions or make general statements. General questions and statements are common when we are trying to start a conversation, as in **1 – 3**, or end a conversation, as in **4 – 6**.

B

OMITTING HELPING VERBS AND SUBJECTS

7 You **seen** my purse? (= Have you seen my purse?)

8 He always **been** this selfish?
(= Has he always been this selfish?)

9 How you **been**? (= How have you been?)

10 **Been** married long? (= Have you been married long?)

In casual conversation, speakers sometimes omit the helping verbs *have* and *has* from the present perfect, as in **7 – 9**. This is especially common with the main verb *be*.

Speakers may also omit the subject, as in **10**.

C

COMPARE

11a Computers **have gotten** a lot better.
(= Computers have become a lot better.)

11b **Have** you **gotten** your paycheck yet?
(= Have you received your paycheck yet?)

11c **I've got to** leave. (= I must leave. It is necessary.)

11d **I've got** some money. (= I have some money.)

Be careful not to confuse these forms:

• *have / has gotten* (the present perfect of *get*), as in **11a – 11b**

• the phrasal modal *have / has got to* (similar in meaning to *must* or *have to*), as in **11c**

• *have / has got* for possession, as in **11d**

26 | Starting a Conversation Complete these conversation starters with the words in parentheses. Use the present perfect form of the verb. 2.6 A

CONVERSATION STARTERS

1. _Have you been_____ keeping busy? (you/be)

2. _____ any good movies recently? (you/see)

3. How long _____ here? (you/live)

4. _____ any good books lately? (you/read)

5. _____ any good music recently? (you/hear)

6. _____ at any good restaurants lately? (you/eat)

7. _____ any trips this year? (you/take)

Talk about It Use one of the questions above to start a conversation with a partner. Ask more questions to continue your conversation. Then use one of the sentences in the box to end your conversation.

A: Hi, James.
B: Hey, Hassan. How are you? Have you been keeping busy?
A: Well, actually, it hasn't been so bad lately. . . .

> It's been good to talk to you.
> I've enjoyed talking with you.
> It's been great seeing you again.

◀))) 27 | Omitting *Have* and *Has* in Conversation Listen and write the missing words in each casual conversation. After you finish listening, write the complete form of each sentence. **2.6 B**

CASUAL CONVERSATION

1. A: _You always lived_ here?

   B: No, I lived in California before this.

2. A: How long _____ here?

   B: Not long. Just a few minutes.

3. A: _____ OK?

   B: Yeah, not bad.

4. A: How are you?

   B: _____ better.

5. A: _____ here before?

   B: No. Have you?

6. A: Where _____?

   B: At the library.

7. A: _____ outside yet?

   B: No, why?

   A: It snowed last night.

8. A: _____ any good movies lately?

   B: No, I haven't. What about you?

   A: No, I haven't either.

9. A: _____ about Amanda?

   B: No, what?

   A: She's going to marry some guy named Joe.

   B: _____ him long?

   A: Oh, I don't know. A year or so.

10. A: _____ to James recently?

    B: No, why?

    A: I think he has a surprise for all of you.

COMPLETE FORM

1. A: _Have you always lived here?_

   B: No, I lived in California before this.

2. A: _____

   B: Not long. Just a few minutes.

3. A: _____

   B: Yeah, not bad.

4. A: How are you?

   B: _____

5. A: _____

   B: No. Have you?

6. A: _____

   B: At the library.

7. A: _____

   B: No, why?

   A: It snowed last night.

8. A: _____

   B: No, I haven't. What about you?

   A: No, I haven't either.

9. A: _____

   B: No, what?

   A: She's going to marry some guy named Joe.

   B: _____

   A: Oh, I don't know. A year or so.

10. A: _____

    B: No, why?

    A: I think he has a surprise for all of you.

Talk about It Practice the conversations above with a partner.

◀))) 28 | Dictation Listen and write the sentences you hear. Then check (✓) the correct meaning. **2.6 C**

	PRESENT PERFECT OF GET	NECESSITY	POSSESSION
1. _____	☐	☐	☐
2. _____	☐	☐	☐
3. _____	☐	☐	☐
4. _____	☐	☐	☐

	PRESENT PERFECT OF GET	NECESSITY	POSSESSION
5. _____	☐	☐	☐
6. _____	☐	☐	☐
7. _____	☐	☐	☐
8. _____	☐	☐	☐

Talk about It Work with a partner. Choose one of the sentences in Activity 28 and use it to create a short conversation. Present your conversation to the class.

2.7 Using Perfect Forms in Academic Writing

A

WRITING INTRODUCTORY STATEMENTS

1 I **have had** a lot of problems since I came here. During my first month here, I **had** to find a job and a place to live. I **didn't have** anyone to help me, and I **wasn't** familiar with apartment hunting here.

2 You probably **have seen** garlic in the kitchen. It **is** about the size of a small onion, and it **has** a strong flavor. But people **prize** garlic for more than its taste. Doctors in ancient Rome **recommended** garlic for 61 different problems.

Writers often use the **present perfect** to make a general introductory statement or to ask a general question at the beginning of a piece of writing. They then use the **simple present** or the **simple past** to give examples and details, as in **1 – 2**.

B

ESSAY WRITING

3 **Essay Prompt:** Discuss the influence that advertising **has had** on your life.

4 **Answer:** Advertising tries to get us to buy things we don't really need and do things we don't really want to do. Thanks to my parents, I **have learned** to stand up to the power of advertising. . . .

Essay test questions and prompts often use the present perfect to ask how something in your past has affected you or how something has changed, as in **3**.

When you answer, it is often a good idea to use the same form in the first paragraph of your essay, as in **4**.

C

SCIENCE AND RESEARCH WRITING

5 Scientists **have already established** that good-looking people find it easier to get a job and are generally viewed as smarter and more likable. Now a new study **has found** that even parents favor more attractive children.

6 Researchers **observed** interactions between parents and children and **found** that prettier children **received** more attention and care.

Writers use the present perfect to describe important findings and accomplishments in science or research. Using this form emphasizes that the results of an experiment are still true and important now, as in **5**.

When writers describe the specific steps in an experiment, however, they often use the simple past, as in **6**. This is because they are describing actions that took place at a finished time in the past.

D

GIVING BACKGROUND INFORMATION

7 Tori McClure took on the adventure of a lifetime when she attempted to be the first woman to row across the Atlantic Ocean. McClure was no stranger to adventure. She **had** already **skied** across Antarctica and **done** a lot of mountain climbing.

Writers sometimes use the **past perfect** to give background information to support an idea or explanation, as in **7**.

Remember: When we use two past perfect verbs together, it's not necessary to repeat the helping verb *had*.

29 | Supporting General Statements Complete these essay outlines. Give two examples to support each general statement. Provide two or three details to explain each example. Pay special attention to the form of the verbs you use. `2.7 A`

1. GENERAL STATEMENT: Computers have made life easier.

    Example 1: _You can go shopping without ever leaving your home._

    Detail 1: _I now buy most of my books online instead of at a bookstore._

    Detail 2: _Last year I bought most of my holiday gifts online._

    Detail 3: _Some people buy their groceries online. I haven't tried this yet, but it would save me a lot of time._

    Example 2: _____

    Detail 1: _____

    Detail 2: _____

    Detail 3: _____

2. GENERAL STATEMENT: The automobile has created serious problems.

    Example 1: _____

    Detail 1: _____

    Detail 2: _____

    Detail 3: _____

    Example 2: _____

    Detail 1: _____

    Detail 2: _____

    Detail 3: _____

3. GENERAL STATEMENT: Telephones and email have made communication between people less personal.

    Example 1: _____

    Detail 1: _____

    Detail 2: _____

    Detail 3: _____

    Example 2: _____

    Detail 1: _____

    Detail 2: _____

    Detail 3: _____

Write about It Choose one of the general statements above and develop your ideas into a cohesive paragraph or essay.

30 | Answering Essay Questions Think of two ways to begin a response to each essay question using the same verb form that is in the question. Then answer the questions below. `2.7 B`

ESSAY QUESTIONS

1. Have your attitudes changed much in the last few years? Explain.

   My attitudes have changed significantly in the last few years.
   OR
   Over the past five years, I have lived in three different countries. This experience has changed the way I think about my own country.

2. Has the automobile been harmful to our society? Discuss.
3. Television has made the U.S. a nation of watchers, not doers. Do you agree or disagree with this statement?
4. In your opinion, what invention has caused the most important changes in our society? Explain.
5. Have computers made our lives easier or more complicated? Explain.
6. Discuss the influence that advertising has had on your life or the lives of your friends.
7. In what ways has information technology changed work and working practices in the past ten years?

QUESTIONS

a. Why is it a good idea to begin your response to an essay question using the same verb form?
b. Do you always need to do this? Why or why not?

31 | Analyzing Verb Choices Circle the present perfect verbs in these excerpts from newspaper articles. Underline the simple past verbs. Then explain why you think the writer used each form of the verb. `2.7 C`

Does Vitamin C Help Fight the Common Cold?

A large review of medical trials[19] has concluded that Vitamin C is largely ineffective in the prevention and treatment of the common cold.

In 30 trials with 11,350 participants who took at least 200 milligrams of vitamin C a day, researchers found that vitamin C did not reduce the occurrence[20] of the common cold. Vitamin C did slightly reduce the duration and severity[21] of cold symptoms, but the effect was very small.

Lecture or Interactive Teaching? New Study of an Old Issue

Professors have lectured for centuries. But how effective is lecturing to students compared to working with them?

A new study compared two classes of a beginning physics course at the University of British Columbia in Canada. There were more than 260 students in each section. Both were taught by popular and experienced professors.

[19] **trials:** experiments
[20] **occurrence:** something that happens
[21] **severity:** the strength of something

Humans Have Been Making Art for a Lot Longer Than We Thought

A new study has revealed that Spain's El Castillo Cave contains the oldest known cave paintings in Europe, with a handprint dating back 37,300 years.

Instead of testing the paint's age, a team of British and Spanish researchers measured the age of the stone that had formed around the drawings.

Scientists Able to Study Atmosphere of Planet Outside Our Solar System

Scientists have detailed the atmosphere of a planet outside our solar system. The team, based in Chile, was able to measure the amount of carbon monoxide on *Tau Bootis b*—one of the first "exoplanets" discovered back in 1996. They were able to measure the atmosphere without relying on a "transit" of the planet—where it passes in front of its star. That is important as, up to now, astronomers and scientists have had to rely on transits to measure the atmosphere.

32 | Providing Background Information Read these sentences from student essays. Then write another sentence giving background information to support the first one. Use a past perfect form in your new sentence. `2.7 D`

SENTENCES FROM STUDENT ESSAYS

1. Her grandfather was a great businessman.
   He had started his own business at age 24, and he had helped his brothers start their own businesses.

2. The athletes were in great shape when they got to the competition.
   _____

3. He was nervous when he moved here by himself.
   _____

4. When he was a young man, he witnessed something that changed his life.
   _____

5. She was tired, but her first days in this new country were very exciting.
   _____

6. It was a real accomplishment when her mother finally graduated from college.
   _____

7. When she was a child, her father didn't know how to act around her.
   _____

8. When he came to this country, he couldn't get a job.
   _____

A | DISCUSSION Look in a magazine or newspaper for a paragraph that uses a variety of verb forms. Read the paragraph to your classmates. Together, identify the verb forms and suggest why the writer used each form.

Eating Well: Less Science, More Common Sense

Food is life. Food **gives** us energy to **do** everyday activities, but not all food ← simple present

is created equal. Studies **have shown**, for example, that children who eat a nutritious

breakfast do better in school than those with a poor diet. Research **has** also **shown** . . . → present perfect

B | WRITING Write three opinions about someone you know. Then give three reasons or examples to support each opinion. Think carefully about whether you need to use the simple present, simple past, present perfect, past perfect, or some other verb form.

Opinions	Examples
My sister Elena is very smart.	*1. She has several academic degrees.* *2. She has been a teacher for ten years.* *3. She graduated from college at the top of her class.*

C | WRITING Choose one of the essay topics in Activity 30, and write an essay in response. Think carefully about whether you need to use the simple present, simple past, present perfect, past perfect, or some other verb form in your writing.

D | INTERVIEW Choose an interesting or unusual job. What kinds of skills, knowledge, or experience would a person need in order to do this job? Write your ideas. Then make a list of interview questions for this job, and practice interviewing a partner.

Job: a cook on a sailboat
Skills/Experience: has experience on sailboats, likes to cook, has cooked for large groups of people . . .
Interview Questions: Have you ever been on a sailboat? Do you like to cook? Have you ever cooked in a very small kitchen? Have you ever cooked for a large group of people?

2.8 Summary of Perfect Forms

SIMPLE

PRESENT PERFECT	I You We They	have gone. 've gone. have not gone. haven't gone.
	He She It	has gone. 's gone. has not gone. hasn't gone.

PAST PERFECT	I You He She It We They	had left 'd left had not left hadn't left	by 6.

USES We use the present perfect to describe something that:
- started in the past and continues to the present
- happened in the past but has an effect on the present

USES We use the past perfect to show that one event in the past took place before another past time or event.

PROGRESSIVE

PRESENT PERFECT PROGRESSIVE	I You We They	have been waiting. 've been waiting. have not been waiting. haven't been waiting.
	He She It	has been waiting. 's been waiting. has not been waiting. hasn't been waiting.

PAST PERFECT PROGRESSIVE	I You He She It We They	had been waiting. 'd been waiting. had not been waiting. 'd not been waiting. hadn't been waiting.

USES We use the present perfect progressive to emphasize that something happened:
- repeatedly in the past and has an effect on the present
- continuously from a time in the past up until now

USES We use the past perfect progressive to show that an earlier activity in the past was ongoing or repeated.

FUTURE

FUTURE PERFECT	I You He She It We They	will have finished. 'll have finished. will not have finished. won't have finished.

FUTURE PERFECT PROGRESSIVE	I You He She It We They	will have been sleeping. 'll have been sleeping. will not have been sleeping. won't have been sleeping.

USES We use the future perfect to describe something that will be completed by or before a time in the future.

USES We use the future perfect progressive to emphasize that something will be ongoing until a time in the future.

3 Modals

If we are not ashamed to think it, we should not be ashamed to say it.

—MARCUS TULLIUS CICERO,
ROMAN STATESMAN
(106–43 BCE)

Talk about It What does the quotation above mean? Do you agree or disagree?

WARM-UP

A | Match the beginnings and endings of the quotations. Which quotation is the most memorable to you? Why?

Famous Quotations

1. A man **should** look for what is, ___*f*___

2. You **must** be the change ___

3. If you want to understand today, ___

4. An inch of time is an inch of gold, ___

5. No one **would** have crossed the ocean ___

6. While we **may not be able to** control all that happens to us, ___

7. The less one **has to** do, ___

a. you wish to see in the world.
   (Mahatma Gandhi, Indian statesman)

b. if he **could** have gotten off the ship in a storm.
   (Charles Kettering, U.S. inventor)

c. the less time one finds to do it in.
   (Lord Chesterfield, British statesman)

d. we **can** control what happens inside us.
   (Benjamin Franklin, writer, scientist, and statesman)

e. but you **cannot** buy that inch of time with an inch of gold. *(Chinese proverb)*

f. and not for what he thinks **should** be.
   (Albert Einstein, physicist)

g. you **have to** search yesterday. *(Pearl S. Buck, U.S. novelist)*

B | The words in green in the quotations above are simple modals. The words in blue are phrasal modals. Based on the examples, check (✓) *True* or *False* for these sentences.

	TRUE	FALSE
1. Simple modals are followed by the base form of the verb.	☐	☐
2. A simple modal changes form after different subjects.	☐	☐
3. A phrasal modal changes form after different subjects.	☐	☐
4. We can place a simple modal next to a phrasal modal in a sentence.	☐	☐
5. Some simple modals and phrasal modals have similar meanings.	☐	☐

C | Look back at the quotation on page 70. Identify any modal forms.

3.1 Overview of Simple Modals and Phrasal Modals

We can use **simple modals** and **phrasal modals** (+ the base form of a main verb) to express different beliefs and attitudes about what we say.

A

1 He **can speak** English very well already.

2 He **has to take** an English class. It's a requirement.

3 He really **should take** an English class.

4 You **might want to take** an English class, too.

5 **Could** you please **help** me with my English homework?

6 They're **allowed to take** English if they want to.

7 He's **going to take** English 101 next fall.

8 He **may take** an English class in the fall—I'm not sure.

9 She **should be** here by 7:00. She left an hour ago.

We use simple modals and phrasal modals to express different social purposes, such as:

- ability, as in **1**
- obligations, as in **2**
- advice, as in **3**
- softening advice, as in **4**
- requests, as in **5**
- permission, as in **6**

We also use these forms to express how sure or likely an event is, as in **7 – 9**.

B

10 Students **should get** a good night's sleep before exam day.

11 She **may be** at work right now. I'm not sure.

12 He **must be taking** a shower. I can hear the water.

13 They **might arrive** at 7:00 instead of 6:00. Their flight is late.

14 I'll **take** those to the office for you.

15 She **has to get** up at 5:00 tomorrow. Work starts at 6:00.

16 We **won't be able to meet** on Monday. Anne is sick.

Most **simple modals** can refer to things that are:

- generally true, as in **10**
- true or in progress at the moment, as in **11 – 12**
- future actions, as in **13 – 14**

When we use modals to refer to past time, we use verb forms in a special way. See Charts 3.3, 3.5, 3.6, and 3.9.

Unlike simple modals, **phrasal modals** include a helping verb, *have* or *be*. We show time by using the correct past, present, or future form of the helping verb, as in **15 – 16**.

 GO ONLINE

1 | Identifying Simple Modals in a Passage Underline each simple modal and its main verb in this passage. **3.1 A**

Choosing a Major . . . and a Career

At many universities, students <u>can choose</u> from dozens of majors and minors. Nowadays, when they are making that important decision, students often focus on the subjects that can provide the best careers because they want to be sure they have jobs after they graduate. But some experts say that students should think about doing something they love instead. Research has shown that students may not do well at studies they don't care about. Before you choose a major, ask yourself: Would you really enjoy doing this as a career? If you don't have a strong interest in the topic, you might want to consider a different choice. For the moment, it may not be clear where your interest will lead you, but passion[1] inspires hard work, which often leads to success.

[1] **passion:** a strong feeling of excitement for something

2 | Identifying Speakers' Attitudes Match each statement on the left with a description on the right. **3.1 A**

1. "They'll bring the potato salad." __e__
2. "He might not remember how to get here." ____
3. "I have to call my sister tonight." ____
4. "You can stay out until 11 p.m." ____
5. "You might want to try a different approach." ____
6. "You shouldn't eat so much sugar." ____
7. "She can do advanced mathematics." ____
8. "Could you please send me a copy of that?" ____

The speaker is:

a. giving advice
b. not sure about something
c. making a request
d. saying that something is necessary
e. sure about something
f. softening advice
g. talking about ability
h. giving permission

3 | Identifying Time References Circle the simple modal and phrasal modal forms in these conversations. Then check (✓) the time that the modal(s) refer to. **3.1 B**

	PRESENT/ GENERAL TIME	FUTURE
1. A: Are you calling the store? B: Yes, but they're not answering. They (must be closed).	✓	☐
2. A: Where are you going on vacation? B: We might go to Hawaii.	☐	☐
3. A: Seems as if Alex always eats pizza for lunch. B: He must really like it.	☐	☐
4. A: I can't decide which one to buy. B: You should get the blue one.	☐	☐
5. A: We won't be able to get reservations this late. B: Let's go tomorrow, then.	☐	☐
6. A: People shouldn't be so quick to judge each other. B: That's true.	☐	☐
7. A: Is he here? I don't hear any noise from his room. B: He might be sleeping.	☐	☐
8. A: The company may have to change its hiring policies. B: I hope so. We'll see what happens.	☐	☐
9. A: What does the handbook say? B: It says, "Employees must report any problems to the proper authorities."	☐	☐
10. A: You can come over after lunch if you want to. B: Great! I'll see you then.	☐	☐
11. A: Did you hear that Sheila quit yesterday? B: Wow, I can't believe that. I thought she liked it here.	☐	☐
12. A: How does your brother feel? Any better? B: Yeah, actually, I think he may be feeling pretty good. He went to work today.	☐	☐

4 | Usage Note: Simple Modal vs. Phrasal Modal Sentence Patterns Study the note. Then do Activities 5–6.

We use the base form of a main verb after simple modals.

Phrasal modals include *to* before the base form of a main verb.

STATEMENTS

	subject	modal / phrasal modal	base form of main verb	
1	I	can(not)	understand	the problem.
2	The manager	is (not) supposed to	tell	us about the problem.

***YES/NO* AND *WH-* QUESTIONS**

	wh- word	modal / first helping verb	subject	other parts of phrasal verb	base form of main verb	
3		Should	we	—	meet	at 7?
4		Are	you	allowed to	leave	early?
5	When	can	we	—	go	home?
6	How	is	she	able to	communicate	with him?

5 | Error Correction Correct any errors in these sentences. (Some sentences may not have any errors.)
`3.1 A`

1. You must to think about that a little more carefully.

   You must think about that a little more carefully.

2. Sal should calls the office in the morning.
3. When do I should place the order?
4. They can to see both sides of the argument.
5. I think the corporations should trying a little harder to solve this problem.
6. Passengers don't must stand near the doors when they are opening and closing.
7. Do students supposed to eat and drink in the library?
8. That color might not is the best choice for you.
9. When we can take another break?
10. If they practice, they might to do a little better next time.

6 | Forming Negatives and Questions Read these sentences. Write a new sentence with a similar meaning. Use the **bold** modal form. (More than one answer may be possible.) `3.1 A`

1. I don't believe I **can** come over tonight.

   I can't come over tonight.

2. Did someone say we **could** wait here?
3. Do you think I **will** be able to finish later?
4. I don't believe the plan **will** work.
5. I don't think I **may** be ready for the test.
6. Is it true that you **can** eat more and lose weight?
7. I don't think we **should** go out tonight.
8. Is it possible that we **could** talk now?

3.2 Willingness and Intent

A

STATEMENTS OF INTENT WITH *WILL*

1 A: I can't understand this problem.
B: **I'll help** you.

2 A: You were late again today.
B: **I'll be** on time tomorrow, I promise.

3 A: Do you want to stay and finish?
B: No, **I'll come** back tomorrow.

4 **In Academic Writing: I will describe** the experiment in more detail later.

In informal conversation, we use **will** to make offers, promises, or general statements of intent, as in **1 – 3**. We usually contract *will* to **'ll**.

Speakers and writers also use *will* in academic contexts to describe something they intend or plan to do later, as in **4**.

For more information on the use of *will*, see Unit 1, page 23.

B

PRESENT AND FUTURE COUNTERFACTUAL STATEMENTS WITH *WOULD*

5 **I'd help** you, but I just don't have any time.
(= I want to help you but I can't.)

6 Following this plan **would reduce** greenhouse gases in the atmosphere.
(= This plan hasn't been followed.)

A counterfactual statement can describe something that will not happen. We use **would** (**not**) to describe:

- something that someone wants to do, but can't, as in **5**
- the results of something that has not been done, as in **6**

We often contract *would* to **'d**.

C

PAST COUNTERFACTUAL STATEMENTS WITH *WOULD*

7 We **would have gone** to the show, but we didn't have enough money.
(= We didn't go to the show.)

8 I **would have stayed** later, but I got too tired.
(= I didn't stay later.)

We can also use counterfactual statements to describe something we were willing to do in the past, but did not actually do, as in **7 – 8**. We use **would** (**not**) + **have** + the **past participle of a main verb**.

In past counterfactual statements, it is possible to contract *I would* to *I'd*, but it is not common.

GO ONLINE

---

7 | Making Statements with *Will* Work with a partner. Complete each conversation with a statement of intent, promise, or offer, using *I'll*. Then practice with your partner. `3.2 A`

1. A: Can you bring something for the potluck dinner?

   B: Sure. _I'll make a salad._

2. A: Amal is late. I wonder where he is.

   B: I don't know. _____

3. A: How will I know what time to show up?

   B: Don't worry. _____

4. A: Bye! It was nice seeing you again.

   B: You too! _____

5. A: Please don't tell anyone I said this.

   B: I promise. _____

6. A: How are you going to find a job?

   B: Well, _____.

7. A: I don't think Sara can do this alone.

   B: That's OK. _____

a potluck dinner

8. A: I don't have time to make all those copies.

   B: I have time. _____

9. A: Are you sure you can go? You look tired.

   B: I _____. I promise.

Think about It Is each statement you wrote in Activity 7 an offer, promise, or general statement? Write *O* (offer), *P* (promise), or *G* (general statement) next to each one.

8 | Using *Will* to State Intentions Write eight meaningful sentences telling what an essay will be about. Use *will*, a verb from Column 1, and phrases from Columns 2 and 3. (Many different answers are possible.) `3.2 A`

SENTENCES FROM ACADEMIC ESSAYS

1	2	3
address describe discuss explore focus on outline refer to	how the virus spreads the effects of an unhealthy diet the government's policies the important points of the novel the process of cell division the relationship between the two countries the research on carbohydrates two of Shakespeare's sonnets[2]	below in depth[3] in the following section in this paper throughout this essay

I will focus on two of Shakespeare's sonnets in depth.

Talk about It Share the sentences you wrote above with a partner. Which of these subjects is each one about?

biology	English literature	nutrition	political science

A: I will focus on two of Shakespeare's sonnets in depth.
B: That's about English literature.

9 | Distinguishing *Will* from *Would* Complete these conversations with *'ll* (will) or *'d* (would). Then practice with a partner. `3.2 A–B`

1. A: Your essay was due today.

   B: I know. I ____ do it tomorrow, when I have time.

2. A: You need to work on your essay.

   B: I know. I ____ do it today, but I don't have time.

3. A: Tomas couldn't make it?

   B: No, I'm sorry. He ____ be here if he could.

4. A: I can't decide what to order.

   B: I ____ have the chicken. That looks delicious.

5. A: Where is Alexander?

   B: He ____ be here any minute.

6. A: I have no interest in that movie.

   B: Really? I ____ love to see it.

7. A: Where are the extra blankets?

   B: Hmm. Ask Rafa. He ____ know.

8. A: I'm sorry we're out of time.

   B: Me too. I ____ stay longer if I could.

Think about It What helped you choose between *would* and *will* in the sentences above? Share ideas with your classmates.

---

[2] **sonnets:** 14-line poems   [3] **in depth:** deeply

10 | Using *Would* to Describe Possible Results The left column of this chart contains proposals for new laws. Use *would* to write possible positive and negative results of each law. **3.2 B**

Proposals for new laws	In favor	Against
1. Make cigarettes illegal.	*Stores would not sell cigarettes, so people would smoke less.*	*Some people would smoke anyway.*
2. Require all citizens to vote.		
3. Don't allow cars in downtown areas.		
4. Allow advertising on school websites.		
5. Increase taxes on gasoline.		
6. Stop the sale of candy at children's schools.		
7. Spend public money on a high-speed railway.		
8. Raise the minimum wage.		

Talk about It Share your ideas above with a partner. Do you agree about the possible results?

11 | Using Counterfactual *Would Have* Complete these conversations with *would have* and the past participle of the verb in parentheses. Then practice with a partner. **3.2 C**

MAKING EXCUSES

1. A: You know, I was in Toronto last weekend.

   B: I didn't know you were in town! I _____would have invited_____ you over for dinner. (invite)

2. A: We missed you at the concert last night.

   B: I _____, but I had a lot of homework. (go)

3. A: I didn't see you in class yesterday.

   B: I know. I _____, but I didn't hear my alarm go off. (come)

4. A: Selena was here yesterday.

   B: Oh, I didn't know that. I _____ her. (call)

5. A: How'd you do on the test?

   B: Not too well. I _____ more, but I left my book in the library. (study)

6. A: I walked all the way over here.

B: Why didn't you call me? I _____ you up! (pick)

7. A: We're out of apples.

B: Oh, I didn't know. I _____ some when I was at the store. (buy)

8. A: Whew! That was hard!

B: Why didn't you tell me? I _____ you. (help)

12 | Using *Will*, *Would*, or *Would Have* Complete the conversations below with *will*, *would*, or *would have* and the correct form of a verb from the box. Use contractions where you can. (More than one answer is possible.) Then practice with a partner. `3.2 A–C`

be	call	come back	eat	have	like	pay	stay

CAFÉ CONVERSATIONS

1. A: Sorry I'm late. I ___*would have called*___ you, but my

    phone is dead[4].

    B: That's OK.

2. A: So what are you getting?

    B: I think I _____ the garden salad.

3. A: This place is kind of expensive.

    B: Don't worry. I _____ for this.

4. A: Are you leaving already?

    B: I _____, but I have a class in 15 minutes.

5. A: This place is fantastic.

    B: Yeah, I know I didn't know about it or I _____

    here before.

6. A: Could you excuse me for a moment? I _____ right back.

    B: Of course.

7. A: So what did you think of this place?

    B: It was great. I _____ absolutely _____ again.

8. A: I think I'll get dessert.

    B: I _____ some pie, but I don't have time.

Think about It What helped you choose between *will*, *would*, and *would have* in the conversations above? Share ideas with your classmates.

---

[4] **dead:** not working or not charged

3.3 Possibility with *Can* and *Could*

<table>
<tr><td rowspan="3" align="center">A</td><td>POSSIBILITY WITH CAN AND COULD

1 Spinal cord injuries can severely damage the central nervous system.
(= Severe damage is possible, but it doesn't always happen.)
2 This treatment could really help you.
3 The manager can do an inspection whenever he wants to. He could do an inspection today.</td><td>We use can(not) and could to suggest that something is possible or impossible, as in 1 – 3. We often use:

• can to talk about general possibilities
• could to talk about the possibility of a particular thing happening in the present or future

WARNING! Don't confuse this meaning of could with the meaning of past general ability: In the old days, people couldn't stay in touch so easily.</td></tr>
</table>

<table>
<tr><td rowspan="2" align="center">B</td><td>PAST POSSIBILITY (COUNTERFACTUAL)

4 A: That driver wasn't even looking. She could have hit us!
B: Thank goodness she didn't.
5 A: Sorry I forgot to tell you about the movie!
B: That's OK. I couldn't have gone anyway. I was working.</td><td>Sometimes we use could (not) have + the past participle of a main verb to say that something was possible in the past but didn't happen, as in 4.

We also use it to say that something was not possible in the past, as in 5.

WARNING! We also use could (not) have to express a past possibility that is NOT counterfactual. This use of couldn't have is discussed in Chart 3.5.</td></tr>
</table>

13 | Using *Can* for Possibility The verbs underlined in the first paragraph of this passage are too definite. Rewrite them using *can*. In the second paragraph, use your own ideas to decide which verbs should use *can*. `3.3 A`

WHAT CAN WE EAT?

We all want to be healthy and to look good, and we all know that exercise and a healthy diet are essential. But specific advice about food and nutrition <u>is</u> overwhelming[5] at times. Research shows that high-fat foods
can be
like red meat <u>raise</u> cholesterol[6], which leads to heart disease. And refined carbohydrates[7], like white flour and white rice, <u>raise</u> blood sugar levels. Many foods, like milk, nuts, eggs, and fish, <u>cause</u> serious allergies.

In addition to these more serious problems, some people think that foods like onions, garlic, and cabbage give you bad breath. Others believe that eating meat and refined carbohydrates leads to bad body odor. Tomatoes, citrus fruits, and chocolate make your stomach hurt. Coffee keeps you awake, but dairy products and bananas make you sleepy. If you drink soda and eat candy, you damage your teeth.

[5] **overwhelming:** so much that you don't know how to react to it
[6] **cholesterol:** a substance found in blood, fat, and most body tissues
[7] **carbohydrates:** sugars or starches found in foods such as bread, rice, and potatoes

Talk about It What can people eat to stay healthy? Share your ideas with your classmates.

Write about It What do you know about the effects of these behaviors? Write two or three sentences about each topic with *can*. If necessary, research your topic online.

drinking plenty of water	eating a lot of vegetables	exercising every day

Exercising every day can increase your energy level.

14 | Using Counterfactual *Could Have* Complete these sentences with *could(n't) have* and the past participle of the verb in parentheses. `3.3 B`

1. We _____ could have seen _____ the movie last night, but we weren't in the mood. (see)

2. It was a beautiful day, so we _____ a walk on the beach. (take)

3. I don't know where my parents are, but they _____ very far. (go)

4. I _____ you last weekend. I wasn't in town. (help)

5. I _____ to the office, but I decided to stay home. I just wasn't feeling well. (go)

6. We _____ soccer today. We just didn't have time. (play)

7. I didn't know the restaurant was going to be crowded. We _____ at home instead. (eat)

8. The concert was fantastic. I _____ to them for another hour. (listen)

9. I _____ Jon, but I didn't think he'd want to come with us. (call)

10. Thank you for all your help. I _____ this without you. (do)

Write about It Write two sentences about plans you had that didn't happen. Use *could(n't) have*.

15 | Present Possibility vs. Past Possibility Which sentences refer to the present or future, and which refer to the past? Circle the modal forms and check (✓) the correct column. `3.3 A–B`

	PRESENT/FUTURE POSSIBILITY	PAST COUNTERFACTUAL
1. A fall from that height could result in a broken arm.	☐	☐
2. He could have hurt himself.	☐	☐
3. We could get a raise this year.	☐	☐
4. The new policies could have a good effect on our neighborhood.	☐	☐
5. They say it could rain.	☐	☐
6. He could have been a very important man.	☐	☐
7. You really could have told me about this before.	☐	☐
8. She could take the day off to relax.	☐	☐

Think about It For each counterfactual sentence above, what *didn't* happen?

Write about It Rewrite the present and future sentences above using a past form. How does the meaning change?

16 | Error Correction Correct any errors in these sentences. (Some sentences may not have any errors.)

1. I'm so tired that I can fall asleep right now.
2. It's too bad he didn't try a little harder yesterday. He could win that race.
3. My brother could got a job anywhere after he graduated.
4. I would buy tickets, but I just couldn't afford them.
5. There is a lot left to do. This job can take seven or eight more days.
6. The team could have went to the finals this year, but Rodriguez broke his leg.
7. The neighbors could move out later this year.
8. In many areas around the world, earthquakes can causing major damage.

3.4 Degrees of Certainty about the Present and Future

We can use **simple modals** and **phrasal modals** to show how certain we are that something is true or is likely to happen, as in **1 – 15**. We often provide evidence or a reason for what we are saying. Notice that some modals show different degrees of certainty in positive and negative sentences.

		POSITIVE	NEGATIVE
STRONGER CERTAINTY	*will/won't*	1 She'll be home at 6:00. Her schedule never changes.	3 She won't get home early. She has too much work to do.
	be going to/ be (not) going to	2 She's going to be home at 6:00. She told me so.	4 She's not going to come home early.
	*must/ must not**	5 She's not here, so she must be at work.	6 She must not be at her desk— I called and she didn't answer.
	can't	—	7 She can't be home already. I saw her at work five minutes ago.
	couldn't		8 She couldn't be home already. I just saw her.
EXPECTATION	*should/ shouldn't*	9 She should be at work by now. It usually takes her 30 minutes.	10 She shouldn't be home yet. She usually works until 7:00.
WEAKER CERTAINTY	*may/ may not**	11 She may be there already— she left before we did.	14 She didn't get paid. She may not have enough money to go out.
	*might/ might not**	12 They might visit tomorrow. I have to call to find out.	15 They might not visit tomorrow after all.
	could	13 I don't know him. He could be a new student, I guess.	—

*We don't usually contract *must not*, *may not*, and *might not*.

 ONLINE

17 | Identifying Degrees of Certainty Circle the Speaker B response that indicates a higher degree of certainty. 3.4 A

1. A: Why haven't they gotten here yet?
   B: They may not know about the time change.
   B: They must not know about the time change.

2. A: I wonder if he's coming to the lecture.
   B: He'll come.
   B: He might come.

3. A: Do you think we'll get a raise next year?
   B: We could.
   B: Oh, we're going to get a raise.

4. A: Does he have enough money?
   B: He may.
   B: He should.

5. A: I don't think I know her.

  B: You must know her! You took a class together.

  B: You might. You took a class together.

6. A: I think we should get Diana the chocolate cake.

  B: She won't like chocolate. Let's get vanilla.

  B: She might not like chocolate. Let's get vanilla.

7. A: That's Koji's car.

  B: It couldn't be Koji's. His car is in the shop.

  B: It could be Koji's. It looks just like it.

8. A: Why is he so tired?

  B: He shouldn't be. He slept for ten hours.

  B: He might not sleep well.

Talk about It Practice the conversations in Activity 17 with a partner. Choose either answer. Try to also show certainty or uncertainty with your voice, facial expression, and body language.

Think about It Which of the statements in Activity 17 are about the future? Which are about the present?

18 | Expressing Degrees of Certainty Write responses to these statements. Use a variety of modals to show different degrees of certainty. Try to provide a reason as well. **3.4 A**

GIVING REASONS

1. A: Why is the classroom empty?

  B: _It's almost 4. The class must be over already._____

2. A: Why is everyone outside?

  B: _____

3. A: Why is the store closed?

  B: _____

4. A: Why does Tara look so confused?

  B: _____

5. A: Why does the soup taste funny?

  B: _____

6. A: Why isn't there anything good on TV?

  B: _____

7. A: Why is Arif reading so much?

  B: _____

8. A: Why is Sarah so pale[8]?

  B: _____

Think about It Take turns reading the responses you wrote above to a partner. Do your partner's reasons match the modal he or she used? Could you use a different modal with the same reason?

Write about It Which of the responses you wrote above could you rewrite using *maybe*?

> **WARNING!**
>
> *Maybe* is an adverb similar in meaning to *may*. We usually use *maybe* at the beginning of a sentence.
>
> He **may have** a new address.
> **Maybe he has** a new address.

---

[8] **pale:** having skin that is lighter than usual

19 | Writing about Degrees of Certainty Choose five topics from this box and write sentences about events in your life. Use modals to show how certain you are about the events. Try to add an explanation or reason for your statements. Then share some of your statements with the class. 3.4 A

a celebrity	events in the news	technology	the weather	your country
a sporting event	politics	the environment	your city	your school

My school might raise tuition rates next year. They are building a new library, so they must need money.

3.5 Past Certainty

We can use **modal** + *have* + the **past participle of a main verb** to express probability in the past, as in **1 – 8**. As with present and future modals, we often give evidence or a reason for our degree of certainty.

A

		POSITIVE	NEGATIVE
STRONGER CERTAINTY	*must have/ must not have**	**1** They **must have seen** us. We were only a few feet away from them.	**2** She's not up yet. She **must not have set** her alarm clock.
	couldn't have	—	**3** It was the first time you met her. You **couldn't have known** about her problems.
WEAKER CERTAINTY	*may have/ may not have** *might have/ might not have** *could have*	**4** I'm not sure why he went home early. He **may have been** tired. **5** You **might have seen** him. Did you notice a guy in a blue jacket? **6** The temperature differences **could have affected** the data, but we're not sure if they did.	**7** She **may not have noticed** the stop sign. It was very dark. **8** They didn't do the project correctly. They **might not have understood** the directions. —

*We don't usually contract *must not*, *may not*, and *might not*.

ONLINE

20 | Identifying Time Frames Circle the modal forms. Then check (✓) the time frame. 3.5 A

GLOBAL WARMING	PAST	PRESENT	FUTURE
1. We might see more extreme weather in the coming years.	☐	☐	☑
2. The earth's temperature may have risen too much to stop the effects of climate change.	☐	☐	☐
3. Past human activity must have helped change the climate.	☐	☐	☐
4. Natural weather cycles could also have contributed.	☐	☐	☐
5. The Arctic ice should continue to melt at the same speed.	☐	☐	☐
6. New energy policies could affect the speed of global warming.	☐	☐	☐
7. Although the earth is warmer, the weather can be colder in particular areas.	☐	☐	☐
8. Climate may be difficult to predict, so scientists have developed complicated models to help them with predictions.	☐	☐	☐

Think about It What kinds of information in each sentence above helped you identify the time frame?

21 | Degrees of Certainty with Modals Match the statements with the responses. Then practice with a partner. 3.5 A

PHONE PROBLEMS

1. I can't find my phone. ____
2. My phone keeps freezing⁹. ____
3. Whose phone is this? ____
4. She never answered my text message. ____
5. He's not answering. ____
6. I forgot to call you! ____
7. My battery is almost dead. ____
8. I must have left her five messages! ____

a. He might have turned off his ringer.
b. It must be Tina's.
c. You must have forgotten to charge it.
d. It's OK. You couldn't have anyway. I left my phone at home.
e. She may not have gotten it.
f. You might need to update the software.
g. She may not check her voicemail.
h. It should be in your bag. I saw you put it there.

Think about It Which responses above refer to past time? Which refer to present or future time?

Talk about It With a partner, write a short conversation (five to six sentences) about a problem with a phone. You can use one of the statements in the left column above to start the conversation. Read your conversation to another pair.

A: I must have left her five messages!
B: She might be busy.
A: It shouldn't take that long to check her voicemail.
B: Well, maybe she doesn't want to talk to you.
A: Gee, thanks.

> **FYI**
>
> We can also use **should**(*n't*) or **can't** + **have** + **past participle** to talk about past certainty, but it is less common.
>
> She **should have called** by now. I wonder where she is.
>
> He **can't have called** them already! It's too early.

22 | Usage Note: Different Uses of *Could* and *Could Have* Read the note. Then do Activity 23.

We can use **could** (*not*) and **could** (*not*) **have** to express many different present, past, or future meanings.

PRESENT OR FUTURE TIME

A Possibility: This class **could** really **help** you with your writing.
B Weaker certainty: He **could be** at work now, but it's pretty early. He's probably still at home.
C Strong negative certainty: She **couldn't be** the manager. She's too young!

PAST TIME

D General ability: When I was a kid, I **could understand** Spanish.
E Possibility (counterfactual): We **could have visited** my parents but we didn't have time.
F Weak certainty: I don't know how many people were at the lecture. There **could have been** 20 or 30 maybe.
G Strong negative certainty: They **couldn't have fit** more people in the lecture hall. It was really crowded.

⁹**freezing:** stopping movement; becoming still

23 | Identifying Meanings of *Could* Label each sentence *A, B, C, D, E, F,* or *G* according to the meanings in Activity 22. `3.5 A`

1. I guess I didn't study enough. I could have passed that test easily. _E_

2. They say it could snow tomorrow. ____

3. I don't see the dictionary. Malai could have taken it to school. ____

4. He could lift a hundred pounds easily when he was younger. ____

5. I'm not sure who ate the cookies. It could have been my brother. ____

6. Don't eat that. It could be spoiled. ____

7. I could start working tomorrow. ____

8. She could have a lot of money in the bank, but I doubt it. ____

9. In those days, you could travel many miles without seeing a city. ____

10. She's exhausted. She couldn't have worked any harder last night. ____

11. She couldn't have written that. That's not even her handwriting. ____

12. That looks like my sister, but it couldn't be her. She doesn't even live in this town. ____

13. We really got lucky. That accident could have a caused a lot of problems. ____

14. He couldn't have any money left now. He spent a fortune last night! ____

I didn't study enough.

24 | Using *Could/Could Have* Work with a partner. Write B's responses. Use *could* or *could have* and your own ideas. Then practice with your partner. `3.5 A`

1. A: I wonder why Marcos is so happy today.
   B: _____

2. A: What should we do tomorrow?
   B: _____

3. A: Who is that man?
   B: _____

4. A: Did you go home last weekend?
   B: _____

5. A: What were you good at when you were a kid?
   B: _____

6. A: Is that woman a doctor?
   B: _____

7. A: What happened to the computer?
   B: _____

8. A: What was that noise?
   B: _____

Talk about It Look at the responses you wrote above. Could you have written a response in a different time frame or with a different meaning of *could/could have*? Discuss the possibilities with a partner.

25 | Error Correction Correct the errors with modals in these sentences. Some sentences have errors in form, and some have errors in meaning.

1. They might go to the celebration last night, but I didn't see them there.

2. He could have gone to work tomorrow. He's not very sick at all.

3. I don't know where your keys are. They must be in the kitchen.

4. It's a good thing she raised so much money. Otherwise, she could lost the election.

5. It's 9 a.m. The store can be open, but I'm not sure.

6. This book is torn. The baby could do it. He was looking at it this morning.

7. We saw someone who looked like you on Friday, but we knew it can't be you.

8. They may not had enough time to finish yesterday.

3.6 Advisability with *Should*, *Ought To*, and *Had Better*

A

ADVISABILITY IN THE PRESENT/FUTURE

1 A: You **should get** a haircut.
B: Yeah, I probably **should**.

2 Future research **should investigate** the effects of air pollutants.

3 A: I think that we **ought to have** a choice about this.
B: I agree. We **should**.

4 You **had better get** ready for this storm. It's going to be bad.

5 I'd **better hurry** or I'm not going to get there on time.

We use the modal *should* (*not*) to give and request advice. We use *should* in informal speech, as in **1**, and in academic writing, as in **2**.

Ought to has a similar meaning to *should*, but we use it much less frequently. We usually use *ought to* in positive statements, as in **3** (but not usually in negative or question forms).

Had better (*not*) is a very strong form of advice. We often use it to say that something should happen soon, as in **4**. We also often use it to talk about things we should do ourselves, as in **5**.

We usually contract *had better* to *'d better* in speaking.

B

ADVISABILITY IN THE PAST (COUNTERFACTUAL)

6 The other team members **should have asked** her for her opinions. Instead, they ignored her.

7 I'm sorry about waking you up. I **shouldn't have called** so early.

8 **Should** I **have contacted** Greg? I didn't call him because I thought someone else was going to.

Should + *have* + the **past participle of a main verb** means that something was advisable, but didn't happen, as in **6**.

We often use *should* / *shouldn't have* to express regret, as in **7**. We can also ask questions with *should* / *should have*, as in **8**.

It is possible to use *ought to have* but it is not very common: *They ought to have helped him, but they didn't.*

 ONLINE

26 | Giving and Requesting Advice Complete the questions and advice with *should* (*not*) + a verb from the box. Include a subject if necessary. Then practice with a partner. **3.6 A**

ACADEMIC ADVISOR

1. Advisor: You need to take Writing for Business and Economics 101.

   Student: Which one _____*should I take*_____ first?

2. Student: When _____ for an internship[10]?

   Advisor: You really should do that in your junior year.

STORE CLERK

3. Clerk: You _____ our accessories[11] table. Everything is on sale.

   Customer: That's OK. I'll just take this.

4. Customer: Where _____ to return an item?

   Clerk: You can do that at the register.

CUSTOMER SERVICE AGENT

5. Customer: Where _____ this item?

   CSA: I can help you with that.

6. Customer: What number _____ for technical service?

   CSA: I'll transfer you.

apply
bring
call
change
contact
go
look at
put
return
take

FYI

In speaking, we often use ***really*** together with ***should*** when we give advice.

A: He really **should see** a doctor.

B: I know. I'm worried about him.

---

[10] **internship:** a job that a student has for a short time in order to get experience

[11] **accessories:** small clothing items, like jewelry or belts

BANK TELLER

7. Customer: What documents _____?

   Teller: You just need your ID and your account number.

8. Teller: We'll stop the check, but you _____ the merchant.

   Customer: OK. I'll do that.

REPAIRPERSON

9. Customer: How often _____ the oil?

   Repairperson: Every three months.

10. Repairperson: You _____ too much laundry in the dryer.

    Customer: I'll keep that in mind.

Write about It Write one more question you could ask each person in Activity 26. Role-play asking and answering your questions with a partner.

27 | Expressing Opinions with *Should* or *Ought To* Write a positive and a negative opinion statement in response to each question. Use *should (not)* or *ought to*. `3.6 A`

ADVICE FOR SUCCESS

1. How should colleges prepare students for the future?

   Colleges ought to provide students with a general education and teach them a variety of skills. They shouldn't just focus on career preparation.

2. How should parents prepare their children for the future?
3. What should a new restaurant do to attract customers?
4. What should teachers do to keep students interested in class?
5. What should people do to meet new friends?
6. What should people do to maintain contact with old friends?
7. What should cities do to attract tourism?
8. What should airlines do to improve the customer experience?
9. What should people do to be happy?
10. How should a person spend his/her early twenties?

Talk about It Share the statements you wrote above with a partner. Do you agree?

28 | Using *Had Better* Write a response to each statement with *had ('d) better* or *had ('d) better not*. `3.6 A`

1. A: It looks like it's going to rain.

   B: _We'd better get inside._

2. A: What did your father say?

   B: _____

3. A: Tom's boss is pretty mad at him right now.

   B: _____

4. A: Marta got sick at that restaurant.

   B: _____

5. A: It looks like the store is going to close soon.

   B: _____

6. A: That might be my boss calling.

   B: _____

7. A: The president of my bank was just caught in a big scandal[12].

   B: _____

8. A: Uh-oh. I forgot about my sister's birthday tomorrow.

   B: _____

FYI
Often we use **had better** to report what other people have said.

He called me and told me **I'd better get** moving.

We may use *had better* when someone else is putting pressure on us.

29 | Expressing Regret with *Should(n't) Have* Write one or two regrets for each situation. **3.6 B**

REGRETS

1. Tony stayed up late watching TV and overslept this morning.

   He shouldn't have stayed up so late. He should have turned off the TV earlier.

2. Kara didn't read the directions carefully and failed the test.
3. Sarah turned her application in late, so she didn't get an interview.
4. Kate lost touch with her best friend. Now she misses her.
5. John didn't accept the job offer. Now the company is doing really well.
6. Mika didn't write down the address. Now she doesn't know where to go.
7. Angela bought a new TV last week. This week the price dropped by 20 percent.
8. Khalid left his laptop on a table in the library. Somebody took it.

Talk about It Tell a partner your own regrets. Talk about two things you should or shouldn't have done when you were younger and two things you should or shouldn't have done recently.

30 | Using Past and Present Advisability with *Should* Complete these conversations with *should/shouldn't* or *should have/shouldn't have* and the verb in parentheses. Then practice with a partner. **3.6 A–B**

1. A: You forgot to buy bananas.

   B: Darn! I _____*should have made*_____ a list before I went to the store. (make)

2. A: Are you going shopping?

   B: Yeah, in a few minutes. I _____ a list first, though. (make)

3. A: I'm so glad we finally talked.

   B: Me too. We _____ this earlier. (do)

4. A: Ken didn't look very happy this morning.

   B: I know. Maybe I _____ him about the layoffs. (tell)

5. A: You don't look very well.

   B: I'm not. I _____ that fish. (eat)

6. A: My interview is tomorrow. I'm so nervous!

   B: You _____ so much. You'll do fine. (worry)

[12] **scandal:** something that is shocking, upsetting, or unacceptable

7. A: Sounds as if you guys had a lot of fun.

    B: We did. You really _____ with us. (come)

8. A: We're not going to get there on time.

    B: I know, I know. We _____ earlier. (leave)

Think about It What helped you choose between *should* and *should have* in the conversations in Activity 30? Share ideas with your classmates.

31 | Usage Note: Different Uses of *Should* and *Should Have* Read the note. Then do Activity 32.

We can use **should** and ***should have*** to express many different present, past, or future meanings.

PRESENT OR FUTURE TIME

A Advisability: She's sick. She **should go** home and rest.
B Expectation (not met): He left work an hour ago. He **should be** here by now. Where is he?
C Expectation (strong certainty): Ask Benny that question. He **should know** the answer.

PAST TIME

D Past advisability (counterfactual): We **should have brought** more cash. They don't take credit here.

32 | Identifying Uses of *Should* and *Should Have* Label each sentence *A*, *B*, *C*, or *D* according to the meanings in Activity 31. `3.6 A–B`

1. You're under a lot of stress. You should relax and take some time for yourself. ____

2. I'm sorry we missed the beginning of the show. We should have come earlier. ____

3. What have you been doing all day? You should be finished with your work by now! ____

4. Try SuperMart. They should have the brand you're looking for. They have a huge selection. ____

5. I've been saving all year. I should have more money than this! ____

6. You should have seen the moon last night. It was beautiful. ____

7. She should call her father. I think he's lonely. ____

8. Just wait here, please. He should be available in a couple of minutes. ____

33 | Pronunciation Note: Modal + *Have* Listen to the note. Then do Activity 34.

When we use *have* after a modal, we usually pronounce it as /əv / or /ə/.

1 She **couldn't have** known.	*sounds like*	"She couldn'tuv known."	or	"She couldn'tuh known."
2 They **should have** called earlier.	*sounds like*	"They shoulduv called earlier."	or	"They shoulduh called earlier."
3 I **would have** told him.	*sounds like*	"I woulduv told him."	or	"I woulduh told him."

You don't have to use the reduced form, but you need to understand it in conversation.

34 | Using *Could Have*, *Would Have*, and *Should Have* Listen and write the complete verb for each sentence. Then listen again and repeat. `3.6 B`

1. Marcia ___*should have come*___ to dinner with us.

2. She _____ enough money.

3. I _____ with you.

4. You _____ out for the team.

5. They _____ ready.

6. He _____ that.

7. She _____ that.

8. You _____ surprised.

9. He _____ me.

10. She _____ that.

11. You _____ me.

12. Carlos _____ it.

Write about It Work with a partner. Write a short conversation for each sentence in Activity 34. Make clear what happened or did not happen in each situation. Read your conversations to another pair.

1. *A: Marcia should have come to dinner with us.*
   B: She couldn't. She had to work.

3.7 Obligation and Prohibition

We can use **must** (**not**), (**don't / doesn't**) **have to**, and **has / have got to** for strong obligation (requirement) or prohibition, as in **1 – 10**.

	EXAMPLES OF OBLIGATION / PROHIBITION	USE
must (not)	**1** Employees **must sign in** when they arrive. (= necessary) **2** Visitors **must not enter** the employee area. (= not allowed)	• Rare in speaking, but common in writing. • Usually refers to present or general time. • The question form is not common.
has to / have to **had to**	**3** They just **have to accept** his decision, whether they like it or not. (= necessary) **4** You **don't have to bring** your laptop. Computers will be provided. (= not required) **5 Does** she **have to talk** so loudly? **6** I **had to accept** the decision. **7** He **didn't have to go**. **8** We'll **have to leave** early today.	• Common in speaking, but rare in writing. • Can refer to past, present, or future time. • Used in positive, negative, and question forms.
has got to / **have got to**	**9** You've just **got to be** tough. (= necessary) **10** She's **got to finish** soon. Time is almost up! (= necessary)	Usually only used: • in speaking. • in simple present positive statements. • in the contracted form ('s / 've got to).

COMPARING OBLIGATION / PROHIBITION TO CERTAINTY

We use **must** (**not**), **have to**, and **have got to** for obligation / prohibition, but we can also use them to express strong certainty, as in **11 – 15**.

	EXAMPLES OF CERTAINTY	USE
must (not)	**11** You **must be** new here. (present time) **12** The new land **must not have looked** very promising to the settlers. (past time)	• Commonly used in speaking to express strong certainty. • Also commonly expresses strong certainty in academic writing. • Can refer to past, present, or future time.
has to / have to **had to**	**13** He's not here so he **has to be** at work. (present time) **14** She **has to have written** it. I recognize her handwriting. (past time)	• Common in speaking, but rare in writing. • Can refer to past or present time. • Usually only used in positive statements.
has got to / **have got to**	**15** He's **got to be** there already—I saw him leave hours ago. (present time)	Usually only used: • in speaking. • in simple present positive statements. • in the contracted form.

See Charts 3.4 and 3.5 for more information on the use of modals for certainty.

35 | Using *Must* for Obligation in Writing Work with a partner. Complete these sentences with *must* (*not*) + a verb from the box. Then match each sentence with a source below. `3.7 A`

SENTENCES FROM WRITTEN SOURCES

be	reach
boil	reconsider
cut	resign
have	retake
pay	use

_e_ 1. For this reaction to occur, temperatures _____must reach_____ 80 degrees.

____ 2. The potatoes _____ dry before you put them in the oil.

____ 3. The government _____ the sales tax on luxury items. We need the revenue[13], and the tax only affects people who can afford it.

____ 4. Hundreds of students _____ the test this year.

____ 5. Students _____ university computers in unlawful[14] ways.

____ 6. The human body _____ a good supply of oxygen.

____ 7. The administration _____ the campus parking rules.

____ 8. The mayor is terrible and _____ immediately.

____ 9. The cream sauce _____ or it will be ruined.

____ 10. Undergraduates _____ their full tuition by October 15.

◄ **80°** Celsius

a chemical reaction

a. cookbook	b. political blog	c. school newspaper	d. school policy handbook	e. science text

Write about It Choose two or three sources from the box above. Search online for sentences from that source that use modals for obligation.

36 | Using *Have To* Complete the conversations with a form of (*not*) *have to* and an appropriate verb. `3.7 A`

1. A: _____ late last night?

   B: Yeah, I did. Jason never showed up for his shift.

2. A: Where's Sun-Hee?

   B: She left about an hour ago. She _____ to class.

3. A: What is Carlos so happy about?

   B: He _____ the final exam tomorrow because he has an A in the class.

4. A: _____ the manager _____ tonight?

   B: Yeah, he does. And he's not happy about it!

5. A: Thank you. That's so nice! You _____ me a present.

   B: I know, but I wanted to.

6. A: I _____ the window. It's so hot in here.

   B: I wish you wouldn't. It's really cold outside.

7. A: I'm so glad I _____ that medicine anymore.

   B: Oh, that's good. It was making you sick, wasn't it?

8. A: Emma has been going to the gym a lot lately.

   B: She _____ in shape for the big game.

Think about It Which two sentences above could be restated with *have got to*?

[13] **revenue:** money that a government or company receives   [14] **unlawful:** not legal

37 | Usage Note: Other Ways to Express Obligation and Prohibition Read the note. Then do Activities 38–40.

> We can express obligation or prohibition with other **phrasal modals**.
>
> **OTHER WAYS TO EXPRESS OBLIGATION AND PROHIBITION**
>
> *be required to* + base form of main verb (similar to *have to*)
> **1** Jillian is required to attend all practices and home games during the season.
> **2** Participants were required to rate their agreement with each statement on a 6-point scale.
>
> *be not allowed to* + base form of main verb (similar to *must not*)
> **3** You're not allowed to bring food on the plane.
> **4** We were not allowed to enter the building.
>
> *be supposed to* + base form of main verb (similar to *should*)
> **5** Students are supposed to take three years of a foreign language.
> **6** I was supposed to take a test yesterday, but I stayed home because I was sick.
>
> > We use these forms to describe external obligations or prohibitions—things that come from an outside authority. These phrasal modals do not describe internal obligations such as *I must try to be more positive* or *She has to think about the effects of her actions.*

38 | Using *Be Required To* and *Be Not Allowed To* These activities are required or permitted at many workplaces. For each activity, write a "work rule" for employees using *be required to* or *be not allowed to*. Choose a job from the box or use your own ideas. **3.7 A**

WORK RULES

1. accept gifts from students

   Teachers are not allowed to accept gifts from students.

2. call a substitute for absences
3. eat or drink in the work area
4. shred[15] many documents
5. talk about work to people outside the company
6. wash their hands before returning to work
7. wear jewelry or loose clothing
8. wear protective clothing

> JOBS
> chemists
> engineers
> factory workers
> government employees
> machine operators
> public service workers
> restaurant servers
> teachers

Write about It Compare the sentences you wrote above with a partner. Then write two more rules for another job using your own ideas.

39 | Using *Be Supposed To* Complete these sentences with information that is true for you. Include the correct form of *be supposed to* if one isn't provided. **3.7 A**

1. When I was younger, I _____, but sometimes I didn't.
2. Recently, I _____, but I didn't because _____.
3. I _____ every day, but sometimes I don't.
4. Tomorrow I _____.
5. My _____ was supposed to _____, but _____.
6. My _____ is supposed to _____, but _____.
7. _____ were supposed to _____, but _____.
8. The _____ was supposed to _____, but _____.

[15] **shred:** to cut or tear into small pieces (usually with a machine called a shredder)

40 | Expressing Prohibition and Obligation Write a sentence for each rule. Use *must, have to, be required to, be not allowed to,* or *be supposed to*. Then compare with a partner. `3.7 A`

RULES FOR STUDENTS

1. try your best to succeed

   You must try your best to succeed.

2. bring all materials to every class
3. don't get discouraged if you fall behind
4. don't copy writing from the Internet
5. be considerate and polite to classmates
6. make wise decisions about how to spend your time
7. believe in yourself
8. attend class regularly

41 | Identifying Meanings of *Must (Not)*, *Have To*, and *Have Got To* Circle the modal forms. Then check (✓) *Strong Certainty* or *Obligation* for each sentence. `3.7 B`

AT THE AMUSEMENT PARK	STRONG CERTAINTY	OBLIGATION
1. "Do you hear those people screaming? That ride must be scary!"	☐	☐
2. "You must be over four feet tall to go on this ride."	☐	☐
3. "You've got to try this roller coaster. It's really fun."	☐	☐
4. "They must employ thousands of people here. This place is huge."	☐	☐
5. "You look exhausted. You must have been here all day."	☐	☐
6. "I'm not surprised they charge so much. It has to cost a lot to maintain this place."	☐	☐
7. "We'll have to stand in that long line if we want to go on the new ride."	☐	☐
8. "This has got to be the most exciting place in the world for little kids."	☐	☐

3.8 Combining Modals

A

SIMPLE MODAL + PHRASAL MODAL

1 I **would be willing to pay** for better service.

2 We **may be able to develop** strategies to overcome this problem.

3 Students **should be allowed to form** their own groups.

4 Have you called your cousin? He **might be able to fix** that computer for you.

5 Physicians **must be permitted to practice** medicine the way they choose.

6 City workers **will have to wait** until next year for a salary increase.

We generally do not use two simple modals together. However, we can use most **simple modals** together with a **phrasal modal**, as in **1 – 6**.

SIMPLE MODALS		PHRASAL MODALS
can	could	be able to
may	might	be allowed to
will	would	be permitted to
—	should	be required to
must	—	be willing to
		have to

WARNING! We do not usually combine *can/could* with *be able to* or *can* with *have to*.

42 | Using Combinations of Modals Work with a partner. Complete these sentences with a positive or negative phrasal modal. (More than one answer may be possible.) `3.8 A`

Facing a Water Shortage

1. In the near future, citizens may _____ pay fines if they use too much water.

2. Homeowners will _____ water their lawns or wash their cars.

3. Each member of the household will _____ take one shower every day.

4. Every one of us should _____ make these changes for the good of the community.

5. City officials must _____ enforce these rules.

6. In some instances, individuals might _____ apply for an exemption[16] from the water limitations.

7. People who are growing fruits and vegetables could _____ use more water.

8. If you have an exemption, you should _____ pay over-use fines.

Think about It What other modal combinations could be used in each sentence? Share ideas with your classmates.

Write about It Choose one of these events. Write four sentences about the effects of this event on the community. Use combinations of modals.

- The Olympics are coming to town.
- A very important person is going to visit your school.
- City officials are putting in a large park near the city center.
- There will be a lot of road construction in the area this summer.

43 | Using Combinations of Modals Complete these sentences with your own ideas. `3.8 A`

OPINIONS

1. Our teacher may not be able to _take a vacation soon_____.

2. Students should be able to _____.

3. I would be willing to _____.

4. I would never be willing to _____.

5. Teenagers should sometimes be permitted to _____.

6. University students must be allowed to _____.

7. Any good friend would be willing to _____.

8. Pretty soon, people in this country will have to _____.

9. All companies should have to _____.

[16]**exemption:** official permission not to do something or pay for something

94

10. Children shouldn't be permitted to _____.

11. The government might have to _____.

12. Someday, people won't be able to _____.

Talk about It Rewrite each statement you wrote in Activity 43 as a question. Ask a partner the questions. Do you and your partner agree?

A: *Do you think our teacher will take a vacation soon?*
B: *Maybe, but she might not be able to until the summer.*

F Y I

We do not usually ask questions with *might* or *may* (for degrees of certainty). You can ask those questions with *will*.

3.9 Modals with Progressive Verb Forms

A

MODALS OF CERTAINTY OR PROBABILITY

1 The medical treatment **must be working**. She's getting better.

2 This is an old address. He **may not be living** there anymore.

3 It **might be confusing** at first, but you'll get it eventually.

4 The company is going bankrupt. Thousands of employees **could be losing** their jobs soon.

5 She didn't hear the phone ring. She **might have been sleeping**.

6 The government shut that company down. It **must have been operating** illegally.

7 He **must know** that already. (NOT: ~~He must be knowing . . .~~)

We can use **progressive verb forms with modals** to express degrees of certainty, as in **1 – 6**. This form is more common in speaking than in writing. For present forms, we use:

| modal | + | *(not)* | + | *be* | + | the *-ing* form of the main verb |

For past forms, we use:

| modal | + | *(not)* | + | *have been* | + | the *-ing* form of the main verb |

We don't usually use non-action verbs such as *believe*, *own*, and *know* in the progressive, as in **7**.

B

MODALS OF ADVISABILITY

8 You **should be spending** more time on your work.

9 I don't know why they're upset. They **ought to be celebrating**.

10 You **should have been listening** while the teacher was talking!

We can also use the progressive verb forms with *should* and *ought to* when we are:

- giving advice or making recommendations in the present, as in **8 – 9**
- making past counterfactual statements, as in **10**

---

44 | Using Modals for Certainty in the Present Read the Speaker A statement. Then circle the appropriate response. **3.9 A**

1. A: He's been on the computer for quite a while.
   B: He might be writing an essay.
   B: He might write an essay.

2. A: The meeting is going long[17].
   B: They must be arguing about the budget.
   B: They must argue about the budget.

3. A: That guy seems to really know what he's doing.
   B: He must be coming here a lot.
   B: He must come here a lot.

[17] **go long:** to last longer than expected

4. A: Mark looks really frustrated.

   B: He must be having trouble with his assignment.

   B: He must have trouble with his assignment.

5. A: Someone said they're going to close the store.

   B: They might have been talking about the one on Hill Street.

   B: They might have talked about the one on Hill Street.

6. A: Mina never wants to go to the games.

   B: She may think sports are boring.

   B: She may be thinking sports are boring.

7. A: What was she doing at the park?

   B: I'm not sure. She might have been playing soccer.

   B: I'm not sure. She might have played soccer.

8. A: How did she finish the game so quickly?

   B: She must be playing a lot.

   B: She must play a lot.

Write about It Work with a partner. Write a new response for each Speaker A statement in Activity 44. If possible, use a progressive form with a modal.

45 | Using Modals for Certainty in the Past

Choose verbs from the box to complete these conversations. Use a modal of certainty with *have* + a past participle verb form or *have* + *been* + an *-ing* verb form. Then practice with a partner. **3.9 A**

1. A: I lost my keys.

   B: You _____ *must have left* _____ them in the car.

2. A: Sara's eyes are all puffy and red.

   B: Yeah, I noticed. She _____ before class.

3. A: All the lights are off.

   B: They _____ early.

4. A: I saw Tony at the lake on Saturday.

   B: He _____.

5. A: Do you think this chicken is still good?

   B: I wouldn't eat it. It _____ there for hours.

6. A: Why did she buy that ugly sweater?

   B: I don't know. She _____ it as a gift.

7. A: Why didn't they hear me knocking?

   B: They _____ to music.

8. A: Why isn't there any cereal in the cabinet?

   B: David _____ it.

| close |
| cry |
| eat |
| fish |
| get |
| leave |
| listen |
| sit |

46 | Expressing Opinions with *Should* Choose a verb from the box to complete each statement below. Use *should* and a progressive verb form. (More than one answer may be possible.) Then check (✓) whether you agree or disagree with each statement. **3.9 B**

ask	cut	eliminate	hire	lower	offer	provide	spend

HOW TO IMPROVE THE ECONOMY   YES   NO

1. Our government officials ____*should be hiring*____ people to build roads and bridges.   ☐   ☐

2. They _____ taxes so people have more money to spend.   ☐   ☐

3. They _____ money on education so that young people can find better jobs.   ☐   ☐

4. They _____ unemployment benefits so people are motivated to work.   ☐   ☐

5. They _____ tax incentives to companies to encourage growth.   ☐   ☐

6. They _____ low-interest loans to people with good business ideas.   ☐   ☐

7. They _____ many government programs to save money.   ☐   ☐

8. They _____ people to spend instead of save.   ☐   ☐

Talk about It Compare your answers above with a partner and discuss. Suggest some other ideas for improving the economy.

Write about It With a partner, brainstorm a list of problems that your school, community, or country is currently facing. Write eight sentences about what leaders should be doing right now to deal with the problems.

47 | Using *Should* to Express Opinions about the Past Work with a partner. Complete each response. Use *should* with *have* + a past participle verb form or *have* + *been* + an *-ing* verb form. Then practice with your partner. **3.9 B**

CRITICIZING OTHERS

1. A: Mark lost some money yesterday. It fell out of his pocket.

   B: Well, he _____*should have put*_____ it in his wallet.

2. A: Sue spent all morning ordering stuff online instead of working. Ed caught her and now he's furious.

   B: What does she expect? She _____.

3. A: Poor Julia worked nine hours last night and now she's even sicker.

   B: I'm not surprised. She _____.

4. A: Paul caught Misha reading his email last night.

   B: That's terrible! He _____ someone else's email.

5. A: Ana started looking for a summer job last week. She hasn't found anything yet.

   B: Why did she start so late? She _____ for the last month.

6. A: Yuri got rear-ended yesterday. He was texting and didn't notice the light had changed.

   B: Well, he _____ in the car.

   A: True, but the other driver _____ attention.

7. A: Hassan called at the last minute to cancel.

   B: I know. He _____ us yesterday.

8. A: Mary threw the book to me and knocked over my cup of coffee.

   B: She _____ the book.

3.10 Other Ways to Express Modality

A

ORDER OF ADVERBS OF CERTAINTY

POSITIVE STATEMENTS

	subject	be or first helping verb	adverb	main verb	
1	She	was	probably	—	frustrated.
2	This	will	most likely	change	later.
3	The people	can	certainly	decide	themselves.
4	He	—	definitely	knows	the answer.

NEGATIVE STATEMENTS

	subject	—	adverb	helping and main verbs	
5	Listeners	—	obviously	can't understand	her.
6	The phone	—	clearly	isn't working.	

We sometimes use **adverbs** to express degrees of certainty. We can place these adverbs:

- after a positive *be* verb, as in **1**, or the first helping verb, as in **2 – 3**
- before positive main verbs (besides *be*), as in **4**
- in negative sentences before any verb, including *be*, as in **5** and **6**

ADVERBS OF CERTAINTY

STRONG CERTAINTY	certainly clearly definitely	evidently obviously
MODERATE CERTAINTY	most likely probably	
WEAK CERTAINTY	possibly	

B

PREPOSITIONAL PHRASES

7 **In a way,** I understand their decision. But I don't agree with it.

8 He has grown up a lot, but he has the same personality and character. **In a sense,** he hasn't changed at all.

9 Their jobs are different, but they both achieved success quickly. **In some respects,** their careers have followed the same path.

With some **prepositional phrases**, we can suggest that a statement is only partly true, as in **7 – 9**.

We often use these prepositional phrases at the beginning of a sentence.

GO ONLINE

48 | Using Adverbs of Certainty Rewrite these sentences using the adverb in parentheses instead of the modal. **3.10 A**

Restaurant Reviews

1. This might be the best fish stew I've ever had. (possibly)

   This is possibly the best fish stew I've ever had.

2. The chef must have trained in France. (obviously)

3. These strawberries must have just been picked. (clearly)

4. This has to be one of the best restaurants in town. (definitely)
5. They must be offering some new dishes this week. (evidently)
6. Soon they might start serving lunch as well as dinner. (possibly)
7. This place must get excellent reviews from everyone. (probably)
8. I should come back very soon. (most likely)

49 | Placing Adverbs of Certainty in a Sentence Write a complete sentence in response to each question. Include an adverb of certainty. `3.10 A`

MODERN LIFE

1. Do most people spend too much time online?

   Some people clearly spend too much time online, but most people don't.

2. Do social media do more good than harm?
3. Is television better today than it was in the past?
4. Can you learn any useful skills from video games?
5. Is it important for everyone to have a smartphone?
6. Should a 13-year-old have a smartphone?
7. Should people have to pay for online newspaper subscriptions?
8. Is it a good idea to buy brand-new technology?

Talk about It Share the sentences you wrote above with a partner. Explain the reasons for your opinions.

"There are obviously people who spend too much time online. They just look at a screen all day and it's not healthy. But most people I know do other things, too."

50 | Using Adverbs and Prepositional Phrases of Certainty Complete these sentences with your own ideas. Share your sentences with a partner. `3.10 A–B`

1. In a way, the past year _____.
2. The people in my classes are clearly _____.
3. _____ will obviously _____ very soon.
4. _____ should definitely _____.
5. In some respects, _____ and _____ are very similar.
6. In a sense, my friends are _____.
7. Tomorrow, I probably _____.
8. Next week, I'm most likely to _____.
9. In a way, I really like _____.
10. In some respects, _____ was the best _____.

3.11 Using Modals in Speaking: Modals for Social Purposes

A	**POLITE SUGGESTIONS** **1** A: I'm having trouble with my math class. B: You **could always get** a tutor. **2** A: I can't get to sleep at night. B: You **may want to stop** drinking coffee. **3** A: I keep running out of money. B: **Maybe** you **should ask** your boss for more hours. **4** A: I don't know anyone here. B: You **may as well introduce** yourself to a few people. Maybe you'll make a new friend.	We sometimes use **modals with other words** to soften suggestions, as in **1 – 4**. Some phrases that make suggestions a little less direct and more polite include: You could always . . . You may want to . . . You might want to . . . Maybe you should . . . You might as well . . . You may as well . . .
B	**SOFTENING SUGGESTIONS WITH NEGATIVE QUESTIONS** **5** A: I'm afraid she's not going to see this email in time. B: **Can't** you **text** her instead? **6** A: **Shouldn't** you **call** your brother today? B: You're right. I should.	Asking questions with *can't*, *couldn't*, and *shouldn't* is another way to soften suggestions, as in **5 – 6**.
C	**OTHER SOCIAL USES OF MODALS** **7** **Could I have** another fork, please? **8** **Would** you **mind** turning the music down? **9** **Can I help** you with that? **10** **May I speak** to you for a moment?	We often use the modals *can*, *could*, *would*, and *may* in speaking for: • requests, as in **7 – 8** • offers, as in **9** • permission, as in **10**

51 | Using Softening Strategies to Make Suggestions Write a suggestion for each problem. Use a polite form with a modal. `3.11 A`

PROBLEMS WITH SOLUTIONS

1. "I don't have time to exercise."

   Maybe you could start walking to school.

2. "I can't stop eating chocolate."
3. "I always oversleep in the morning."
4. "I'm really shy."
5. "I have trouble getting organized."
6. "I'm always late to class."

7. "I can't decide what to major in."
8. "I can't find a job."
9. "I have a friend who is constantly calling and texting me."
10. "I want to ask for a raise, but I'm nervous."
11. "This class is really hard for me."
12. "I can barely afford to pay my rent these days."

Talk about It Compare the advice you wrote above with a partner. For each problem, which piece of advice is the most helpful?

52 | Using Negative Questions to Make Suggestions Work with a partner and take turns. One of you reads a statement in Activity 51 aloud. The other uses negative questions to give advice for the situation. `3.11 B`

A: I don't have time to exercise.
B: Couldn't you walk to school in the morning?

53 | Using Modals for Requests, Offers, and Permission Write a short conversation for each situation. Use *can, could, would,* or *may.* `3.11 C`

AROUND TOWN

At a restaurant

1. Customer: Ask for permission to exchange a menu item.

   A: Could I get fresh fruit instead of potatoes?
   B: Yes, of course.

2. Customer: Request a new table.
3. Server: Offer to clean up a spill on the table.

At work

4. Employee: Ask for permission to take a day off.
5. Co-worker: Offer to help a co-worker with a big job.
6. Employer: Request that the employee do some additional work.

At a clothing store

7. Customer: Ask to see a different item.
8. Customer: Ask for permission to try something on.
9. Clerk: Ask if the customer wants to pay with a credit card.
10. Clerk: Offer to show other styles.

At an acquaintance's house

11. Visitor: Ask for permission to look at the garden.
12. Visitor: Offer to help with dinner preparations.
13. Host: Request that a guest put his or her jacket/purse in the bedroom.

3.12 Using Modals in Academic Writing

To **hedge** a statement means to make it less definite. Hedging is a very common way we use **modals** in academic writing, where it's necessary to be precise.

A

COULD / MIGHT

1 You **could say** that they have run out of ideas.
2 One **might conclude** that no peaceful options remain. But that is not the case.

We sometimes use *could* or *might* to make a less definite conclusion, as in **1**. Sometimes we use them to introduce an idea that we are going to argue against, as in **2**.

MAY

3 After the procedure, patients **may notice** an increase in energy levels.

We can use *may* in writing to show that something is possible, as in **3**. *May* shows a higher degree of certainty than *might* or *could*.

WOULD

4 We **would argue** that the point is valid.
5 I **would suggest** that we need to review this topic.
6 One **would assume** that the answers are obvious.

We can use *would* with verbs like *say, suggest, assume,* and *argue* when we are making a point that others might disagree with, as in **4 – 6**.

SHOULD

7 Our experiment **should show** the effects of carbon monoxide.
8 These studies **should demonstrate** the usefulness of our procedure.

We can use *should* to describe our expectations, as in **7 – 8**. It shows more certainty than *might* or *may*, but less than *will* or statements without modals.

GO ONLINE

54 | Identifying Hedges with *Could* and *Might* Underline the hedging expressions. Then match the statements with the conclusions. `3.12 A`

DRAWING CONCLUSIONS

1. The two birds look extremely similar. ____
2. This is the author's most well-known novel. ____
3. She rarely left the house and avoided all contact with strangers. ____
4. The mice began to solve the maze more quickly. ____
5. Six months after the shopping center was built, stores along Main Street began to close. ____
6. The company's closure affected the lives of hundreds of people. ____
7. Every year, more students are passing the entrance examination. ____
8. The two documents have a similar writing style and use much of the same vocabulary. ____

a. One <u>could say</u> that it's also his most important work.
b. One might assume that she was deeply depressed during this period.
c. We might assume that the new diet was increasing their intelligence.
d. One could say it is the worst disaster this city has ever faced.
e. This might suggest that they were written by the same person.
f. We might conclude that secondary schools are doing a better job of preparing them.
g. This might suggest that customers feel little loyalty to local business owners.
h. We could conclude that they are closely related.

Write about It Choose three sentences from this box to write a conclusion about. Hedge your conclusions with *could* or *might*, using three of the phrases you underlined above.

> 1. Gas prices have risen in the last two years.
> 2. High-end televisions have gotten cheaper.
> 3. Computing power has increased rapidly over the last five years.
> 4. More and more businesses have moved into this area recently.
> 5. The traffic problems downtown continue to get worse.
> 6. The number of students applying to the university goes up every year.

55 | Hedging with *May* Write two to three sentences about possible results for each situation. Use *may*. Share your sentences with a partner. `3.12 A`

LIFESTYLE

What happens when people . . .

1. take long naps in the afternoon

   They may have difficulty sleeping at night.

2. sit at the computer for hours every day
3. begin a dance class
4. move to a new city
5. lose a job
6. get plenty of exercise
7. become very famous
8. start college

56│Hedging with _Would_ Write an opinion statement about each issue. Use _would argue that,_ _would suggest that, would assume that,_ or _would say that._ 3.12 A

SOLVING CAMPUS PROBLEMS

1. There is an increase in the number of students cheating on exams.

   I would suggest that we need to put cameras in the classrooms.

2. Student residences are overcrowded.
3. Students are not happy with the food choices in the cafeteria.
4. There are long lines in the bookstore at the beginning of every semester.
5. The registration process is confusing.
6. There is not enough for students to do on weekends.
7. Some of the classrooms are old and lack modern technology.
8. Classes often fill up very quickly.

Write about It Think of a real problem on your campus. Suggest an idea for a solution. Use _would._

57│Hedging with _Should_ Rewrite these statements with _should_ to make them less certain. 3.12 A

1. The patient's quick recovery will demonstrate the usefulness of the procedure.

   The patient's quick recovery should demonstrate the usefulness of the procedure.

2. Our research will show the negative effect of the oil spill on wildlife.
3. This treatment will make the patient much more comfortable.
4. The new software will solve most of the problems we have been experiencing.
5. The presentation is going to help students understand the material.
6. The team will finish the first research by early next year.
7. The new fertilizer[18] will add nutrients to the soil.
8. Our profits will increase over the next year.

Write about It Complete these sentences with your own ideas. Write about your expectations.

1. _____ should show _____.
2. _____ should make _____.
3. _____ should finish _____.

WRAP-UP Demonstrate Your Knowledge

A│ROLE-PLAY Work with two partners. Role-play these situations. Use _can, could, might want to, have to,_ _will, should,_ or _be going to._ Take turns being Student A.

1. Student A: You are going on a two-week vacation. You will be staying in three different hotels and taking public transportation. It's summer. Ask your friends for advice.

   Students B and C: Give advice.

2. Student A: You want to look for a new job but aren't sure when to tell your boss. Ask for advice.

   Students B and C: Give advice about when to tell the boss and about how to find a new job.

[18]**fertilizer:** something added to soil to make plants grow more successfully

3. Student A: You want to buy a birthday gift for a friend, but it can't be too expensive. Ask for advice.

Students B and C: Give advice about what to buy and how to celebrate the birthday.

4. Student A: You have visitors coming to town, and you want to show them the perfect weekend in your city. Ask for advice.

Students B and C: Give advice about where to go, what to do, and what to eat.

B | SENTENCES Write a paragraph for each picture to answer these questions. Use various verb forms with modals.

1. What probably happened?
2. What should have happened?

3. What should happen now?
4. What might happen next?

Her child must have left the toy on the floor....

C | SURVEY Work with a partner. Write an opinion statement about each group of people in this chart. Use modals and *be required to, be permitted to, (not) be allowed to,* or *be supposed to.* Then read your statements to your classmates. Find out how many people agree or disagree with you.

	Do you agree with these statements?	Yes	No
professional athletes	*Professional athletes should not be allowed to participate in the Olympics.*		
drivers			
flight attendants			
landlords			
parents			
politicians			

3.13 Summary of Modals

SIMPLE MODALS

She **can speak** English well. →
She **could speak** Chinese when she was a child. →
They say it **will rain** tomorrow. →
They said it **would rain**, but it didn't. →
Employees **must arrive** on time. →
Employees **may take** two 15-minute breaks. →
We **might finish** by 4:00, but I'm not sure. →
He **should help** his mother. →

PHRASAL MODALS

Many immigrants **are able to speak** English very well.
She **was able to speak** Chinese when she was a child.
They say it's **going to rain** tomorrow.
They said it **was going to rain**, but it didn't.
Employees **have to arrive** on time.
Employees **are permitted to take** two 15-minute breaks.
—
He **is supposed to help** his mother.

SOCIAL PURPOSE MEANINGS

CAN(NOT)
Ability I **can swim**.
Permission We **can stay** for a few more hours.
Prohibition You **can't stay** any longer.
Offer **Can** I **help** you?

WILL
Offer I'**ll help** you with that.

MUST (NOT)
Obligation Employees **must sign in** when they arrive.

SHOULD (NOT)
Advice You **should take** Walker Boulevard.

MAY (NOT)
Permission **May** I **continue**?
Prohibition You **may not talk** during the test.
Offer **May** I **help** you?

MIGHT (NOT)
Suggestion You **might want to try** calling him again.

COULD
Permission **Could** I **sit** here?
Suggestion We **could try** that new restaurant downtown.
Request **Could** you **say** that again?

DEGREE OF CERTAINTY / LOGICAL PROBABILITY MEANINGS

CAN(NOT)
General possibility Honey **can make** your throat feel better.

very certain / very likely strong probability

WILL / WON'T
They **will come** home soon.
They **won't be** out much longer.

MUST / CAN'T / COULDN'T
She has so many flowers. She **must love** to garden.
That **can't be** our train. It's too early.

SHOULD (NOT)
I **should be** home by 5:00. I **shouldn't be** late.

MAY (NOT)
I **may take** accounting next year. I haven't decided.

MIGHT (NOT) / COULD
They **might drop by** tomorrow, but I'm not sure.

The meeting **could last** for an hour.

WOULD (NOT)
Counterfactual I **would help** you, but you
     haven't asked.

not certain / not likely weak probability

OTHER WAYS OF SHOWING PERMISSION / PROHIBITION / OBLIGATION

Permission On Fridays, we **were allowed to wear**
     casual clothing at work.
You **are permitted to turn** right on a red light here.

Prohibition Employees **are not allowed to eat** at
     their desks.

Obligation He **is required to take** a final exam for
     this class.
Children **are supposed to obey** their parents.

OTHER WAYS OF SHOWING CERTAINTY / UNCERTAINTY

ADVERBS
Strong certainty They are **certainly / definitely / clearly** going to
     enjoy this wonderful meal.
Moderate certainty He is **probably / most likely** going to come
     home tomorrow.
Weak certainty They are **possibly** going to get new uniforms.

PREPOSITIONAL PHRASES
In way, this is the most difficult class I've ever taken.
In a sense, he is representing the class.
In some respects, nothing has changed.

4 The Passive

Nothing great was ever achieved without enthusiasm.

—RALPH WALDO EMERSON,
ESSAYIST, POET,
AND PHILOSOPHER
(1803–1882)

Talk about It What does the quotation above mean? Do you agree or disagree?

WARM-UP

A | Match each time on the timeline with an event. Then compare answers with your classmates. How many do you agree on?

TIMELINE OF GREAT ACHIEVEMENT

1839   1895 1903   1928   1952 1954 1960   the future

1. The first open-heart surgery **was attempted** in _1952_ .

2. The first airplane **was flown** by the Wright brothers in _____ .

3. The camera **was invented** in _____ .

4. Penicillin, the first antibiotic, **was discovered** by accident in _____ .

5. The first nuclear power plant **was built** in _____ .

6. The first motion pictures **were shown** to a paying audience in _____ .

7. Lasers **had been developed** by about _____ .

8. A cure for cancer **will** probably **be found** in _____ .

RESEARCHERS FIND
CURE FOR CANCER
_____
_____
_____
_____

B | The verb in **blue** in each sentence above is a passive verb form. Based on these examples, what can you say about passive verb forms? Check (✓) *True* or *False*.

	TRUE	FALSE
1. A passive verb form has a form of the verb *be*.	☐	☐
2. In a sentence with a passive verb form, the subject causes the action.	☐	☐
3. A sentence with a passive verb form always has *by* + a noun phrase.	☐	☐

C | Look back at the quotation on page 106. Identify any passive forms.

4.1 Comparing Active and Passive Sentences

A

ACTIVE

subject (agent)	verb	direct object (receiver)
1 Shakespeare	wrote	the play *Hamlet*.

PASSIVE

subject (receiver)	verb	(agent)
2 The play *Hamlet*	was written	by Shakespeare.

3 *Hamlet* **was written** between 1599 and 1601.

In most sentences, the subject is the performer of the action, or agent, as in **1**. When the subject performs the action, we call the sentence an **active sentence**. The direct object is the receiver of the action.

A **passive sentence** lets us change the focus to what happened or who received the action, as in **2**.

- The receiver of the action becomes the subject of the sentence.
- When the agent is included, it follows the word *by*.

In passive sentences, however, the agent is usually omitted, as in **3**.

B

We form the passive with **be** + the **past participle of the main verb**. The form of *be* signals the time frame we are talking about.

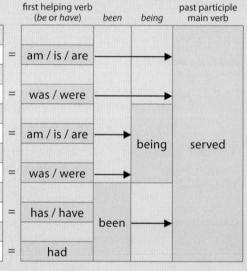

				first helping verb (*be* or *have*)	*been*	*being*	past participle main verb
SIMPLE PRESENT	Active	The waiters serve the food quickly.					
	Passive	The food **is served** quickly.	=	am / is / are			
SIMPLE PAST	Active	The waiters served the food.					
	Passive	The food **was served**.	=	was / were			
PRESENT PROGRESSIVE	Active	The waiters are serving the food now.					
	Passive	The food **is being served** now.	=	am / is / are		being	served
PAST PROGRESSIVE	Active	The waiters were serving the food.					
	Passive	The food **was being served**.	=	was / were			
PRESENT PERFECT	Active	The waiters have already served the food.					
	Passive	The food **has** already **been served**.	=	has / have	been		
PAST PERFECT	Active	The waiters had just served the food.					
	Passive	The food **had** just **been served**.	=	had			

For a list of past participles of irregular verbs, see the Resources, page R-3.

GO ONLINE

1 | Performer or Receiver of the Action? Decide if each **bold** subject is the performer of the action or the receiver of the action. Write *P* (performer) or *R* (receiver) above the subject. **4.1 A**

FACTS ABOUT WILLIAM SHAKESPEARE

1. *P*
   Many people think that William Shakespeare was the greatest writer in the English language.

2. **Nobody** knows Shakespeare's actual birthday, but scholars think he was born on April 23, 1564.

3. As far as we know, **Shakespeare** never went beyond grammar school.

4. **Shakespeare and his wife** had three children: Susanna and twins Judith and Hamnet.

5. Although **Shakespeare's son Hamnet** died at age 11, **his name** lives on.

6. **The name Hamnet** was sometimes written as *Hamlet*, the title of one of

   Shakespeare's greatest plays.

7. **"Shakespeare"** was spelled 80 different ways, including "Shaxpere"

   and "Shaxberd."

8. **Shakespeare's work** has been translated into many languages.

9. **His plays** are read in at least 80 languages.

10. **Shakespeare** is thought to be the author of 39 plays. **About half of them** were printed before his death.

11. **Some of Shakespeare's most famous works** were not published until after his death.

F Y I

Passive forms are
much more common in
academic writing and
news reporting than in
conversation.

Think about It Which of the sentences in Activity 1 are passive? How do you know?

2 | Noticing Passive Forms Read this email message and underline the passive forms. Then write each verb under the correct group in the chart below. [4.1 B]

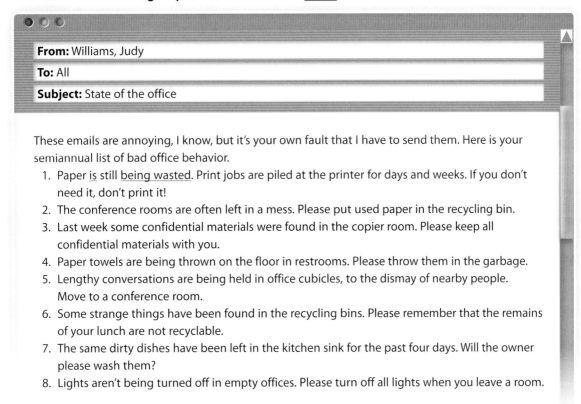

From: Williams, Judy

To: All

Subject: State of the office

These emails are annoying, I know, but it's your own fault that I have to send them. Here is your semiannual list of bad office behavior.

1. Paper is still <u>being wasted</u>. Print jobs are piled at the printer for days and weeks. If you don't need it, don't print it!
2. The conference rooms are often left in a mess. Please put used paper in the recycling bin.
3. Last week some confidential materials were found in the copier room. Please keep all confidential materials with you.
4. Paper towels are being thrown on the floor in restrooms. Please throw them in the garbage.
5. Lengthy conversations are being held in office cubicles, to the dismay of nearby people. Move to a conference room.
6. Some strange things have been found in the recycling bins. Please remember that the remains of your lunch are not recyclable.
7. The same dirty dishes have been left in the kitchen sink for the past four days. Will the owner please wash them?
8. Lights aren't being turned off in empty offices. Please turn off all lights when you leave a room.

Simple present passive	Simple past passive	Present progressive passive	Present perfect passive
am/is/are + past participle of verb	*was/were +* past participle of verb	*am/is/are + being +* past participle of verb	*have/has + been +* past participle of verb
		is being wasted	

Talk about It What other examples of bad office behavior can you think of? Share ideas with your classmates.

Think about It Why do you think the writer used the passive forms in the sentences in Activity 2?

3 | Forming Simple Present Passive Sentences Complete these sentences with the simple present passive form of the verbs in parentheses. `4.1 B`

IT'S A FACT!

1. Every year, about 70 million tons of fish and other sea animals _____*are caught*_____ in the oceans. (catch)

2. Nuclear energy _____ when atoms of a nuclear fuel, such as uranium, _____ apart. (produce/split)

3. There is enough food in the world for everybody. The problem is getting it where it _____. (need)

4. More than half of the world's languages _____ by less than 1 percent of the population. (speak)

5. When land _____ by water on three sides, it _____ a peninsula. (surround/call)

6. Modern bridges _____ with materials that can expand and contract[1] as the temperature changes. (build)

7. When air _____, it expands and takes up more space. (heat)

8. One large body of water covers about 71 percent of the earth. It _____ by scientists into four oceans: the Pacific, the Atlantic, the Indian, and the Arctic. (divide)

9. A tide is the movement of water toward and away from land. Ocean tides _____ mostly by the pull of the moon's gravity on the earth's water. (cause)

10. Reykjavik, Iceland, is located in a cold northern climate. Buildings in this city _____ by the hot-water springs in the ground below. (heat)

11. Ice covers about 10 percent of the earth's land surface. Nearly all of it _____ in Greenland and Antarctica. (find)

12. About 80 percent of microwaves from mobile phones _____ by your head. (absorb[2])

13. Trees _____ just for wood. They do many other important things such as releasing oxygen for us to breathe. (not need)

14. A battery uses special chemicals to make electricity. When the chemicals _____, the battery stops working. (use up)

15. Three of Switzerland's official languages are German, French, and Italian. All national laws _____ in these three languages. (publish)

Talk about It Which facts above were new to you? Which was the most interesting to you? Why?

[1] **contract:** to become smaller

[2] **absorb:** to take something in like liquid or heat and hold it

4 | Using Simple Past Passive Verb Forms Complete these sentences with the simple past passive form of the verbs in parentheses. 4.1 B

FAMOUS FIRSTS

1. The first pulley ___was___ probably ___invented___ in ancient Greece. Pulleys _____ first _____ to help construct buildings. (invent/employ)

2. Toothbrushes _____ probably first _____ in Egypt and Babylonia about 3500 BCE. (use)

3. The first books _____ in China and Korea about 700 CE. (print)

4. The first English newspaper _____ in 1621, but it wasn't until 1643 that the first newspaper with pictures _____. (publish/print)

5. The first photograph of land from above _____ from a balloon over a village in France in 1858. (take)

6. The first record player _____ a phonograph, and it played cylinders³ instead of discs⁴. (call)

pulley

7. The first gasoline _____ about 1864, but it wasn't until the automobile _____ in 1885 that gasoline became really useful. (produce/invent)

8. Wristwatches _____ about 1890, but for many years they _____ only _____ by women. (introduce/wear)

9. The first contact lenses⁵ _____ by a Swiss doctor. They were thick and not very comfortable. (develop)

10. The first plastic _____ "Parkesine" because it _____ by a scientist named Alexander Parkes. (call/invent)

11. The first World Cup _____ in 1930, and Uruguay _____ to host it. (hold/choose)

12. In 1797, André-Jacques Garnerin made the first parachute jump ever. He _____ from a balloon at about 3,200 feet above Paris. (drop)

phonograph

13. The world's first skyscraper _____ in Chicago in 1885. This ten-story building _____ inside and outside by a metal frame. (complete/support)

14. The first photograph _____ in 1826 by a French scientist. It's a picture of the view from an upstairs window of his house. (take)

Talk about It What other famous inventions or discoveries do you know about? When were they invented or discovered?

---

³ **cylinders:** long, round shapes like tubes or cans
⁴ **discs:** flat, round objects

⁵ **contact lenses:** small, round pieces of plastic that you wear in your eyes so you can see better

5 | Using Different Forms of the Passive Which monument does each sentence describe? Check (✓) your answers. Then rewrite each sentence to make it passive. Leave out the agent (the performer of the action) in your passive sentence. **4.1 B**

TWO FAMOUS MONUMENTS

	PYRAMID OF GIZA	EIFFEL TOWER
1. Today, people recognize it as a symbol of France.	☐	✓
Today, it is recognized as a symbol of France.		
2. The builders used more than 2.3 million stone blocks to build it.	☐	☐
More than 2.3 million stone blocks _____.		
3. The builders completed it more than 4,500 years ago.	☐	☐
4. People built it for a world's fair.	☐	☐
5. It opened in 1889.	☐	☐
6. People designed it as a tomb[6] to protect a king's body.	☐	☐
7. In 1909, the government almost tore it down.	☐	☐
8. They covered it with limestone.	☐	☐
9. The government repaints it every seven years.	☐	☐
10. The United Nations has identified it as a World Heritage Site.	☐	☐
11. In ancient times, people considered it one of the Seven Wonders of the World.	☐	☐
12. Architects are completely redesigning the first floor.	☐	☐

Think about It What verb form did you use in each sentence above? Why?

[6] **tomb:** a place where a body is buried after the person dies, often with a large decorated stone

6 | Pronunciation Note: Sentence Rhythm Listen to the note. Then do Activity 7.

English speakers usually stress the content words (nouns, verbs, adjectives, adverbs, etc.) in a sentence. They don't usually stress function words (articles, helping verbs, prepositions, etc.). The length of time it takes to say a sentence depends on the number of STRESSED syllables—not the length of the sentence. Notice:

——— TAKE THE SAME AMOUNT OF TIME TO SAY ———

1 The WAITers SERVED DINner at SIX.

Number of syllables in the sentence: 8
Number of stressed syllables: 4

2 The WAITers are going to SERVE DINner at SIX.

Number of syllables in the sentence: 11
Number of stressed syllables: 4

Notice that a passive sentence may have more syllables than an active sentence, but the two sentences take about the same amount of time to say.

3 Active: AMANda MADE the deCIsion.

Number of syllables in the sentence: 8
Number of stressed syllables: 3

4 Passive: The deCIsion was MADE by AMANda.

Number of syllables in the sentence: 10
Number of stressed syllables: 3

7 | Pronouncing Passive Sentences Count the number of syllables in each sentence, and write the number. Then underline the stressed syllables in each sentence, and write the number on the next line. Finally, listen and check your answers. **4.1 B**

	NUMBER OF SYLLABLES IN THE SENTENCE	NUMBER OF STRESSED SYLLABLES
1. a. John finished it.	4	2
b. It was finished by John.	___	___
2. a. A switch turns on the light.	___	___
b. The lights are turned on by a switch.	___	___
3. a. Toni Morrison wrote the novel *Sula*.	___	___
b. The novel *Sula* was written by Toni Morrison.	___	___
4. a. The workers are cleaning the streets today.	___	___
b. The streets are being cleaned by the workers today.	___	___
5. a. The storm destroyed the house.	___	___
b. The house was destroyed by the storm.	___	___
6. a. A friend introduced them.	___	___
b. They were introduced by a friend.	___	___
7. a. Their employer is organizing a conference.	___	___
b. A conference is being organized by their employer.	___	___
8. a. The committee has recently honored Dr. Bell.	___	___
b. Dr. Bell has recently been honored by the committee.	___	___
9. a. One of his students made the furniture.	___	___
b. The furniture was made by one of his students.	___	___
10. a. Scientists have discovered other stars with planets.	___	___
b. Other stars with planets have been discovered by scientists.	___	___

Think about It There are more syllables in each passive sentence, yet it takes about the same amount of time to say the active sentence. What do speakers do differently when they say the passive sentences?

8 | Error Correction Correct any errors in these sentences. (Some sentences may not have any errors.)

1. This picture is painted about 100 years ago, but it still looks very modern.

2. My father was left the country after the war ended, and he didn't go back until he was in his sixties.

3. All of the work was finish before noon, but we were told to stay anyway.

4. This photo taken by my parents in 1990. You can see my sister next to the car and my brother with a soccer ball.

5. My grandfather was very important to me when I was a child. He was the only person who were helped me.

6. When my father was a young man, he was ask to set up a school in my city. This school has become one of the best schools in the area.

7. My sister admires by many of her friends because she has appeared on national TV several times.

8. After the storm, our house was surround by water. We weren't able to get into town for over a week, and even then we had to walk.

9. My parents were always willing to give me advice, but they are encouraged me to make my own decisions.

4.2 Using the Passive

Passive sentences are much less common than active sentences, but they are very useful when we want to focus on what happened and to what or whom. The first sentence in **1** below focuses on the agent or performer of the action (*My brother*) and uses an **active verb form**. The second sentence in **1** focuses on what happened (*was designed*) and to what/whom (the *house*) and uses **passive verb forms**.

1 My brother just **bought** an unusual house. It **was designed** and **built** in the 1950s.

A

2 Their car **was stolen.** (by someone unknown)

3 Dr. Henry, one of our most prominent scientists, **was honored** with an award last night.
(We aren't interested in who gave the award.)

4 What **is** this **called** in English? (by everyone)

5 Sam Edwards, 32, **was arrested** at his home last night.
(by the police)

We often use the passive because the agent:

- is unknown, as in **2**
- is unimportant in a particular context, as in **3**
- refers to people in general, as in **4**
- is obvious from the context, as in **5**

B

COMPARE

6a David didn't notify anyone about the meeting.
6b No one **was notified** about the meeting.

7a We have made many mistakes in this war.
7b Many mistakes **have been made** in this war.

We sometimes use the passive:

- to avoid blaming someone for something, as in **6b**
- to avoid taking responsibility for something, as in **7b**

C

8 Ega is an endangered language. It **is spoken** in Ivory Coast **by only 300 people.**

9 The engine **is started** by an electric device.

Because the focus of a passive sentence is on what happens and to what / whom, we rarely mention the agent. The few times that we do, it is because the agent is worth noticing. This might be because the agent is:

- new, unique, or unexpected, as in **8**
- nonhuman, as in **9** (We expect agents to be human.)

9 | Using the Passive Complete the sentences below with the passive form of the verbs in parentheses. Then explain why the writer wanted to focus the sentence on what happened or to whom. Write one or more reasons from the box. `4.2 A`

> **REASONS TO USE THE PASSIVE**
> a. because the agent is unknown
> b. because the agent is unimportant
> c. because the agent refers to people in general
> d. because the agent is obvious from the context

HOT CHOCOLATE   REASON(S)

1. The Aztec emperor Montezuma drank hot chocolate every day. The hot chocolate   _a, b_
   _____was made_____ with chili peppers and dyed red. (make)

2. Hot chocolate was valued very highly by the Aztecs; in fact, cocoa beans   _____
   _____ in place of money. (use)

3. In some Central American villages back then, no one under the age of 60   _____
   _____ to drink hot chocolate. (allow)

TEA

4. Over the years, tea _____ as part of different ceremonies. (serve)   _____

5. When tea _____ in the American colonies, many people served the   _____
   tea leaves with sugar and threw away the water. (introduce)

6. Tea was so expensive in seventeenth-century Europe that it _____   _____
   in locked boxes. (keep)

COFFEE

7. The beans of one entire coffee tree _____ for a single pound of   _____
   ground coffee. (require)

8. The amount of coffee you can safely drink _____ yet.   _____
   (not/determine)

9. Today, coffee _____ commercially in more than 50 countries. (grow)   _____

Think about It Which passive verb forms did you use in the sentences above? Write them under the correct group in this chart. Then explain why you chose each verb form.

Simple present passive	Simple past passive	Present perfect passive
	was made	

10 | Using the Passive Rewrite each sentence to avoid blaming someone or taking responsibility. [4.2 B]

1. I think Anna broke the window on purpose.

   I think the window was broken on purpose.

2. My best friend broke my arm during a soccer game.

   _____

3. I can't believe the parents left their children at home alone.

   _____

4. Emma hasn't returned the keys.

   _____

5. The car seat is all wet because James left the window open.

   _____

6. Rob left the door open and the dog got out.

   _____

7. I didn't lock the front door this morning.

   _____

8. Matt accidentally deleted all the files.

   _____

9. Kate didn't pay the bill on time.

   _____

10. We didn't clean up the room after the meeting.

   _____

Think about It For each sentence you wrote above, decide if the speaker uses a passive form to avoid blaming someone or to avoid taking responsibility for something.

11 | Identifying the Agent Match the beginning of each passive sentence on the left with the agent that best completes the sentence. Then listen to the news reports and check your guesses. [4.2 C]

1. Much of the city was destroyed __c__	a. by a park.
2. A swimmer was hurt ____	b. by a crowd of cheering fans.
3. In the 1800s, the city was surrounded ____	c. by a fire.
4. The movie has been ignored ____	d. by a shark.
5. The house is heated ____	e. by the critics.
6. The winning team was met ____	f. by a dog.
7. The music was written ____	g. by a ten-year-old girl.
8. A man in the park was attacked ____	h. by the sun.

Think about It Why do you think the speaker included the agent in each sentence above? Is the agent new, unique, or unexpected, or is the agent nonhuman?

Talk about It Think of three different ways to complete each sentence above.

1. *"Much of the city was destroyed by a flood. Much of the city was destroyed by the enemy. Much of the city was destroyed by an earthquake."*

4.3 Transitive and Intransitive Verbs

Many verbs need a direct object in order to be complete, as in **1 – 2**. We call these verbs **transitive verbs**. Most (but not all) transitive verbs can be used with a **passive form**, as in **3 – 4**. Some verbs make sense without an object, as in **5 – 6**. These verbs, called **intransitive verbs**, cannot be used with a passive form.

A

TRANSITIVE VERBS

ACTIVE FORM

subject	verb	direct object
1 Scientists	**have discovered**	a new planet.

subject	verb	direct object
2 Someone	**took**	my book.

PASSIVE FORM

subject	verb
3 A new planet	**has been discovered.**

subject	verb
4 My book	**was taken.**

For a list of common transitive verbs, see the Resources, page R-5.

INTRANSITIVE VERBS

ACTIVE FORM

subject	verb	adverbial
5 Everyone	**arrived**	early.

subject	verb
6 Something	**happened.**

NO PASSIVE FORM

For a list of common intransitive verbs, see the Resources, page R-6.

B

COMPARE

subject	verb	direct object	
7a We	**'re going to smoke**	the fish.	(transitive use)

subject	verb	
7b That pile of leaves	**is smoking.**	(intransitive use)

8a I **can't run.** I'm too tired. (intransitive use)
8b The same family **has run** the company for 50 years. (transitive use)
8c The company **has been run** by the same family for 50 years. (passive form / transitive use)

We can use many verbs both transitively and intransitively, as in **7a – 7b**.

The transitive and intransitive uses of the same verb may have different meanings, as in **8**. Only when you are using the transitive meaning of the verb can you use a passive form, as in **8c**.

C

VERBS WITH TWO OBJECTS

subject	verb	indirect object	direct object
9 Someone	**gave**	the library	a lot of books.

subject	verb	direct object	indirect object
10 Someone	**gave**	a lot of books	to the library.

subject	verb	indirect object
11 A lot of books	**were given**	to the library.

subject	verb	direct object
12 The library	**was given**	a lot of books.

Some transitive verbs can have two objects: an indirect object and a direct object, as in **9**. With many of these verbs, the indirect object can come before or after the direct object, as in **9 – 10**. For example:

ask	give	offer	pay	read	serve	teach
bring	lend	owe	promise	send	show	tell

With the verbs above, either the direct object or the indirect object can become the subject of a passive sentence, as in **11 – 12**. However, it is more common for the direct object to become the subject.

GRAMMAR TERM: Verbs with two objects are also called **ditransitive verbs**. The indirect object is the person/thing to or for whom the action was performed.

D

CORRECT THE COMMON ERRORS (See page R-11.)

13 ✗ They thought she was died.
14 ✗ These things were happened on Friday evening.
15 ✗ The paintings appeared several people.
16 ✗ Three people injured in the accident.

12 | Transitive or Intransitive Verb? Circle the verbs in these paragraphs. Then write each verb under the correct group in the chart below. `4.3 A`

BIOGRAPHIES

1. Naomi Shihab Nye (grew up) in St. Louis, Missouri, and Jerusalem and now lives in San Antonio, Texas. A graduate of Trinity University, Nye has published nearly two dozen books including *Come with Me: Poems for a Journey*, *Fuel*, and *Habibi*. Daughter of a Palestinian father and an American mother, she has edited six prize-winning collections of poetry for young readers. She has worked as a visiting writer in schools for 37 years.

2. Julia Alvarez was born in New York City but spent part of her childhood in the Dominican Republic before returning to the United States, and her Spanish-speaking heritage[7] has influenced her literary work in English. She has published novels, poetry, and books for young readers. Alvarez received a BA degree from Middlebury College in Vermont and master's degrees from Syracuse University and the University of Illinois. She has held teaching positions at the University of Vermont and George Washington University. She currently has a position as writer-in-residence at Middlebury College.

Transitive verb (needs/has an object)	Intransitive verb (doesn't need/have an object)
	grew up

Write about It Choose another person, and write a similar paragraph with biographical information. Read your paragraph to the class, and ask your classmates to identify the transitive and intransitive verbs.

[7] **heritage:** important traditions, history, and culture of a country

13 | Usage Note: Understanding Linking Verbs Read the note. Then do Activity 14.

Linking verbs such as **be**, **become**, **remain**, and **seem** are neither transitive nor intransitive. Linking verbs are followed by a complement—a noun phrase, adjective, or adverb that refers back to the subject—not by a direct object. For this reason, we don't use linking verbs with a passive form.

subject	verb	complement
She	**was**	a great president.

She = a great president

subject	verb	complement
He	**became**	my best friend.

He = my best friend

subject	verb	complement
They	**remained**	behind.

They = behind

For a list of linking verbs, see the Resources, page R-2.

14 | Identifying Transitive Verbs Underline the verbs in these sentences. Then decide if each verb is a transitive verb, an intransitive verb, or a linking verb. Write *T*, *I*, or *L* above the verb. `4.3 A`

Albert Einstein

1. When Einstein $\overset{L}{\underline{was}}$ 5 years old, his father showed him a simple compass[8]. This sparked his interest in science.

2. A physics journal published his articles when he was just 26 years old.

3. He became a citizen of Switzerland in 1901 and a citizen of the U.S. in 1940.

4. Einstein often had a pipe[9] in his mouth. Wherever he went, a trail of smoke followed him.

5. Albert Einstein won the Nobel Prize in 1921.

6. Einstein spent the last 22 years of his life at Princeton University in the U.S.

7. He died in 1955.

Pablo Picasso

8. The artist Pablo Picasso grew up in Spain.

9. He completed his first painting at the age of 9.

10. His father sent him to the Royal Academy of San Fernando in Madrid to study art.

11. He was very smart but he wasn't a very good student.

12. Picasso's paintings were unconventional.

13. His unconventional painting style annoyed his father.

14. Picasso's paintings influenced the direction of modern art.

Write about It Where possible, rewrite the sentences above to make them passive.

---

[8] **compass:** a tool for finding direction, with a needle that always points north

[9] **pipe:** a tube with a small bowl at one end that is used for smoking tobacco

15 | Distinguishing Transitive and Intransitive Verbs Write each verb from this box under the correct group in the chart below. Then use each word in a sentence. `4.3 A`

allow	come	die	find	happen	involve	occur	say	stare
bring	describe	exist	go	include	mean	pull	smile	wait

Transitive verb	Sample sentence	Intransitive verb	Sample sentence
allow	*My parents allowed me to drive their car.*		

Think about It Where possible, rewrite the active sentences you wrote above as passive sentences.

16 | Transitive or Intransitive Meaning? Decide if the verb in each sentence has a transitive or an intransitive meaning. Write *a*, *b*, or *c*. `4.3 B`

1. The children opened the door. _a_
2. The door opened in front of us. ____

open	—*tr*	**a.** to cause (something) to no longer be covered
	—*intr*	**b.** to move and no longer cover something

3. She spoke at our annual meeting. ____
4. He speaks English and Spanish. ____
5. She always speaks clearly. ____

speak	—*tr*	**a.** to use or be able to use
	—*intr*	**b.** to give a speech
	—*intr*	**c.** to communicate by voice

6. The movie starts at 9:00. ____
7. I started that book a month ago. ____

start	—*tr*	**a.** to begin work on
	—*intr*	**b.** to begin

8. I usually walk to work. ____
9. I need someone to walk my dog tomorrow. ____

walk	—*tr*	**a.** to cause to travel on foot; to lead
	—*intr*	**b.** to travel on foot

10. We leave for Brazil next week. ____

11. I think I left the door open. ____

leave	—tr	**a.**	to cause or allow someone or something to stay in a particular place or condition
	—intr	**b.**	to depart

12. Did I hurt you? ____

13. My neck hurts. ____

hurt	—tr	**a.**	to cause pain
	—intr	**b.**	to feel pain

14. Bananas are selling for a dollar a pound. ____

15. The neighbors finally sold their car. ____

sell	—tr	**a.**	to exchange money for goods and services
	—intr	**b.**	to have a specific price

Think about It Where logical, rewrite the active sentences in Activity 16 as passive sentences.

17 | Using Verbs with Two Objects Rewrite each complaint in two ways. Use passive forms. `4.3 C`

COMPLAINTS ABOUT A COMPANY

1. The company doesn't pay the employees a fair salary.

   The employees aren't paid a fair salary. A fair salary isn't paid to the employees.

2. My company doesn't offer employees health insurance.

   _____

   _____

3. This company doesn't give people proper training.

   _____

   _____

4. The company hasn't always told the workers the truth.

   _____

   _____

5. The company has never paid overtime[10] to its employees.

   _____

   _____

6. The company didn't give employees a bonus last year.

   _____

   _____

7. The company gave a huge raise to the president.

   _____

   _____

8. The company promises a lot of things to the employees.

   _____

   _____

RESEARCH SAYS...

The choice of indirect object or direct object as the subject of a passive sentence often depends on which is mentioned in the previous sentence.

The company doesn't treat its **employees** well. For example, **they** aren't paid a fair salary.
(vs. *A fair salary isn't paid to them.*)

CORPUS

[10] **overtime:** extra time you spend at work

18 | Error Correction Correct any errors in these sentences. (Some sentences may not have any errors.)

1. My father is the person who grew me.
2. In this photograph appears all of my relatives at home.
3. It was a very bad accident and two people were died.
4. A strange thing happened me yesterday.
5. How did you injure?
6. What was appeared on the screen when you turned on your computer?
7. When was the accident occurred? Does anyone know?
8. The money was meant to be payment for my work.
9. After the war started, my brothers were run away to the countryside.
10. All my photographs, school assignments, and telephone numbers saved on my computer.

4.4 The Passive with Modals

We often use the passive with modal and phrasal modal forms, as in **1b – 13b**.

MODAL + *BE* + PAST PARTICIPLE

WILL	Active	**1a** The organizers **will hold** the meeting tomorrow at 10:00.
	Passive	**1b** The meeting **will be held** tomorrow at 10:00.
SHOULD	Active	**2a** Somebody **should deliver** the package in two weeks.
	Passive	**2b** The package **should be delivered** in two weeks.
MUST	Active	**3a** Somebody **must tell** him soon.
	Passive	**3b** He **must be told** soon.
CAN	Active	**4a** We **can prevent** heart disease.
	Passive	**4b** Heart disease **can be prevented**.
MAY	Active	**5a** No one **may copy** any part of this publication.
	Passive	**5b** No part of this publication **may be copied**.
MIGHT	Active	**6a** They **might make** this offer again.
	Passive	**6b** This offer **might be made** again.
COULD	Active	**7a** The writer **could improve** this essay.
	Passive	**7b** This essay **could be improved**.
WOULD	Active	**8a** They said they **would hold** the election as promised.
	Passive	**8b** They said the election **would be held** as promised.

PHRASAL MODAL + *BE* + PAST PARTICIPLE

BE GOING TO	Active	**9a** They **are going to give** us another chance to play.
	Passive	**9b** We're going to **be given** another chance to play.
BE SUPPOSED TO	Active	**10a** We **are supposed to keep** this outside.
	Passive	**10b** This **is supposed to be kept** outside.
HAVE TO	Active	**11a** Somebody **has to do** something.
	Passive	**11b** Something **has to be done**.
BE ABLE TO	Active	**12a** Teachers **are** easily **able to use** this method in all schools.
	Passive	**12b** This method **is able to be used** easily in all schools.
BE ALLOWED TO	Active	**13a** No one **is allowed to take** photographs.
	Passive	**13b** No photographs **are allowed to be taken**.

A

19 | Active or Passive? Decide if the underlined verb is a passive or active form. Write *P* above the passive verb forms. Write *A* above the active forms. Then choose the correct sport. `4.4 A`

Describing Sports

1. This sport <u>can be played</u> indoors or outdoors, but it <u>has to be played</u> on a hard surface.
   Each team <u>is made up</u> of five players.
   a. baseball   b. basketball   c. soccer

2. Players of this sport <u>wear</u> a protective jacket, or *hogu*. This jacket <u>is able to be fitted</u> with sensors
   that <u>signal</u> hits to the body.
   a. boxing   b. diving   c. tae kwon do

3. Jumps and turns <u>have to be performed</u> perfectly to win at this sport. You definitely <u>aren't supposed</u>
   <u>to fall</u> down—you <u>lose</u> points for that.
   a. archery   b. cycling   c. figure skating

4. In this sport, athletes <u>are supposed to be judged</u> on their takeoff, flight, and entry.
   The score <u>is</u> then <u>multiplied</u> by a degree of difficulty factor.
   a. diving   b. judo   c. weight-lifting

5. Women <u>were allowed to participate</u> in the Olympics for the first time in 1900, but they <u>could only</u>
   <u>play</u> these two sports.
   a. golf and lawn tennis   b. canoeing and sailing   c. figure skating and badminton

6. In this sport, gloves <u>must be worn</u>, and a punch[11] <u>must be landed</u> with the white part of the glove.
   a. boxing   b. fencing   c. judo

7. In this sport, a serve <u>must be made</u> from below the waist, with the racket head below the hand and
   with both feet on the ground.
   a. badminton   b. table tennis   c. tennis

8. This sport <u>has been played</u> at every Olympic Games though the rules <u>have changed</u> over the years.
   Today, penalties[12] <u>can be awarded</u> for deflecting hits with the hand or refusing to salute one's
   opponent.
   a. archery   b. fencing   c. volleyball

9. This sport <u>can be played</u> on a soft or hard surface. Players <u>are supposed to hit</u> the ball back and
   forth over a net without letting it touch the ground. Any part of the body above the waist
   <u>may be used</u> to hit the ball, but the ball <u>isn't allowed to be held</u>.
   a. basketball   b. football   c. volleyball

10. In this sport, 85 percent of the bat or racket <u>is supposed to be made</u> of wood. The other 15 percent
    <u>can be made</u> of other materials.
    a. football   b. table tennis   c. water polo

---

[11] **punch:** a hit with a closed hand

[12] **penalties:** punishments for one team and advantages for another team when a player breaks a rule

Talk about It Work with one or more classmates. In three minutes, think of as many sports as you can for each category. Then compare ideas with your classmates.

It's played with a ball but players aren't allowed to kick it.	It can be played indoors or outdoors.	Special shoes have to be worn.
tennis		

It is supposed to be played by teams of 11 people.	It isn't going to be played at the next Olympic Games.	It must be played on ice.

Write about It Write several sentences about a sport, but don't identify the sport. Try to use the passive with modal or phrasal modal forms. Then read your sentences to your classmates and let them identify the sport.

20 | Using the Passive with Modals Complete these descriptions with the passive form of the words in parentheses. 4.4 A

> ## Course Descriptions
>
> 1. **ENGL 242 English Grammar and Conversation I**
>
>   This course _____*is intended*_____ to help foreign students in acquiring fluency in spoken English.
>   (intend)
>   All four language skills (listening, speaking, reading, and writing) _____.
>   (will / practice)
>
> 2. **ENGL 243 English Grammar and Conversation II**
>
>   This course is a continuation of ENGL 242. It _____ prior to ENGL 256.
>   (should / take)
>   Some students whose assessment scores qualify them for ENGL 256 _____
>   (may / advise)
>   to take this course as a companion course.
>
> 3. **ENGL 245 Advanced Conversation**
>
>   Students discuss current events in English. Pronunciation, vocabulary development, and group
>
>   discussion skills _____. This course _____ concurrently[13]
>   (stress)   (may / take)
>   with other English courses.
>
> 4. **ENGL 256 Grammar and Composition**
>
>   This intermediate course in English grammar and composition _____ to help
>   (design)
>   students acquire a greater facility in written English. This course is for the student who is pursuing
>
>   a college career. It _____ with ENGL 243 or 245.
>   (can / take)

Think about It Passive forms are common in course descriptions. Why might this be?

---

[13] **concurrently:** at the same time

21 | Using the Passive with *Can*, *Can't*, *Could*, and *Couldn't* Write the passive form of each sentence using *can*, *can't*, *could*, or *couldn't* + the past participle of the verb in parentheses. [4.4 A]

1. These questions were unanswerable. (answer)
   These questions couldn't be answered.

2. This place was indescribable. (describe)
   _____

3. Her absence is inexcusable. (excuse)
   _____

4. The problem was solvable. (solve)
   _____

5. The results were measurable. (measure)
   _____

6. War is preventable. (prevent)
   _____

7. Sometimes delays are unavoidable. (avoid)
   _____

8. The consequences were unpredictable. (predict)
   _____

9. His goal is achievable. (achieve)
   _____

10. These walls are movable. (move)
    _____

> **F Y I**
> The most common modals used with the passive are *can* and *could* (for possibility).

Write about It Choose three verbs used in the passive sentences above, and write your own sentences.

4.5 Special Passive Structures

A

ACTIVE VERB + *THAT* CLAUSE

1 At one time, people **believed** that the earth was flat.

2 In the 1600s, Europeans **thought** that tomatoes were poisonous.

PASSIVE FORM + *TO*-INFINITIVE

3 At one time, the earth **was believed** to be flat.

4 In the 1600s, tomatoes **were thought** to be poisonous.

We use certain verbs (e.g., *believe, consider, say, think, understand*) to identify a common belief. In an **active** sentence, we often use a ***that* clause** after these verbs, as in **1 – 2**. In these sentences, the *that* clause functions as a kind of direct object.

In a **passive** sentence, we sometimes use a **to-infinitive** after these verbs, as in **3 – 4**.

For more information on *that* clauses, see Unit 12.

B

IT + PASSIVE FORM + *THAT* CLAUSE

5 It **has been reported** that this year will be warmer than usual.

6 It is commonly **believed** that children are better language learners than adults.

7 In Shefley (1999), **it is argued** that children are better language learners than adults.

We sometimes use **it + passive form + *that* clause**, as in **5 – 7**. Verbs used with this pattern include:

argue	estimate	report	suppose
believe	expect	say	think
consider	know	show	

In academic writing, this pattern is sometimes used to introduce an argument, as in **7**.

22 | Using the Passive to Identify Common Beliefs Match the sentence beginnings with the sentence endings. (More than one answer may be possible but only one is correct.) `4.5 A`

COMMON BELIEFS

1. Tobacco was once considered __a__
2. Carrots were once thought ____
3. The planet Venus was once believed ____
4. Television was once thought ____
5. Earth was once believed ____
6. Bathing was once considered ____
7. Thinking was once understood ____
8. Centuries ago, a child was said ____
9. Your personality was once thought ____

a. to be a cure[14] for a toothache.
b. to be related to your blood type.
c. to be the death of the movie industry.
d. to be covered with oil.
e. to be a small adult.
f. to be the center of the solar system.
g. to take place in the heart.
h. to be bad for your health.
i. to improve your vision.

Think about It Why does it make sense to use passive rather than active forms in the sentences above?

Write about It Identify three more things that were thought to be true in the past and write sentences about them. Read your sentences to the class.

23 | Using *It* + Passive Form + *That* Clause Rewrite each sentence using *it* + a passive verb form. Pay special attention to the form of the verb. `4.5 B`

MEDICAL BELIEFS

1. Experts say that more than 20,000 different plants are used for health purposes.
   It is said that more than 20,000 different plants are used for health purposes.

2. For a long time, people believed that the evil "influence" of the stars caused influenza, or the flu.
   _____

3. In sixteenth-century England, people thought the color red helped sick people get well.
   _____

4. Doctors have reported that some dogs are able to smell skin cancer.
   _____

5. Researchers believe that doctors prescribe antibiotics[15] too frequently.
   _____

6. Researchers estimate that one in two Americans will get cancer.
   _____

7. Many people think cancer is the most frightening disease.
   _____

8. Many people expect that researchers will find a cure for AIDS.
   _____

Think about It Why might a writer choose to use the passive rather than the active form in the sentences above?

---

[14] **cure:** something that makes an illness go away   [15] **antibiotics:** medicines that fight illness in a person's body

4.6 Passive Form or *Be* + Adjective?

A

PASSIVE FORM

1 The door **is locked** every evening at 9:00.
(= Someone locks the door every evening.)

2 The atoms **were excited** by the X-rays.
(= The X-rays excited the atoms.)

BE + ADJECTIVE

3 I **was exhausted** after the hike.

4 I can't sleep. I'm too **excited**.

5 The front door **is** always **locked** in the evening.
(= appears locked or is locked by someone)

A **passive verb form** is made with *be* + past participle, as in **1 – 2**. In these sentences, the past participles *locked* and *excited* describe actions.

A past participle can also function as an **adjective**, as in **3 – 4**. In these sentences, the past participles *exhausted* and *excited* follow *be* and describe a state—how something is. In these sentences, you can often use *very* before the past participle.

Sometimes it is difficult to tell whether a past participle is an adjective (describes a state) or a true passive form (describes an action), as in **5**.

B

PASSIVE WITH *BY* + AGENT

6 She **was frightened by** the loud noise.
      agent

7 Everyone **was confused by** the instructions.
      agent

BE + ADJECTIVE + PREPOSITION

8 He's **interested in** science.

9 The table **was covered with** a dark cloth.

10 The committee **is composed of** instructors from each faculty.

Remember: In a passive sentence, we sometimes use the preposition *by* to introduce the agent, as in **6 – 7**.

However, when a past participle functions as an adjective, we use other prepositions, as in **8 – 10**. Common *be* + participle + preposition combinations include:

be annoyed with	be dressed in	be known for
be bored with	be excited about	be made of
be composed of	be filled with	be opposed to
be concerned about	be finished with	be pleased with
be covered with	be interested in	be satisfied with
be dedicated to	be involved in	be worried about
be disappointed with/in		

 GO ONLINE

---

24 | Passive Verb Form or *Be* + Adjective? Decide if the underlined words in these sentences are passive verb forms or *be* + adjective. Check (✓) your answers. **4.6 A**

Rudolph Nureyev

	PASSIVE	BE + ADJECTIVE
1. Rudolf Nureyev, the famous dancer, <u>was born</u> in a train in 1938.	☑	☐
2. From an early age, Nureyev <u>was interested</u> in music and ballet.	☐	☐
3. When he was 17, he <u>was accepted</u> at a famous ballet school in Leningrad.	☐	☐
4. His instructor, Alexander Pushkin, <u>was renowned</u> in the world of ballet.	☐	☐

	PASSIVE	BE + ADJECTIVE
5. Pushkin's students <u>were not scolded</u>[16] when they made mistakes.	☐	☐
6. In 1958, at the age of 20, Nureyev <u>was asked</u> to join the Kirov Ballet.	☐	☐
7. For the most part, his colleagues at the Kirov Ballet <u>were unimpressed</u> with his dancing.	☐	☐
8. Nureyev's early style <u>was unrefined</u>.	☐	☐
9. In early films of Nureyev, his shoulders <u>are hunched</u>[17] and his landings[18] are heavy.	☐	☐
10. Nureyev <u>was dedicated</u> to ballet and he worked hard to become one of the best dancers in the world.	☐	☐

RESEARCH SAYS...

Some verbs are almost always used in the passive form. Examples include:

be approved
be associated with
be based on
be born
be classified as
be composed of

CORPU

Think about It Which of the underlined verb forms in Activity 24 were easy to classify as a passive form or *be* + adjective? Why? Which were difficult?

25 | Listening for Past Participles Read these conversations and guess the missing past participle. (Many different answers are possible.) Listen and check your guesses. Then practice with a partner. `4.6 A`

1. A: What's the matter? You look _____*bored*_____.

   B: I am. There's nothing to do.

2. A: What happened to this chair? It's all wet.

   B: Yeah, it was _____ outside in the rain last night.

3. A: Look. You've made your sister cry. You should be _____!

   B: Sorry, Mom.

4. A: I hear your brother didn't get that job.

   B: Yeah. They gave it to someone with more experience.

   A: He must have been very _____.

   B: Yeah, he was.

5. A: Why are you so _____ about money?

   B: Because I don't have any.

   A: That's a good answer.

6. A: Do you want to go with us to the lecture?

   B: Thanks, but no thanks. I'm really not _____.

7. A: It's getting late. Are you _____?

   B: I'm just putting on my shoes.

   A: OK. I'll wait for you downstairs.

---

[16] **scold:** to tell a person in an angry way that he or she has done something wrong

[17] **hunched:** bent over
[18] **landings:** acts of coming down onto the ground

8. A: How did your speech go?

   B: It was all right. At least the audience seemed _____.

9. A: Did you hear? Carlos and Sarah are getting married.

   B: I'm not _____. They've been talking about it for months.

10. A: Are you going to the conference next spring?

    B: I hadn't thought about it. Where is it being _____?

    A: In London.

11. A: I heard there was an accident last night.

    B: Yeah, a car went through a red light and hit another car.

    A: Was anyone _____?

    B: Luckily, no.

Think about It In which conversations in Activity 25 does a speaker use a passive form?

26 | Choosing the Correct Preposition Complete each sentence with the correct preposition. Then check (✓) *True* or *False* for you. 4.6 B

ALL ABOUT ME	TRUE	FALSE
1. I am very interested ___*in*___ politics.	☐	☐
2. I am concerned _____ the state of the world.	☐	☐
3. I am engaged _____ a wonderful person.	☐	☐
4. I have never been involved _____ a car accident.	☐	☐
5. I am known _____ my generosity.	☐	☐
6. I am opposed _____ gun control.	☐	☐
7. I am pleased _____ my progress at school this year.	☐	☐
8. I am worried _____ the environment.	☐	☐
9. I am dressed _____ casual clothes today.	☐	☐
10. I am satisfied _____ the amount of money I have.	☐	☐
11. I have never been annoyed _____ anyone.	☐	☐
12. My parents were never disappointed _____ my schoolwork.	☐	☐
13. My bedroom is filled _____ books.	☐	☐
14. My shoes are made _____ leather.	☐	☐
15. I am bored _____ the news about climate change.	☐	☐
16. I am excited _____ my plans for this coming weekend.	☐	☐

Write about It Write three statements about yourself using *be* + participle + preposition. Make two of your statements true and one false. Read your statements to the class, and ask your classmates to identify the false statement.

Today, I'm dressed in my best clothes.
I'm interested in chess.
I'm satisfied with my life so far.

4.7 Using the Passive in Speaking

A

1 A: Who **got offered** the job?
B: I haven't heard.

2 A: What happened to Jeremy?
B: He **got caught** skipping class.

3 A: How did you **get hurt**?
B: I **got hit** by a golf ball.

4 A: Are you going to Yan's dinner?
B: No, I **didn't get invited**.

5 Did she **get fired**? (= Was she fired?)

6 They **didn't get paid** for their work.
(= They weren't paid for their work.)

In conversation, we sometimes use **get + past participle** instead of *be* + past participle for the passive, as in **1 – 2**. We usually use *get* + a past participle to express a change of situation or condition. For example:

get asked	get fired	get left
get blamed	get hit	get offered
get caught	get hurt	get paid
get done	get invited	get promoted
get elected	get killed	

The passive with *get* is often (but not always) used when there is a negative result, as in **3 – 4**.

Notice that we use the helping verb *do* in questions and negative statements with *get*, as in **5 – 6**.

27 | Listening for *Get* Passives Read these conversations and guess the missing past participle. (Many different answers are possible.) Listen and check your guesses. 4.7 A

1. A: Did you hear about the accident?
   B: Yeah, it was on the news.
   A: Did anyone get ___hurt___?
   B: I don't think so.

2. A: Why don't you stay home today?
   B: Are you kidding? I could get _____.

3. A: Why are you driving so slowly?
   B: Because I've already gotten _____ by the police once today.

4. A: Why are you celebrating?
   B: Because Toshi just got _____.
   A: Really? That's great!

5. A: What's that smell?
   B: I think it's the trash. It didn't get _____ out yesterday.

6. A: What are you looking for?
   B: My dark-blue shirt.
   A: Look in the closet. It just got _____.

7. A: Do you know if the lights got _____ off?
   B: Yeah, I'm pretty sure they did.

8. A: How did you break the window?
   B: I didn't do it. Why do I get _____ for everything?

9. A: I wonder why we haven't received those books yet. It's been three weeks.
   B: Maybe they got _____ to the wrong address.

WARNING!

We use *get* in a number of expressions that don't have a passive meaning. In these contexts, *get* means *become*. The word used with *get* is an adjective.

get dressed	get lost
get engaged	get married
get involved	get tired

10. A: Can I borrow some money?

    B: Again? I thought you just got _____.

    A: I did but I had some bills to pay.

11. A: Are you going to vote tomorrow?

    B: Yes, but I'm not sure why. No one I vote for gets _____.

12. A: Don't forget to wash the car today.

    B: I'm not sure I can do it today. Is tomorrow OK?

    A: As long as it gets _____ this week, I'm happy.

Talk about It Practice the conversations in Activity 27 with a partner.

28 | Using *Get* Passives Rewrite these questions with the *get* passive. `4.7 A`

1. Were you ever punished as a child?

   Did you ever get punished as a child?
   _____

2. Were you ever yelled at by an adult?

   _____

3. Were you ever caught cheating on a test?

   _____

4. Were you ever treated unfairly by someone?

   _____

5. Were you ever hit by someone?

   _____

6. Were you ever elected to something?

   _____

7. Were you ever sent home from school?

   _____

8. Were you ever blamed for something you didn't do?

   _____

> **WARNING!**
>
> We don't normally use *get* in the passive with non-action verbs (*hate, know, like, own, see, want,* etc.).
>
> You were seen at the beach. (NOT: ~~You got seen at the beach.~~)

Talk about It Ask a partner the questions you wrote above. If your partner answers yes, ask a follow-up question.

A: *Did you ever get punished as a child?*
B: *Sometimes.*
A: *When?*
B: . . .

A	**MAKING WRITING COHESIVE** **1** Dr. Bell is one of our most prominent scientists. His research focuses on the role of the environment in the development of cancer. Because of the importance of his work, Dr. Bell **was honored** with a research award last night. **2** The researchers selected 209 compositions for the study. All of the compositions **were written** in 50-minute class sessions.	In a cohesive paragraph, each sentence connects smoothly to the sentences before and after it. The passive is one of several techniques that writers can use to make a connection between sentences, as in **1 – 2**. • In **1**, the writer connects the sentences by keeping the focus on the same topic: *Dr. Bell / His research / Dr. Bell*. To do this, the writer uses a passive form in the third sentence. • In **2**, the writer connects the sentences by using the new information in the first sentence (*209 compositions*) as the subject of the next sentence (*All of the compositions*). To do this, the writer uses a passive form in the second sentence. For more information on cohesion, see Units 5, 6, and 7.
B	**USING THE PASSIVE IN ACADEMIC WRITING** **3** For this study, 107 young adults **were divided** into three groups. For three weeks, they all they drank the same type of coffee. Then the participants **were randomly assigned** to different groups. Each of these groups **was given** a different type of coffee.	The passive is often used in academic writing, especially in the sciences where the focus is more on what happened than on who did something, as in **3**. Using the passive gives the impression that the person doing the research is unimportant. It suggests that the results of the research will be the same for anyone.
C	**USING PARALLEL STRUCTURE** **4** For each composition, the errors **were counted**, **classified**, and later **analyzed**. (NOT: For each composition, the errors were counted, classified, and ~~later they analyzed them.~~)	In a sentence with a series of verbs, it's important to be consistent or parallel, as in **4**. Use all passive or all active verbs.

29 | Using the Passive to Connect Sentences Check (✓) the sentence in each pair that best follows the first sentence. **4.8 A**

1. Several people complained about the new schedule.

   ☑ a. The first complaint was made by a member of the school committee.

   ☐ b. A member of the school committee made the first complaint.

2. This year's graduation celebration cost $6,549.

   ☐ a. The parents of the graduates raised this money.

   ☐ b. This money was raised entirely by the parents of the graduates.

3. Frederick Tyler designed the new furniture for the town library.

   ☐ a. One of his students made it.

   ☐ b. It was made by one of his students.

4. Football has a long history in Europe.

   ☐ a. In fourteenth-century England, authorities banned the sport for being too violent.

   ☐ b. In fourteenth-century England, it was banned for being too violent.

5. A typical grocery store in 1928 stocked about 870 items.

   ☐ a. Today's supermarkets carry up to 30,000 items.

   ☐ b. Today, up to 30,000 items are carried.

6. For many years, bicycle racers wore leather helmets. Then, in the mid-1980s, they started wearing helmets made of strong, dense materials.
   - ☐ a. Engineers designed them to protect the racers' heads if they fell.
   - ☐ b. They were designed to protect the racers' heads if they fell.

7. Pollution causes poor air quality.
   - ☐ a. It can be bad for your health.
   - ☐ b. Your health can be affected by it.

8. Antibiotics are important tools in the fight against illness, but some bacteria change.
   - ☐ a. Therefore, we need new medicines to kill them.
   - ☐ b. Therefore, new medicines are needed to kill them.

9. There are two types of fats: saturated and unsaturated. Saturated fats, such as butter and coconut oil, are solid at room temperature. Unsaturated fats, such as olive oil and corn oil, are liquid at room temperature.
   - ☐ a. Doctors consider unsaturated fats better for you.
   - ☐ b. Unsaturated fats are considered better for you.

10. The first U.S. flag had 13 white stars.
    - ☐ a. A new star has been added for every new state.
    - ☐ b. The government has added a new star for every new state.

11. The president is the head of the executive branch of the government.
    - ☐ a. He or she is elected by the entire country.
    - ☐ b. The entire country elects the president.

12. There are nine justices, or judges, on the U.S. Supreme Court.
    - ☐ a. The president nominates them and the Senate approves them.
    - ☐ b. They are nominated by the president and approved by the Senate.

13. In this study, French researchers looked at more than 7,000 men and women.
    - ☐ a. They recorded information on their education, income, and tobacco use, among other factors.
    - ☐ b. Information on their education, income, and tobacco use, among other factors, was recorded.

14. Michelle Kwan became famous when she was quite young.
    - ☐ a. She was asked to represent the U.S. as a skater when she was just 13 years old.
    - ☐ b. The U.S. Olympic team asked her to represent the U.S. as a skater when she was just 13 years old.

15. In this study, researchers tested students both outdoors in natural settings and inside buildings.
    - ☐ a. The students were found to have more energy after spending time in nature.
    - ☐ b. Spending time in nature increased the students' energy level.

16. Although he worked as an engineer in the U.S. for 20 years, Gilberto Cetina never forgot the food of his native country.
    - ☐ a. Eleven years ago, a restaurant was opened by Gilberto and his son.
    - ☐ b. Eleven years ago, he and his son opened a restaurant.

Write about It What do you think the third sentence in each item above might be?

Several people complained about the new schedule. The first complaint was made by a member of the school committee. This person felt that the new schedule didn't give students enough time for lunch.

30 | Identifying Reasons for Using the Passive An obituary is a news report on someone's death. Underline the passive verb forms in this obituary. Then tell why the writer used the passive in each case. Choose one or more reasons from the list on the right. [4.8 A]

Marmaduke Hussey, Former Chairman of the BBC, Dies Aged 83

By Mark Herlihy and Chris Peterson

Dec. 27 (Bloomberg)—Marmaduke Hussey, the former chairman of the BBC and managing director of Times Newspapers, has died at the age of 83.

Hussey, who lost a leg in in World War II, <u>was educated</u> at Trinity College, Oxford. He was trained as a journalist and worked as chief executive and managing director of Times Newspapers, owner of the Times of London, from 1971 to 1980.

"He will be remembered for his great vision, his integrity and his forthrightness, but also for his great personal kindness," BBC Director General Mark Thompson said in an e-mailed statement today. His contribution to public life was immense, Thompson said.

Hussey was appointed chairman of the BBC in 1986 thanks in part to his connections to the then ruling Conservative Party under the leadership of Margaret Thatcher. During his time as BBC chairman, he sacked Alasdair Milne as director general in 1987 after a series of rows with the government over the BBC's independence.

Hussey was made a life peer in 1996, following his retirement from the BBC. He was married to Lady Susan Waldegrave, a lady in waiting to Queen Elizabeth II and godmother to Prince William, who is next in line to the throne after Prince Charles.

> **REASONS**
> 1. because the agent is unknown
> 2. because the agent is unimportant
> 3. because the agent refers to people in general
> 4. because the agent is obvious from the context
> 5. to keep the focus on the same topic
> 6. to use new information in the previous sentence as the subject of the following sentence

Think about It Compare your answers above with your classmates. Was it difficult to choose between reasons for any of the passive uses? Why?

31 | Analyzing Passive Forms in Academic Writing Read this text from a psychology textbook. Underline any passive forms. Then answer the questions on page 135. [4.8 A–B]

A STUDY OF STEREOTYPES

It <u>has recently been shown</u> that stereotypes can have negative, long-lasting effects on the people who experience them. A new study has found that people who experience negative stereotypes and insults in one situation may continue to experience the effects of those insults in a later, unrelated situation. "Past studies have shown that people perform poorly in situations where they feel they are being stereotyped," said lead researcher Michael Inzlicht of the University of Toronto in Canada. "What we wanted to do was look at what happens afterwards." Inzlicht's study asked if there are any lasting effects of prejudice and if being stereotyped has an impact after the moment when the stereotyping occurs.

The researchers divided female participants into two groups. The women were asked to take a test that would determine their math abilities. One group of women was exposed to negative stereotypes about women and their math abilities. After the test began, the researchers made negative statements about women in order to make them feel more stress. In contrast, another group of women was given the same test, but they were offered strategies to deal with the stress of taking the exam. The researchers were very supportive with this group. After the math test ended, both groups of women were given ice cream samples and were asked to describe the flavors. Next, they were asked to play a video game that allowed them to shoot other players with a loud noise for as long as they wanted.

The women who were discriminated against performed more poorly on the math test. They also ate more ice cream than the women in the supported group, and they showed more hostility and aggression when they played the video game than the other group. These effects were particularly noticeable for the women who experienced negative stereotypes during the math test.

In the end, the study results show that stereotypes have negative effects, even for individuals who leave the environments where they experienced the stereotyping. These effects can be long-lasting. When people are affected by negative stereotyping, they are more likely to be aggressive and show a lack of self-control. After they've faced prejudice, they have trouble making good decisions, and they are more likely to make unhealthy food choices and overeat. Researchers hope the study will make people more aware of these effects of stereotyping. They hope this will help people to better manage their emotions and thoughts when they are faced with stereotypes so that they can show more self-control in later situations.

QUESTIONS

1. How many passive verb forms did you find in this text? Compare answers with your classmates.
2. How many of these passive forms appear with *by* + agent?
3. Did the writer use a passive form to help connect two sentences? Give an example.
4. Did the writer use any intransitive verbs? Which ones?

Write about It Write a one-paragraph summary of the article in Activity 31.

32 | Using a Series of Verbs Complete these sentences with the appropriate form of the verb in parentheses. 4.8 C

1. The letter was written and _____*sent*_____ before the due date. (send)
2. Stone can be carved, chipped, and _____. (smooth)
3. Penicillin was created and _____ to fight infection. (use)
4. Ice reduces the swelling around an insect bite and _____ the itching. (ease)
5. Their children were raised and _____ in London. (educate)
6. The house was designed and _____ in the 1860s. (build)
7. Scientists have already established that good-looking people are paid better

   and _____ as smarter and more likeable. (view)
8. The book was written in 1968 and _____ in 1982. (revise)

WRAP-UP Demonstrate Your Knowledge

A | ANALYZE Look for an interesting news story—a story that focuses on what happened and to whom. Bring the story to class and identify the passive verb forms.

National Zoo Names Panda Cub

WASHINGTON—The giant female panda cub at the Smithsonian National Zoo <u>has been given</u> a name—Bao Bao. The name <u>was selected</u> after it received more than 123,000 votes online from the public.

Panda mother Mei Xiang (may-SHONG) has been caring for her cub since Bao Bao <u>was born</u> on August 23. Bao Bao <u>will be shown</u> for short periods of time beginning early next year.

The public <u>was asked</u> to vote for one of five names for the new cub. The others were Ling Hua (ling-HWA), Long Yun (long-YOON), Mulan (moo-LAHN), and Zhen Bao (jen-BAO). The names <u>were submitted</u> by the Chinese ambassador.

B | WEB SEARCH Complete this question and then look online for the answer. Tell your classmates what you learned.

When and where was the first _____ used?

C | RESEARCH AND REPORT Choose three countries and look for the information to complete this chart. Present your findings to the class.

	Country *Cambodia*	Country _____	Country _____	Country _____
What language is spoken?	*Khmer*			
What percentage of the land is used for agriculture?	*30.9%*			
What is grown or produced there?	*rice, rubber, clothing*			
What natural resources are found there?	*oil, gas, timber, fish*			

D | COMPARE Study the "before" and "after" pictures below. How many changes can you find? Describe them.

The birdhouses were taken out of the room.

4.9 Summary of the Passive

USES

We sometimes use the passive:

- to focus a sentence on what happened and to what or whom
- because we can't or choose not to identify the performer of the action, or agent
- to avoid blaming someone for something
- to avoid taking responsibility for something
- to connect sentences in a paragraph

SIMPLE PRESENT PASSIVE:

BE (AM, IS, ARE) + PAST PARTICIPLE

I	am		
He / She / It	is	paid	twice a month.
We / You / They	are		

SIMPLE PAST PASSIVE:

BE (WAS, WERE) + PAST PARTICIPLE

I / He / She / It	was		
We / You / They	were	paid	last week.

PRESENT PROGRESSIVE PASSIVE:

BE (AM, IS, ARE) + *BEING* + PAST PARTICIPLE

I	am	
He / She / It	is	being helped.
We / You / They	are	

PAST PROGRESSIVE PASSIVE:

BE (WAS, WERE) + *BEING* + PAST PARTICIPLE

I / He / She / It	was	
We / You / They	were	being helped.

PRESENT PERFECT PASSIVE:

HAVE / HAS + *BEEN* + PAST PARTICIPLE

I / We / You / They	have	
He / She / It	has	been helped.

PAST PERFECT PASSIVE:

HAD + *BEEN* + PAST PARTICIPLE

I / He / She / It	
We / You / They	had been helped.

MODALS:

MODAL + *BE* + PAST PARTICIPLE

The package	will should can must may might could would	be delivered	soon.

PHRASAL MODALS:

PHRASAL MODAL + *BE* + PAST PARTICIPLE

The package	is going to is supposed to has to is able to is allowed to	be sent	by air.

5 Adverbs and Adverbials

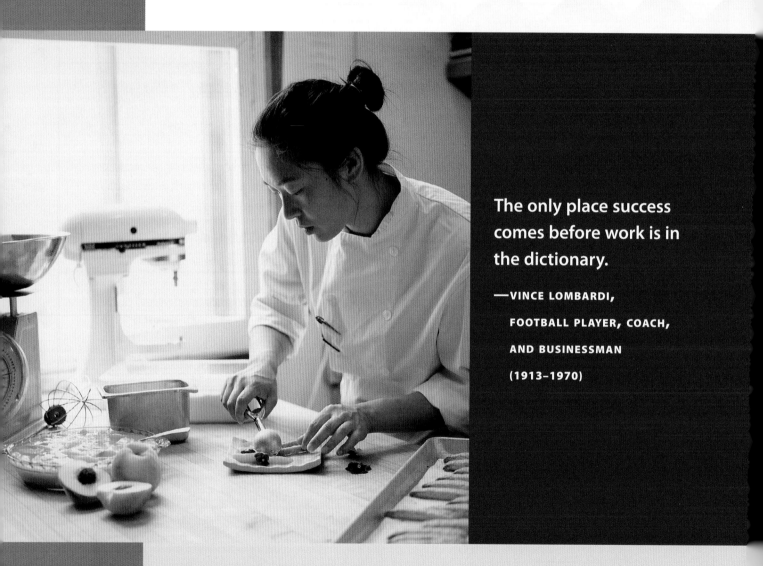

The only place success comes before work is in the dictionary.

—VINCE LOMBARDI,
FOOTBALL PLAYER, COACH,
AND BUSINESSMAN
(1913–1970)

Talk about It What does the quotation above mean? Do you agree or disagree?

WARM-UP

A | Match each description with a topic on the right. (You will not use all of the topics.)

What are they describing?

1. It's a medium-sized place **near my apartment. For very little money,** you can get a sandwich and a bowl of soup. ____

2. There was nothing I could do **to calm my fear.** I squeezed the armrest of my seat **until my knuckles were white.** I drank some bottled water **to settle my stomach.** I tried to read a book and listen to music. No luck. **Finally,** I started talking to an elderly woman **across from me.** ____

3. He had problems with his GPS, and then he had to stop **to change a flat tire.** He traveled **very slowly**—only 10 miles in **five hours**— and **along the way** his camera got destroyed. ____

4. It has **fairly** new tires and **only 2,400 miles on the odometer**[1]. ____

a. a motorcycle
b. a city
c. a classroom problem
d. a plane ride
e. a difficult trip
f. a restaurant

B | The words in green in the descriptions above are adverbials. Based on these examples, what can you say about adverbials? Check (✓) *True* or *False*.

	TRUE	FALSE
1. Adverbials are always single words.	☐	☐
2. A prepositional phrase can be an adverbial.	☐	☐
3. Some adverbials begin with a *to-* infinitive.	☐	☐
4. Adverbials add different kinds of information to a sentence.	☐	☐
5. Adverbials are common in writing.	☐	☐

C | Look back at the quotation on page 138. Identify any adverbials.

[1] **odometer:** an instrument that shows the distance that a car has traveled

5.1 Overview of Adverbs and Adverbials

A

We use some **adverbs** to add information to verbs, adjectives, and other adverbs, as in **1 – 3**.

verb	adverb		adverb	adjective		adverb	adverb
1 Go	ahead.	**2** You look	really	familiar.	**3** She isn't here	right	now.

We use other adverbs to show our feelings or attitude about the information in a clause or whole sentence, as in **4 – 5**.

adverb	sentence		sentence	adverb
4 Unfortunately,	I couldn't call you.	**5** I'm OK,	honestly.	

And we use other adverbs to connect clauses or sentences, as in **6**. (We call these linking adverbs.)

sentence	adverb	sentence
6 Food is not allowed on the trains.	However,	mobile phones can be used.

WARNING! Sometimes the same adverb can be used in different ways.

7 He told me a **really** funny story. (*really = very*; it strengthens the meaning of the adjective *funny*)

8 I don't want to go, **really**. (*really = honestly*; it shows our feelings or attitude about the whole sentence)

B

DIFFERENT KINDS OF ADVERBIALS

9 I'll come **later**.

10 The car is running **much better**.

11 She can't be here **on Tuesday**.

12 Can you come **this weekend**?

13 They're coming **to see you**.

14 **Since everyone is here**, let's get started.

Any word, phrase, or clause that can function like an adverb is called an **adverbial**. Forms of adverbials include:

- one-word adverbs, as in **9** (and **1 – 8** above)
- adverb phrases, as in **10**
- prepositional phrases that function as adverbs, as in **11**
- noun phrases that function as adverbs, as in **12**
- to- infinitive phrases that function as adverbs, as in **13**
- adverb clauses, as in **14**

For information on *to-* infinitives, see Unit 11.
For information on adverb clauses, see Unit 6.

C

15 I think he writes **well**. (adverbial)

16 She doesn't feel **well**. (adjectival)

17 He appeared **on TV**. (adverbial)

18 The man **on TV** was funny. (adjectival)

Sometimes a word or phrase can be **adverbial** in one context but **adjectival** (function like an adjective) in another, as in **15 – 18**.

For more information on the kinds of words and phrases we use to add information to nouns, see Unit 9.

1 | Noticing How Adverbs Add Information Draw an arrow from the **bold** adverbs to the words they describe or connect. Some adverbs may describe a whole sentence or connect two sentences. **5.1 A**

Hurricanes

1. Hurricanes are storms with **extremely** strong winds.

2. In the Indian Ocean, these storms **generally** are called cyclones.

3. A storm **officially** becomes a hurricane when winds reach above 75 miles an hour.

4. Hurricanes **usually** start in the North Atlantic and move **westward**.

5. They move at about 10 miles an hour in the beginning and **gradually** gain speed.

6. A **fully** mature hurricane is **almost** circular.

7. In the center, or eye, the sky **often** looks blue.

8. **Remarkably**, the air is **very** calm in the eye of the hurricane.

9. The Atlantic hurricane season starts on June 1 and ends on November 30.
   However, most hurricanes form between August 15 and October 15.

Think about It What is the purpose of each **bold** adverb in Activity 1? Write each adverb under the correct group in this chart.

Describes a verb	Describes an adjective	Describes the writer's attitude about the information in the sentence	Connects two sentences
	extremely		

2 | Categorizing Adverbials Read the text below. Match each **bold** adverbial with a form from the box. Write the number of the form over the adverbial. `5.1 B`

1. one-word adverb	3. prepositional phrase	5. *to-* infinitive phrase
2. adverb phrase	4. noun phrase	6. adverb clause

My Scariest Experience

The scariest experience I can remember was an airplane flight I took
many years ago. I was **at my university** and decided to spend the
holidays **with my father**. I was studying **in Los Angeles**, and he lived
in a small city near Phoenix, Arizona. My trip was divided into two
flights. **First**, I flew **from Los Angeles to Phoenix**. **Then** I had to change
planes **to fly to the smaller city**. The first flight was on a large jet and
was **very** smooth. **By the time I landed in Phoenix, however**, it was
snowing. I walked **to my connecting flight**, and imagine my surprise
to discover that the plane was small—it **probably** sat ten people.

   We took off **in the middle of a snowstorm**. **From the first moment**, the plane shook **back and forth,
up and down**. There was nothing I could do **to calm my fear**. I squeezed the armrest of my seat **until my
knuckles were white**. I drank some bottled water **to settle my stomach**. I tried to read a book and listen

1. one-word adverb	3. prepositional phrase	5. *to-* infinitive phrase		
2. adverb phrase	4. noun phrase	6. adverb clause		

to music. No luck. **Finally**, I started talking to an elderly woman **across from me**. She didn't seem bothered by the turbulence **at all**. She revealed that, **many years ago**, she had **also** attended my university. **In fact**, she had been its first female graduate! I was so absorbed with her story that I calmed down. **Thankfully**, the flight was short! **When we landed**, I was relieved to be on the ground and I thanked my new friend.

Think about It Which of the **bold** adverbials in Activity 2 show the writer's feelings about the information in the sentence? Which connect two sentences?

3 | Adverbial or Adjectival? Decide if the **bold** words and phrases in these sentences are used in an adverbial or adjectival way. Check (✓) your answers. 5.1 C

	ADVERBIAL	ADJECTIVAL
1. a. The temperature **in there** was unbearable.	☐	☐
b. Don't go **in there** until it cools off.	☐	☐
2. a. Don't you feel **well**?	☐	☐
b. I don't think I did **well** on the test.	☐	☐
3. a Lots of people use their cell phones **at the grocery store**.	☐	☐
b. People **at the grocery store** are always talking on their cell phones.	☐	☐
4. a. I hope this test isn't going to be **hard**.	☐	☐
b. I was breathing **hard** after running for so long.	☐	☐
5. a. On Sundays we usually eat **early**.	☐	☐
b. We usually have an **early** dinner on Sundays.	☐	☐
6. a. There isn't anything **on the table**.	☐	☐
b. The things **on the table** are yours.	☐	☐
7. a. Travelers **without a guide** can't visit this area.	☐	☐
b. You can't travel there **without a guide**.	☐	☐
8. a. There are many opportunities for work and education **in a large city**.	☐	☐
b. Apartments **in a large city** are usually quite expensive.	☐	☐
9. a. **On the radio**, you can hear many different kinds of programs.	☐	☐
b. I can't hear the music **on the radio**.	☐	☐

Write about It Write questions using each of these words or phrases in both an adverbial and an adjectival way. Then ask a partner your questions.

hard	on your desk	well

5.2 Using Adverbials to Explain *When, Where, How,* and *Why*

A

TIME ADVERBIALS

1 **Now** it's my turn. (when)

2 Reports in the natural sciences **often** begin with the results. (how often)

3 She arrived **this morning**. (when)

4 They're going to stay **for a while**. (how long)

We use some **adverbials** as time expressions. Time adverbials answer the question *when, how often,* or *how long,* as in **1 – 4**. The adverbial may be:
- an adverb or adverb phrase, as in **1 – 2**
- a noun phrase, as in **3**
- a prepositional phrase, as in **4**

B

PLACE ADVERBIALS

5 Everyone's **here**. (where)

6 Could I see you **in my office**? (where)

7 He's gone **to England**. (where)

8 They live **ten miles away**. (how far)

Some adverbials indicate location or distance. These place adverbials answer the question *where* or *how far,* as in **5 – 8**. The adverbial may be:
- an adverb or adverb phrase, as in **5**
- a prepositional phrase, as in **6 – 7**
- a noun phrase, as in **8**

C

MANNER ADVERBIALS

9 You need to do something **quickly**. (how)

10 Please handle this **with care**. (how)

11 She talks **like a businessperson**. (in what way / manner)

12 Did you come **by car**? (by what means)

Some adverbials answer the question *how, in what way / manner,* or *by what means,* as in **9 – 12**. We call them manner adverbials. The adverbial may be:
- an adverb or adverb phrase, as in **9**
- a prepositional phrase, as in **10 – 12**

D

REASON/PURPOSE ADVERBIALS

13 Classes were canceled **because of the weather**. (why)

14 **As a result of changing trends**, automobile sales have decreased. (why)

15 There were 50,000 deaths last year **due to car crashes**. (why)

16 **On account of the snow**, he hadn't even gone outside. (why)

17 We called **to invite them to dinner**. (for what purpose / reason)

18 I'm waiting **to finally have some free time**. (why)

We can also use adverbials to answer the question *why* or *for what purpose / reason,* as in **13 – 18**.
- In **13 – 16**, the adverbials are multi-word prepositional phrases.
- In **17 – 18**, the adverbials are *to-* infinitive phrases.

For information on *to-* infinitives, see Unit 11.

4 | Explaining *When, How Often, Where,* and *How Far* Decide if each underlined adverbial answers the question *when, how often, where,* or *how far*. Write your answers in the boxes. **5.2 A–B**

From: Professor Collins

To: All students

Subject: Biology field trip

Hi class,

This is a reminder about the biology field trip <u>next week</u>. We'll be collecting
₁

samples <u>on Thursday</u>, so be sure to write the date <u>on your calendar</u>. We only
₂ ₃

do this <u>once a semester</u>, so you don't want to miss this trip. We'll be meeting
₄

1. *when*

2.

3.

4.

<u>at the entrance to Poplar Pond</u> <u>at 7:30</u>. (See picture below.) Be sure to arrive
    5   6

early. <u>Every year</u> a few students show up <u>late</u> and hold up everyone else.
7   8   9

Don't forget to wear comfortable shoes as we will be walking <u>several miles</u>.
                                                               10

If you have any questions or problems, send me an email <u>before Friday</u>.
                                                          11

I'll be checking my email <u>frequently</u> and will answer you <u>as soon as possible</u>.
                           12   13

You can also come to see me <u>during my office hours</u>.
                            14

EBC

| 5. |
| 6. |
| 7. |
| 8. |
| 9. |
| 10. |
| 11. |
| 12. |
| 13. |
| 14. |

Think about It Is each underlined adverbial in Activity 4 an adverb, an adverb phrase, a noun phrase, or a prepositional phrase?

Write about It Write a formal email message like the one in Activity 4 in which you remind a class of students about an upcoming event. Remember to explain when and where the event takes place.

5 | Explaining *When, How Often,* and *How Long* Match the questions with the answers. `5.2 A`

WHAT DO YOU KNOW?

Questions

1. How many times a day does the human eye blink[2]? _b_
2. How long do the Olympic Games last? ____
3. How often does a presidential election take place in the United States? ____
4. How long does it take to drive across the U.S.? ____
5. How long does it take to become a medical doctor? ____
6. When did the first modern Olympic Games take place? ____
7. How often do strong earthquakes happen worldwide? ____
8. How often do small earthquakes occur? ____
9. How long does it take the earth to go around the sun? ____
10. How often does the earth stop moving? ____

Answers (time adverbials)

a. Four to five days.
b. On average, 17,000 times.
c. In 1896.
d. 365 days.
e. At least 11 years.
f. Never.
g. Every 4 years.
h. Generally for 12 to 17 days.
i. About once a month.
j. Several hundred times a day.

[2] **blink:** to close and open your eyes very quickly

Think about It Identify the form of each adverbial in the answers in Activity 5. Write *A* (adverb), *NP* (noun phrase), or *PP* (prepositional phrase) next to it.

Write about It Try to use a different adverbial to answer each question in Activity 5. Are there any questions that are difficult to answer differently?

1. How many times a day does the human eye blink?
About 17,000 times a day.

Write about It Write five questions that begin with *when*, *how often*, or *how long*. Ask a partner your questions.

A: How often do you eat out?   *A: How long does it take to get from your home to school?*
B: Once a week.   *B: About 20 minutes.*

6 | Explaining *How* Complete each sentence with an adverbial from the box. Then compare answers with your classmates. Which facts were the most surprising? `5.2 C`

FACT FILE

1. The only planet that rolls on its side _____*like a ball*_____ is Uranus.

2. It can take the body over 50 hours to digest[3] food
   _____.

3. A rabbit can see on both sides of itself _____
   _____.

4. The left side of your body is controlled _____
   _____.

5. Eating _____ can improve your ability to remember things.

6. The average cough comes out of the mouth
   _____.

7. It's almost impossible to sneeze _____.

8. When you don't get enough sleep, your brain can't function
   _____.

9. A moderately severe[4] sunburn damages the blood vessels[5]
   _____.

10. A candle flame typically burns _____.

11. In nearly every language, the word for *mother* begins
    _____.

12. Women can identify smells _____ than men.

ADVERBIALS

at 60 miles (96.5 km) per hour
by the right side of your brain
completely
like a ball
well
without moving its head

at about 1000° C
at full capacity
extensively
more easily
with an *m* sound
with your eyes open

Write about It Try to think of a different adverbial to complete each sentence above.

1. The only planet that rolls on its side like a wheel is Uranus.

---

[3] **digest:** to change food in your stomach so your body can use it
[4] **severe:** very bad or strong

[5] **blood vessels:** tubes in the body that blood moves through

7 | Explaining *When*, *Where*, and *How* Decide if each **bold** adverbial answers the question *when*, *where*, or *how*. Write your answers in the boxes. `5.2 A–C`

Letter of Complaint

August 25, 2014

Sound Systems Electronics
Consumer Complaint Division
500 Derby Drive
Cullman, AL 35056

Dear Sir or Madam:

I would like to call your attention to a problem I am having. **Last month**, ¹
I ordered a radio from your company. I paid for the radio **by credit card** ²
when I ordered it. It was my understanding that I would receive the
radio **within five days**. It is now **four weeks later** and I still don't have it. ³ ⁴
However, my records show that you charged my credit card account
on August 1. Enclosed is a copy of my credit card statement as proof. ⁵

   If the radio has not been sent, please deliver it **by September 10**. If ⁶
there is a problem, please contact me **by email at dsmith@arkmail.net**. ⁷ ⁸

Thank you for your attention to this matter.

Sincerely,

David Smith

| 1. *when* |
| 2. |
| 3. |
| 4. |
| 5. |
| 6. |
| 7. |
| 8. |

Write about It Write your own letter of complaint using the example above as a model.

---

8 | Explaining *Why* Choose an adverbial from the box to complete each sentence below. `5.2 D`

as a result of global warming	due to the demands of the workplace	because of quickly changing job markets
as a result of the growth of cities	due to the lack of snow	because of the distractions they cause
as a result of the weak economy	because of a possible problem with the brakes	on account of age
due in part to the animal's diet	because of advances in medicine	on account of darkness

1. The earth's polar regions[6] have begun to change drastically
   as a result of global warming .

2. Many schools have banned cell phones from classrooms

   _____ .

3. The government began an investigation of the car after two people died
   in accidents _____ .

[6] **polar regions:** areas around the top and bottom of the earth

146

4. Human life expectancy[7] has increased steadily, mainly

    _____ .

5. Taking a nap after the midday meal used to be a common practice in many countries. Unfortunately, this practice is now less common

    _____ .

6. Giraffes vary in color from light brown to almost black. The difference is _____ .

7. _____ , housing has become more expensive.

8. In the future, many ski resorts may be unable to operate

    _____ .

9. In the U.S., it's against the law to discriminate[8] against someone

    _____ .

10. The tennis match was stopped at 7 p.m. _____

    _____ .

11. _____ , businesses are hiring fewer people.

12. _____ , education is an ongoing, lifelong process.

Think about It What other adverbials can you find in the sentences in Activity 8? Circle them.

Write about It Write three sentences using *as a result of*, *due to*, *because of*, or *on account of*. Then read your sentences to your classmates.

9 | Identifying *To*- Infinitives of Purpose Match the first part of each sentence with a *to*- infinitive on the right. (More than one answer may be possible.) **5.2 D**

HELPFUL HINTS FOR GIVING A SPEECH

1. Practice your speech several times _d_
2. Just before your speech, do some breathing exercises ____
3. Use pictures and diagrams ____
4. Keep your eyes on your audience ____
5. Use facial expressions and gestures[9] ____
6. Use your voice like a musical instrument ____
7. Increase and decrease the volume of your voice ____
8. Ask questions ____
9. Start your speech with something interesting ____
10. Include some personal stories ____

a. to communicate difficult information.
b. to help communicate your message.
c. to keep the sounds interesting.
d. to hear how it will sound to the audience.
e. to watch for signs of confusion or boredom.
f. to help yourself relax.
g. to emphasize your main points.
h. to get the audience's attention.
i. to add fun to your speech.
j. to involve your audience.

[7]**life expectancy:** how long one is believed to be able to live
[8]**discriminate:** to treat one person or group in a worse way than others

[9]**gestures:** movements of your head or hands to show how you feel or what you want

Think about It Think of different *to-* infinitives to complete the sentences in Activity 9.

Practice your speech several times to find out how much time it will take.

Write about It Choose a different topic and write a list of helpful hints. Try to use *to-* infinitives in your list.

10 | Usage Note: *Because of* vs. *Because* Read the note. Then do Activity 11.

COMPARE

We use the multi-word prepositions *as a result of*, *because of*, *due to*, and *on account of* + a **noun phrase**.

		noun phrase
1a	We didn't go	because of	**the heat.**

		noun phrase
2a	She plays well	due to	**years of practice.**

However, we use *because* when we introduce an **adverb clause**.

		adverb clause
1b	We didn't go	because it was very hot.	(NOT: ~~because of it was hot~~)

		adverb clause
2b	She plays well	because she has practiced for years.	(NOT: ~~due to she has practiced for years~~)

11 | Using Adverbials to Explain *Why* Rewrite each sentence using *as a result of*, *because of*, *due to*, or *on account of*. (Many different answers are possible.) **5.2 D**

1. Classes were canceled because the weather was terrible.

   Classes were canceled because of the terrible weather.

2. Fewer people can travel nowadays because the price of gasoline is very high.

3. A cell phone can last for many hours because it has a rechargeable battery.

4. A lot of people take naps here in the summer because it gets so hot.

5. I wasn't successful in learning Chinese because I lacked self-discipline.

6. Because farms have become more efficient, people here have plenty of food.

7. California is the top producer of food in the U.S. because it has such a great climate.

8. Some scientists say we are having more storms because the weather has gotten warmer.

9. I would like to visit Poland someday because my ancestors lived there.

10. Because they share a lot of experiences, brothers and sisters get to know each other well.

11. Because these scissors are very small, you can carry them in your pocket.

5.3 Degree and Focusing Adverbials

A

DEGREE ADVERBIALS

1 You're **absolutely** right.

2 The bridge is **extremely** unsafe.

3 We are all working **pretty** hard.

4 You look **really** familiar.

5 It's **rather** late to go out, don't you think?

6 You **almost** hit that car.

7 I think it's **about** 50 years old.

8 I'm **fairly** certain about this.

9 Be careful. The floor is **slightly** wet.

We use **degree adverbials** to explain *to what degree*, as in **1 – 9**. Notice that we usually use degree adverbials before an adjective or adverb.

Some degree adverbials make a statement stronger, as in **1 – 5**.

absolutely	extremely	perfectly	really	terribly
completely	highly	pretty	reasonably	totally
considerably	incredibly	quite	significantly	truly
entirely	much	rather	so	very

A few degree adverbials show an approximation, as in **6 – 7**.

about	almost	approximately	nearly

Some other degree adverbials can make a statement weaker, as in **8 – 9**.

a (little) bit	less	somewhat
fairly	slightly	to an extent

B

FOCUSING ADVERBIALS

10 A: Can I help you?
   B: No, I'm **just** looking.

11 Smoking increases the risk of many diseases, **especially** heart disease and cancer.

12 Football is known as soccer **only** in North America.

COMPARE

13a Some people can communicate complicated ideas in **only** a few words.

13b Some people can **only** communicate complicated ideas in a few words.

13c **Only** some people can communicate complicated ideas in a few words.

Sometimes we want to focus attention on one word or phrase in a sentence, as in **10 – 12**. When we use adverbials to do this, we call them **focusing adverbials**. Adverbials used in this way include:

especially	even	just	only	particularly

Focusing adverbials usually come immediately before the words they describe. Changing the position of these adverbials can change the meaning of the sentence, as in **13a – 13c**.

GO ONLINE

12 | Choosing Degree Adverbials Complete each sentence with the correct adverbial in parentheses. (You may want to look up information online.) Then compare answers with your classmates and together agree on the correct answer. **5.3 A**

GEOGRAPHY

1. From the moon, the earth looks _____*very*_____ smooth, like a ball. (very / a bit)

2. China covers an area _____ larger than that of the U.S. (significantly / slightly)

3. The Nile River is _____ longer than the Amazon River. (considerably / a little bit)

4. Mount Everest is _____ higher than Mount Fuji. (considerably / somewhat)

5. Brazil is _____ bigger than Venezuela. (much/a little bit)

6. Annual rainfall varies _____ around the world. (greatly/slightly)

7. An island is _____ surrounded by water. (a little bit/completely)

8. It's _____ cold in Antarctica. In some places the average temperature is -58 degrees Celsius. (extremely/fairly)

9. The population of Mexico City is _____ larger than the population of Paris. (significantly/somewhat)

10. Although the sun doesn't rise on parts of Greenland for three whole months, it is never _____ dark there. (slightly/totally)

Think about It Which adverbials in Activity 12 describe an adjective or adverb? Which describe a verb? Do the adverbials come before or after the words they describe?

13 | Usage Note: Collocations with Degree Adverbials Read the note. Then do Activity 14.

Degree adverbials collocate strongly with specific adjectives, adverbs, and verbs. Notice some of the adverbs that are used with these five adjectives.

adverb + adjective		adverb + adjective		adverb + adjective		adverb + adjective		adverb + adjective	
fairly highly so completely extremely reasonably generally quite pretty totally really relatively entirely truly somewhat very	reliable	fairly extremely totally almost quite really relatively completely perfectly pretty so very	clean	absolutely incredibly quite really so very	beautiful	bitterly extremely pretty quite particularly rather really so terribly very	cold	pretty rather extremely fairly quite very	lively

14 | Using Degree Adverbials Underline the degree adverbials in these sentences. Then rewrite each sentence using a different adverbial. (Don't change the meaning of the sentence.) `5.3 A`

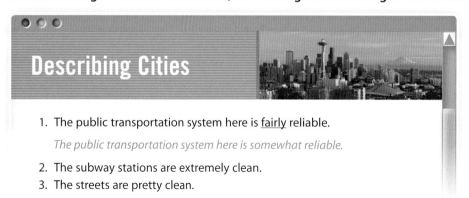

Describing Cities

1. The public transportation system here is <u>fairly</u> reliable.

   The public transportation system here is somewhat reliable.

2. The subway stations are extremely clean.

3. The streets are pretty clean.

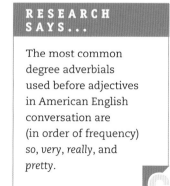

RESEARCH SAYS...

The most common degree adverbials used before adjectives in American English conversation are (in order of frequency) *so, very, really,* and *pretty.*

COR

4. It gets quite cold here in the winter.
5. The buses here are never on time, but the subways are extremely reliable.
6. I stayed in a very lively part of town.
7. It's quite beautiful here in the summertime.
8. The mountains in the distance are incredibly beautiful.
9. Although the city is rather quiet during the week, the streets get pretty crowded on the weekend.
10. Because of the bitterly cold weather in winter, people spend a lot of time indoors.

Write about It Write three sentences describing a city you know. Use a degree adverbial in each sentence.

15 | Noticing Focusing Adverbials Which of the **bold** adverbials in these conversations are focusing adverbials? Circle them. `5.3 B`

1. A: Do you **ever** get homesick?

   B: Sure—(**especially**) on holidays.

2. A: Where's Amanda?

   B: She's **already** gone.

   A: You're kidding! She didn't **even** say goodbye.

   B: I think she was in a hurry.

3. A: Did you tell James about the meeting?

   B: Yeah, but he didn't seem **particularly** interested.

4. A: Do you want something for breakfast?

   B: No, thanks. I **only** eat breakfast **on weekends**.

5. A: Want to go **to a movie tonight**?

   B: Can't we **just** stay **home**?

   A: Sure. That's fine with me.

6. A: Have you heard anything about our new boss?

   B: Not a word. I don't **even** know her name.

7. A: Wow! That was a big bird.

   B: **Really**? I didn't **even** see it.

8. A: Don't you need a rest?

   B: No, why?

   A: **Because you're always doing something**.

   I get tired **just** watching you.

9. A: What did you think of the movie?

   B: It was **pretty** good. I **particularly** liked the ending.

10. A: Want to try some of my macaroni and cheese?

    B: Thanks, but no thanks. I'm not **especially** fond of cheese.

Talk about It Practice the conversations in Activity 15 with a partner.

16 | Usage Note: Adverbials with Multiple Meanings Read the note. Then do Activity 17.

Many adverbials have more than one meaning; the adverbial can function in different ways in a sentence based on the meaning of the word. Notice in this dictionary entry how the word *just* can function as:

- a degree adverbial (definition 1)
- a time adverbial (definition 2)
- a focusing adverbial (definitions 3 and 4)

Sometimes the meanings overlap, and it can be difficult to know how the adverbial is functioning.

> **just** /dʒʌst/ *adverb*
>
> **1.** exactly: *This jacket is just my size.* • *You're just in time.* • *He looks just like his father.*
> **2.** a very short time before: *I just heard the news.* • *Jim isn't here. He just went out.*
> **3.** only: *It's just a small gift.*
> **4.** a word that makes what you say stronger (positive or negative): *Just look at that funny little dog!*

17 | Choosing the Correct Meaning Read the sentences below and choose the correct meaning of *just* from the box. `5.3 B`

1. exactly	3. only
2. a very short time before	4. a word that makes what you say stronger

1. Excuse me for interrupting. I **just** wanted to ask a quick question. __3__

2. This room is **just** a mess. ____

3. No one came to the meeting. It was **just** me and 20 empty chairs. ____

4. It was really cold there **just** as you said it would be. ____

5. John is fine. I **just** talked to him. ____

6. I brought something **just** for you. ____

7. After she was kicked out of school, she **just** disappeared. ____

8. I'm **just** not interested in poetry. ____

9. He cut his leg **just** above the ankle. ____

10. Chicago is **just** north of here. ____

11. We did it **just** for fun. ____

12. I'm not really hungry—I **just** had lunch. ____

Write about It Write four more sentences using each meaning of *just* in the box above.

5.4 Stance Adverbials

We use **stance adverbials** to express our attitude about the information in a clause or sentence.

A

GIVING AN OPINION OR EVALUATION

1 **Unfortunately,** I couldn't contact her.
(= It was unfortunate that I couldn't contact her.)

2 The president believes, **quite rightly,** that we have a serious problem. (= I think the president is right to believe that we have a serious problem.)

We use some stance adverbials to give an opinion or evaluation of what we are saying, as in **1 – 2**.
For example:

(un)fortunately	luckily	thankfully
hopefully	surprisingly	

We often use commas before and after stance adverbials.

B

SHOWING CERTAINTY OR DOUBT

3 They wanted me to be there, but **of course** I had to work.

4 It was **definitely** too late to do anything.

5 **Without a doubt,** Yosemite is one of the most beautiful places in the world.

COMPARE

6a I thought he was here, but **maybe** he went out.
6b I thought he was here, but he **may have gone out**.

We use some stance adverbials to show certainty or doubt about what we are saying, as in **3 – 5**.
For example:

to show certainty			to show doubt
certainly	no doubt	undoubtedly	maybe
clearly	obviously	very likely	perhaps
definitely	of course	without a doubt	possibly
			probably

Notice that stance adverbials are similar to modal verbs in the ways we use them to show certainty or doubt, as in **6a – 6b**.

C

OTHER STANCE ADVERBIALS

7 I **honestly** didn't see anything.

8 **Seriously,** I want you to leave now.

9 Eating too much **actually** reduces your ability to hear.

10 A: Is there an easy way to get downtown?
B: Yes, there is. **In fact,** there's a very easy way.

COMPARE

11a Don't take life too **seriously.** (adverb of manner)
11b **Seriously,** I want you to be home by 10:00.
(stance adverbial)

12a I think something is **really** wrong. (degree adverb)
12b I **really** need to talk to you. (stance adverbial)

Other adverbials that speakers and writers use to comment on the information in a whole clause or sentence include:

actually	really	technically speaking
honestly	seriously	to tell you the truth
in fact		

Remember: An adverbial can function in more than one way, as in **11a – 12b**.

GO ONLINE

---

18 | Using Stance Adverbials to Give an Opinion or Evaluation Choose a stance adverbial from the box to complete each quotation below. (More than one answer may be possible, but only one is correct.) `5.4 A`

QUOTATIONS FROM FAMOUS PEOPLE

fortunately	luckily	sadly	thankfully	to my surprise	unfortunately

1. _Luckily_, in my case, I have managed, by writing, to do the one thing that I always wanted to do. (*Jonathan Coe, novelist*)

2. _____, it's much easier to create a desert than a forest. (*James Lovelock, environmentalist*)

| fortunately | luckily | sadly | thankfully | to my surprise | unfortunately |

3. _____, it doesn't seem to have made a lot of difference to my audience that I'm as bald as a billiard ball! (*James Taylor, musician*)

4. _____, my 70s are nicer than my 60s and my 60s than my 50s, and I wouldn't wish my teens and 20s on my enemies. (*Lionel Blue, clergyman*)

5. Dad taught me everything I know. _____, he didn't teach me everything he knows. (*Al Unser, athlete*)

6. _____, I have my mom and a small group of close friends who are there for me 24/7[10] and whom I can trust and depend on. (*Christina Aguilera, musician*)

James Taylor

| happily | hopefully | luckily | oddly | sadly | unfortunately |

7. I would've loved to have been in a band, but _____ I just wasn't good enough. (*Tony Blair, British prime minister*)

8. I've broken my nose, I've broken ribs. You name it. In fact, we just got back from South America, and I fell over a monitor speaker[11] on the stage and almost ended up in the front row of the audience. I managed to sprain[12] my wrist on that one but _____ nothing was broken. (*Keith Emerson, musician*)

Tony Blair

9. Winning is a habit. _____, so is losing. (*Vince Lombardi, football coach*)

10. I think maybe ten years from now, I'm _____ going to be, in like, Tahiti or something. Kicking back[13] like in my huge mansion, if everything goes right, it's all up to me. (*Corey Haim, actor*)

11. I love having a big family. I think it's easier, _____, in some ways, having three children as opposed to one. (*Patrick Dempsey, actor*)

12. A sense of freedom is something that, _____, comes with age and life experience. (*Diane Keaton, actor*)

Think about It Compare answers with your classmates. In which sentences in Activity 18 could you use more than one adverbial?

19 | Using Stance Adverbials to Show Certainty or Doubt Underline the stance adverbials in these conversations and sentences. Then practice conversations 1–6 with a partner. 5.4 B

IN CONVERSATION

1. A: How was your plane trip?
   B: Scary. Next time I'll <u>definitely</u> go by train.

2. A: Have you eaten at the new restaurant?
   B: Yeah, and I'd definitely go again.

---

[10] **24/7:** 24 hours per day, seven days per week
[11] **monitor speaker:** the part of the audio system where sound comes out; it is used onstage during a performance
[12] **sprain:** to hurt part of your body by turning it suddenly
[13] **kick back:** to relax

3. A: Are you going to the meeting tomorrow?

   B: Probably. What about you?

   A: I don't know yet.

4. A: Do you still want to look at my photos?

   B: Oh, yeah. Sure. Of course.

5. A: I'm going to Matt's house tonight. Maybe you'll come?

   B: No, not tonight.

6. A: How well do you know Rob?

   B: Pretty well.

   A: What's he like?

   B: Well, he's usually good-natured and funny. Of course, he can be a little moody at times.

IN WRITING

7. Clearly, it's both advantageous and enjoyable to have a brother or sister, especially if you are close in age.

8. Some people prefer vigorous exercise, such as running. Others prefer less strenuous[14] activities, such as walking. Of course, more strenuous activities burn more calories.

9. I am especially concerned about the spread of consumer culture[15] in the twenty-first century. There are certainly many other important problems in the world today, but consumerism is one of the least noticed.

10. Students should be encouraged to learn a second and possibly even a third foreign language.

11. Slang and other informal spoken language obviously has no place in school reports.

12. Without a doubt, recreation is essential to a healthy life.

13. The smartphone has changed the way people communicate, and it will surely see many innovations in the future.

Think about It Based on sentences 7–13 in Activity 19, when do writers use a comma after a stance adverbial?

Write about It Rewrite sentences 7–13 in Activity 19 using a different stance adverbial.

20 | Identifying Other Stance Adverbials Underline the stance adverbials in these conversations and sentences. Then practice conversations 1–6 with a partner. 5.4 C

IN CONVERSATION

1. A: I can't believe you wrote this.

   B: But I did, <u>really</u>.

2. A: Will you still be here in an hour?

   B: Actually, I won't. I'm leaving in a few minutes and I won't be back until this evening.

3. A: Is that your money over there?

   B: I don't honestly know. It might be.

4. A: Did you like my speech?

   B: Yeah, it was great. Seriously, I'm kind of jealous. I wish I could speak in public like that.

5. A: Hey, Sam. Do you have a few minutes? I have some questions.

   B: Yeah, I need to talk to you, too. In fact, I've been trying to get in touch with you all week.

6. A: That was a good movie, don't you think?

   B: To tell you the truth, I thought it was really strange.

---

[14] **strenuous:** requiring physical effort and strength

[15] **consumer culture:** the belief that it is good for people to spend a lot of money on goods and services

7. Technically speaking, your brain has the capacity to store everything you experience.

8. Your brain processes pain signals but it doesn't actually feel pain.

9. It may seem impossible to come up with a single definition of psychology, but actually we can: psychology is the scientific study of mental processes and behavior.

10. Many people change careers at some point. In fact, many people have several careers in their lifetime.

11. Humans are social animals. We aren't supposed to live alone. Relationships stimulate our brains—in fact, socializing with others is a great form of brain exercise.

12. The Romans invented indoor plumbing using lead pipes. In fact, the word *plumbing* comes from the Roman word for lead, *plumbum*.

Write about It Write your own sentences using the stance adverbials in Activity 20.

21 | Using Stance Adverbials Rewrite these sentences. Replace the **bold** words with a stance adverbial. (More than one answer may be possible.) `5.4 A–C`

1. **It's not surprising that** your skin is thickest on the bottom of your feet.

   Not surprisingly, your skin is thickest on the bottom of your feet.

2. **It is obvious that** mothers who work outside the home have less time to spend with their children.

3. **I'm going to tell you exactly what I think**. I think you are making a big mistake.

4. **I'm being honest when I say that** I didn't break it.

5. **I'm being truthful when I say** I don't know how long I will be here.

6. **She is lucky that** she didn't break her leg.

7. **I don't doubt that** you will do well on the exam.

8. **Everyone can see that** you aren't happy here.

9. I don't want you to go. **I'm serious about that**.

10. **I'm very thankful that** I didn't have to go.

11. **It's possible that** they will get here in time.

5.5 Sentence Patterns with Linking Adverbials

Linking adverbials have a special function. We use them to link or connect ideas within and across sentences, most often in academic writing. We can connect ideas in a number of different ways. For example:

PATTERN 1

independent clause / period (.) + linking adverbial / comma (,) + independent clause

| **1** | We haven't received the information. | Therefore, | we won't be able to comment on it. | (two sentences) |

PATTERN 2

independent clause / semicolon (;) + linking adverbial / comma (,) + independent clause

A

| **2** | We haven't received the information; | therefore, | we won't be able to comment on it. | (one sentence) |

PATTERN 3

independent clause / semicolon (;) + part of independent clause / comma (,) + linking adverbial / comma (,) + rest of clause

| **3** | We haven't received the information; | we won't, | therefore, | be able to comment on it. | (one sentence) |

WARNING! Not all linking adverbials can be used with each pattern.

GRAMMAR TERMS: Linking adverbials are also called **transition words**, **connecting words**, or **conjunctive adverbials**.

22 | Connecting Sentences in Different Ways Read each sentence. Write the number of the pattern from Chart 5.5 that the writer uses. Then rewrite each sentence using the pattern in parentheses. **5.5 A**

1. The island of Greenland belongs to Denmark. **However,** if it were a separate country, it would be the thirteenth largest country in the world. ___1___

   (Use pattern 2.) _____

   _____

   _____

2. China covers an area only slightly larger than that of the U.S.; the population of China, **however,** is nearly five times greater. ____

   (Use pattern 1.) _____

   _____

3. The gravity[16] of the moon is one-sixth that of Earth; on the moon, **therefore,** you would weigh one-sixth of what you weigh on Earth. ____

   (Use pattern 2.) _____

   _____

   _____

4. We use linking adverbials to connect ideas in writing. **However,** it's important not to overuse them. ____

   (Use pattern 3.) _____

   _____

5. An environmentalist is defined as someone who is interested in preserving[17] the environment; to me, **however,** simply being interested is not enough. ____

   (Use pattern 1.) _____

   _____

   _____

6. The tropical deserts are the hottest places on earth; **however,** nights can be very cold there. ____

   (Use pattern 3.) _____

   _____

7. There isn't much food for animals in Antarctica. **Therefore,** most animals live in or near the sea. ____

   (Use pattern 3.) _____

   _____

8. The acting in this movie was terrible and the plot was entirely predictable; I wouldn't, **therefore,** recommend this movie to most people. ____

   (Use pattern 1.) _____

   _____

   _____

RESEARCH SAYS...

The most common position for linking adverbials is at the beginning of a clause or sentence. This is true in both conversation and academic writing.

CORPUS

[16]**gravity:** the force that pulls everything toward the earth   [17]**preserving:** keeping safe or in good condition

5.6 Linking Adverbials That Signal a Result or Contrast

A

SIGNALING A RESULT OR CONSEQUENCE

1 There is twice as much hydrogen as oxygen in water. **Therefore**, its chemical formula is written as H_2O.

2 The author points out that we value some abilities over others; **as a result**, we often fail to develop our children's potential.

3 My father was born in Italy, but he grew up in California. **Consequently**, he feels more American than Italian.

We use **linking adverbials** to show a connection between two sentences or clauses. Different linking adverbials signal different kinds of connections. Some linking adverbials signal that a result or consequence of something in the first clause or sentence is coming in the second clause or sentence, as in **1 – 3**.

as a result	consequently	therefore	thus

B

SIGNALING A CONTRAST

4 A few years ago it seemed likely that computers would replace books. Now, **however**, most experts think that books are here to stay.

5 A professional cyclist can cover 30 miles in one hour. **In contrast**, the average cyclist covers only 16.

6 Cities are generally noisy, dirty, and expensive. **In spite of that**, the number of people moving to cities is increasing.

7 Many cities are dirty, noisy, and dangerous. **Nonetheless**, many people prefer cities because of the job opportunities and the excitement.

Some linking adverbials signal a contrast between two clauses, as in **4 – 5**.

however	in contrast	on the contrary
in comparison	instead	on the other hand

Certain other linking adverbials signal a contrast that is surprising or unexpected, as in **6 – 7**.

after all	besides	nevertheless
anyhow	in any case	nonetheless
at any rate	in spite of that	still

C

OTHER WAYS TO EXPRESS A RESULT OR CONTRAST

independent clause / comma (,) + *so* + independent clause
8 I'm going to graduate soon, **so** I'll probably relocate.

independent clause / comma (,) + (*and*) *yet* + independent clause
9 Everything was going wrong, **and yet** I was still happy.

independent clause / comma (,) + *but* + independent clause
10 Televisions were expensive at first, **but** they eventually became much cheaper.

GO ONLINE

23 | Using Linking Adverbials to Signal a Result Choose the answer in parentheses that best completes each sentence. **5.6 A**

1. Foldable scissors are very small; consequently, they ___*fit*___ easily in a purse or pocket. (don't fit/fit)

2. I practiced the piano several hours a day. Therefore, I made progress _____. (slowly/quickly)

3. For me, a good job is one where I can help others become smarter. Thus, I can think of nothing better than being a _____. (singer/teacher)

4. Centuries ago, children were considered to be small adults. As a result, _____ done to help address the special emotional needs of young children. (lots of things were/very little was)

5. Much of the surface of Mars is covered by reddish rocks and sand. As a result, people often call Mars the _____ planet. (old/red)

6. Living in another country gave me the opportunity to meet new people and to learn about another culture. As a result, I now _____ to travel to foreign countries. (hate/love)

7. The number of overweight children is increasing. As a result, schools are serving _____ junk food. (less/more)

8. In psychology, the term *behavior* refers to almost any activity. Thus, the blink of an eye _____ an example of a behavior. (is/isn't)

24 | Result or Contrast? Choose the linking adverbial in parentheses that best completes each sentence.
5.6 A–B

1. The tallest tree in the world today is a redwood tree. In the nineteenth century, _____*however*_____, much taller eucalyptus trees existed. (however/thus)

2. Japan is a popular tourist spot for many Koreans. _____, bookstores in Korea carry a lot of travel books for Japan. (as a result/in contrast)

3. Both humans and giraffes have seven neck vertebrae[18]. For giraffes, _____, each one can be more than 10 inches (25.4 centimeters) long. (however/therefore)

4. I've never thought of him as being sad. _____, he seems happy and full of life. (on the contrary/thus)

redwood trees

5. Something always went wrong on our family vacations. One year, everyone got sick. Another year, it rained the whole time. _____, now we look back on these incidents and laugh. (as a result/nevertheless)

6. My sister got into all the schools she applied to. I, _____, didn't get into any of them. (on the other hand/thus)

7. Spanish and Italian male colleagues may embrace when they greet each other. _____, the Japanese usually bow. (consequently/in contrast)

8. The western calendar is based on the length of the seasonal year. The lunar calendar, _____, is based on the cycle of the moon. (as a result/in contrast)

embrace

9. When I first moved to Canada, I was very homesick. _____, once I started school, I made a lot of friends, and I began to feel more comfortable. (as a result/however)

10. Divorce has become common in some countries. _____, the traditional role of the father as wage-earner[19] and the mother as homemaker continues to be viewed as the norm. (consequently/still)

---

[18] **vertebrae:** the small bones that are connected together to form the line down the middle of your back

[19] **wage-earner:** a person who gets money from working

11. The universe is so large that we can't measure it in miles or kilometers.

_____, we measure it in light years. (nevertheless/instead)

12. I am a good judge of character. I can tell if someone is trustworthy.

_____, I am not very organized. (consequently/however)

Think about It In which sentence(s) in Activity 24 is there a surprising contrast?

25 | Other Ways to Express a Result or Contrast Rewrite these sentences using a linking adverbial to connect the clauses or sentences. 5.6 C

Sentences from Student Essays

1. Running your own business can be difficult, but it can prove to be extremely rewarding.

   Running your own business can be difficult; however, it can prove to be extremely rewarding.

2. His mother worked for a university, so they didn't have to pay tuition.
3. Modern technology has freed us from many chores[20], so we have more time to enjoy ourselves.
4. Several years ago I was thinking of taking a trip to Russia. At the time, I was living in California, so it was going to be quite a journey just getting there.
5. She was very young and small, yet she was able to skate beautifully with the eyes of the whole world on her.
6. He worked 20 hours every day to make his business successful, but after several years, he finally gave up.
7. Most people have more than one skill or talent, and yet they stay in the same profession for their whole life.
8. I most often get sick when I am run down, so I try to make sure I eat well, exercise daily, and get plenty of sleep.
9. It's often a difficult decision to leave children in the care of others—and yet millions of women do it.

Write about It Rewrite the second clause in each sentence you wrote above. (You can also use a different linking adverbial.)

1. _Running your own business can be difficult; as a result, many businesses fail during their first year._

---

[20] **chores:** small jobs or routine tasks

5.7 Linking Adverbials That Signal Additional Information

A

SIGNALING AN EXAMPLE

1 Not all plants are gentle on the environment. Cotton plants, **for instance**, are often covered with chemicals.

2 Skilled public speakers use hand gestures for emphasis. **For example**, a speaker may point a finger or use a chopping motion.

We use some **linking adverbials** to signal that an example is coming next, as in **1 – 2**.

for example	for instance

B

SIGNALING NEW RELATED INFORMATION

3 Biking is a good way to get around Berlin because many parts of the city are hard to get to via public transportation. **Moreover**, the city is almost entirely flat, so it is easy to use a bike.

4 The study found that healthy employees are more productive during work hours. **In addition**, they take fewer sick days.

5 Diabetes rates are rising quickly and an increase in heart disease cannot be far behind. **Furthermore**, new evidence suggests that sitting all day is bad for your health.

Some linking adverbials signal that we are adding new information that is related to what we said before, as in **3 – 5**.

furthermore	likewise
in addition	moreover

C

OTHER WAYS TO SIGNAL ADDITIONAL INFORMATION

such as + noun phrase
6 In some countries, activities **such as bullfighting** are part of the culture.

besides + noun phrase
7 Besides being the largest city in Canada, Toronto has a multicultural population.

in addition to + noun phrase
8 In addition to self-discipline, a self-employed person needs to have a lot of motivation.

 GO ONLINE

26 | Adding Examples Match the linking adverbials with the examples they introduce. **5.7 A**

1. Our ears can't hear every sound. For instance, __c__

2. Efforts to use recycled products haven't always been successful. In the 1990s, for example, ____

3. When you visit another country, it's interesting to learn about cultural differences. For example, ____

4. I think that feeling a little stress can be a good thing. For example, ____

5. Rubber is a common material used in sports equipment. For example, ____

6. Because of the Internet, we can find out how people in other countries are dealing with events. For instance, ____

7. Some places have very old laws that don't make any sense. For instance, ____

8. At times it's natural to feel angry. For example, ____

a. worrying about a test might actually make me study harder.

b. we can hear stories from people who have been affected by earthquakes or typhoons[21].

c. ultrasonic sounds are too high-pitched[22] for humans to hear.

d. in one state in the U.S., it is against the law to carry an ice-cream cone in your pocket.

e. recycled wool came and went, mostly because the clothes were very itchy[23].

f. it is the main ingredient in bicycle tires and basketballs.

g. the food may be very different from what you are used to.

h. being treated unfairly upsets most people.

[21] **typhoons:** violent storms with strong winds in hot countries
[22] **high-pitched:** at a very high sound frequency

[23] **itchy:** producing the feeling in your skin that makes you want to scratch it

Think about It Think of another example to complete each statement in Activity 26. Share your ideas with a partner.

27 | Signaling New Related Information Circle the answer that best completes each sentence. **5.7 B**

Hong Kong

1. When you are visiting Hong Kong, Kowloon Peninsula may be a better place to stay because it is less crowded. Moreover, ____

    a. Hong Kong has some great hotels.

    b. it doesn't have as many good restaurants.

    c. it has great museums and good views of the Hong Kong skyline.

Hotel Review

2. The bedrooms are comfortable but very dark. The closets are tiny, so good luck if you want to hang up any clothes. And housekeeping could be better. During our entire stay, the floors were never cleaned. In addition, ____

    a. the staff was very friendly.

    b. the furniture in our room was covered with a thick layer of dust.

    c. the floors were very dirty.

Student Essay

3. Coping with stress is very important, and I have a few main methods of helping myself stay relaxed. The first things I always try to do are to slow down my breathing, quiet my thoughts, and relax my muscles. I also try to speak more calmly and slowly. Furthermore, ____. For me, the best thing to do is to take a quiet walk alone or to exercise.

    a. this isn't always easy to do

    b. I often try to take myself out of the stressful environment

    c. I feel more relaxed when I do this

Think about It What other adverbials can you find in the sentences above? Circle them. Then tell a partner what kind of information they add to the paragraph.

28 | Signaling Additional Information Choose the word or phrase in parentheses that best completes each sentence. Add the correct punctuation if necessary. 5.7 A–C

1. There are many interesting things to do in Washington, D.C. A visitor can tour the White House, the home of the president, visit the many historical museums, or walk around government buildings such as the Supreme Court and the Capitol. _____*Besides*_____ touring the educational sites in the city, visitors can do fun activities such as visiting the zoo. (besides/in addition)

2. In the past, people spent many hours taking care of basic chores _____ cooking and cleaning. (for instance/such as)

3. I would need a very good reason to fire an employee. _____ I would fire an employee who was stealing from the company. (for example/such as)

4. Many forms of exercise, _____ running, playing sports, and swimming, are good for the body. (for example/besides)

5. Cape Town in South Africa is a great place to visit. _____ the spectacular mountains, you will find some beautiful beaches there. (in addition/in addition to)

6. Whatever your profession is, you can find work in a large city. _____ there are many different kinds of schools. (in addition/in addition to)

7. People in different cultures value different things. _____ in some countries people value punctuality—they expect you to be on time. (for instance/such as)

8. You should encourage her to avoid bad habits _____ smoking and drinking. (for instance/such as)

Write about It Rewrite each sentence above using the other word or phrase in parentheses. (You may write one or two sentences.)

1. In addition, visitors can do fun activities such as visiting the zoo.

5.8 Linking Adverbials That Signal a List or Summary

SIGNALING A LIST

A

1 The popularity of Arabic coffee is due to several of its characteristics. **First**, it is easy to grow. More importantly, however, Arabic coffee has the best flavor.

2 It was not a typical lunch. **For one thing**, I was in a small boat. **For another**, my boat was tied to 16 other boats.

Some **linking adverbials** signal that a list or sequence of ideas is coming next, as in **1 – 2**.

first	first of all	to begin with
second	second of all	next
firstly	for one (thing)	lastly
secondly	for another (thing)	finally

SIGNALING A SUMMARY OF PREVIOUS INFORMATION

B

3 . . . **In conclusion**, something must be done to ensure that children's toys are safe.

4 . . . **All in all**, it has been a good year.

We can also use certain linking adverbials to signal that a summary of previous information is coming, as in **3 – 4**.

in sum	in conclusion	all in all
in summary	to conclude	overall
ultimately	to summarize	

29 | Noticing Linking Adverbials Read these paragraphs and underline the linking adverbials. (The number in parentheses indicates the number of linking adverbials in the paragraph.) Then answer the questions below. `5.8 A`

What would you do if you knew that you would die in a few months?

1. If I knew that I would die in a few months, I would stop worrying about long-term goals. I think that knowing I would die soon could help me to focus on the here and now[24]. The first thing that I would do is to stop worrying about jobs and careers; if I am going to die soon, I will have little need for money. Secondly, I would want to spend a lot more time in quiet, either alone or with close friends. I hope that this would make me a wiser and calmer person. Lastly, I would try to share what wisdom I have gained in life with the people I trust most. If I did these things, I think it could help others live happier lives after I'm gone. (2)

What do you want to accomplish in the next ten years?

2. There is a lot that I would like to accomplish in the next ten years. I think that this will be a very busy time for me. The first thing that I will do is complete my education. I will go to college and study to become a teacher. I have always wanted to be a teacher; I think this is because I've always liked school and my teachers have been important figures in my life. Getting my degree will be hard work, but it is very important to me. Once I've received my teaching degree, I will try to find a job in a public school. I think it will be fun to have my own students, and I will work hard to be the best possible teacher. Finally, once I am settled into a teaching career, I will think about starting my own family. I would like to get married and have children someday. Hopefully my future spouse will be easy to find. We will get married, find a home, and settle down. (1)

MAKING LITERATE[25] SOCIETIES

3. There are two primary purposes of this chapter. First, it reviews the development of widespread literacy in various countries, examining the influences that have accelerated this process and, more briefly, those that have hindered[26] it. Second, it examines the broader social context of literacy: how it is learned and practiced in particular social settings, how it serves different individual and group purposes, and how it is influenced by public policies and family circumstances. In particular, the chapter focuses on language issues, literacy practices, and literate environments. (2)

QUESTIONS

1. Writers use different forms to signal a list or sequence, not just adverbials. They do this to give variety to their writing. In the first and second paragraphs above, what other forms does the writer use to signal a sequence or list? Circle them.

2. What other linking adverbials could you use in the paragraphs above? Compare ideas with your classmates.

[24] **here and now:** the present time
[25] **literate:** able to read and write
[26] **hinder:** to make it more difficult to do something

30 | Adding a Summary Statement Read each paragraph and choose the best summary statement.

Paragraphs from Student Essays

1. **Essay Prompt: Do you have the skills to run your own business? Explain.**

   To run your own business, you must be very organized and hard-working. If you are involved in the hiring process, you must also be a good judge of character. I do have some of these skills. I am one of the most hard-working people I know. Even if it isn't necessary, I always try to do a job to perfection. I am also a good judge of character. I can tell when someone is trustworthy or when a person is not. Unfortunately, I am not very organized. I would have a difficult time keeping track of everything related to the business, like legal documents and receipts. In addition, I have a hard time making a budget and keeping to it. This skill is essential for a business owner. In conclusion, ____

   a. I think that I could run my own business, but I would need an assistant and a financial advisor.

   b. I am not a good decision maker and this is a liability in business.

   c. most people do not have the skills to run their own business.

2. **Essay Prompt: Explain why you would or would not want to live in a large city.**

   For me, the choice of whether or not to live in a big city is easy to make: Why would I want to live where there is such a high concentration of people? Why would I want to spend so much money to live in a tiny apartment? And why would I want to be exposed to noise and air pollution? Obviously, you get less for your money in the city. Overall, ____

   a. it's more expensive to live in a large city.

   b. it's not very pleasant to live in a big city.

   c. there are a lot of good reasons to live in a big city.

Think about It Compare your answers above with your classmates. Explain your choice of the best summary statements.

Write about It Write your own answer to one of the essay prompts above.

5.9 Using Adverbials in Speaking and Academic Writing

A

HEDGING

1 A: What do you think of this shirt?
B: I **kind of** like it.

2 A: Do you **by any chance** have a piece of paper?
B: Sure. Just one?

In conversation, we sometimes use an **adverbial** to hedge, or soften, our words, as in **1 – 2**. We often do this to sound more polite.

COMPARE 3A–3B

3a Some people claim they never dream, but that is not true.

3b Some people claim they never dream, but that is **generally** not true.

4 Most scientists think that a sudden event—**perhaps** caused by a crashing meteor or planet—led to the extinction of dinosaurs.

5 The average person spends about nine hours a day using some kind of media. This is **arguably** more than was expected ten years ago.

In academic texts, writers need to make sure their claims are not too strong. A claim that is too strong becomes unbelievable, as in **3a**. Adverbials are one of many tools that writers can use to qualify, limit, or hedge a claim, as in **3b – 5**.

B

CONNECTING IDEAS

6 The coal question remains perhaps the most difficult issue in the energy world. Supporters of solar, wind, and even nuclear power say these are cleaner and safer sources of energy. **On the other hand**, the use of coal continues to climb.

7 A number of experiments suggest that the brain is very malleable. **However**, all were carried out on animals.

In academic writing, linking adverbials are just one of many tools that writers use to connect ideas in a text, as in **6 – 7**.

WARNING! Don't use too many linking adverbials in your writing. This makes the writing choppy. Instead, use linking words, phrases, and clauses together with other cohesive tools like pronouns, repetition of key words, etc.

 GO ONLINE

31 | Hedging a Statement in Speaking Choose a word or phrase from the box to soften each question or response. (Many different answers are possible.) Then compare with your classmates. `5.9 A`

1. You should come back later.

   Maybe you should come back later.

2. You called the wrong number.
3. Are you driving to the meeting tomorrow?
4. She didn't like my essay. In fact, she said it was boring.
5. Aren't you young to own your own business?
6. He has a loud, unpleasant voice.
7. You're mistaken.
8. Is Dr. Martin at home?
9. You upset her.
10. Can I borrow ten dollars?

> by any chance
> kind of
> maybe
> perhaps
> probably
> sort of

Think about It For each sentence above, which expressions do not work well? Why not?

32 | Hedging a Statement in Writing What words do these writers use to hedge, or limit, their claims? Underline them. `5.9 A`

SENTENCES FROM ACADEMIC SOURCES

1. Deserts are dry regions, <u>generally</u> receiving less than ten inches of precipitation a year.
2. Mothers who work outside the home obviously have less time to spend with their children. According to a recent study, however, this does not necessarily have a negative effect on their children.
3. This is arguably the best museum in the whole country.
4. In general, smoking is no longer fashionable in Canada. In many other parts of the world, however, smoking is still growing in popularity.
5. Researchers have found these substances almost everywhere they have looked for them.
6. The risk to humans is uncertain in part because few tests have been done.
7. In most cases, the assumption that wealthy countries have better education systems than poorer countries is correct.
8. Researchers have long suggested that in "noun-friendly" languages including English, infants' attention is focused mainly on objects, typically marked by nouns.
9. The number of farm workers has decreased steadily over the years. This is primarily because the use of sophisticated machines has reduced the need for labor.

Write about It Rewrite the sentences above using a different adverbial to hedge.

33 | Using Linking Adverbials in Writing Choose the linking adverbial in parentheses that best completes each sentence. `5.9 B`

Facts about Japan

1. Many people think Japan is one large island; _____*however*_____, it is actually thousands of islands. (however/thus)

2. Much of Japan is mountainous; _____, there is little farmland. (as a result/in addition)

3. Japan has only a small supply of minerals. It is _____ one of the world's richest nations. (for example/nonetheless)

4. Volcanic eruptions take place frequently. _____, earthquakes are common occurrences. (in contrast/in addition)

5. Japanese trees are often cultivated[27] as miniatures; _____, gardens are often designed as smaller versions of the surrounding landscape. (on the other hand/likewise)

---

[27] **cultivate:** to grow

6. The largest of the main islands, Honshu, is less than 200 miles wide at its greatest width; _____, no part of Japan is more than 100 miles from the sea. (consequently/nevertheless)

7. Few inlets are found on the east coast north of Tokyo; _____, south of Tokyo are many of the best harbors. (however/therefore)

8. Every valley in Japan has a stream; _____, there aren't any long, navigable[28] rivers in Japan. (as a result/however)

9. In the Japanese mountains, there are about 200 volcanoes; _____, only about 60 are still active. (however/moreover)

34 | Choosing Linking Adverbials Choose linking adverbials from the box to complete each textbook excerpt below. (There is one extra adverbial for each text. More than one answer may be possible.) Then answer the questions on page 169. 5.9 B

as a result	consequently	however	in addition

Parenting Styles

There are three basic styles of parenting: permissive, dictatorial, and authoritative. Generally, each style has fairly predictable effects on children.

Permissive parents have very few demands of their children. They don't make many rules, and when they do, they often fail to enforce[29] them. These parents generally act more like friends rather than parents. _____, their children don't learn much about good behavior and the consequences for bad behavior. Children raised in this way can be impulsive[30] and irresponsible.

Dictatorial parents are inflexible. They make strict rules and demand obedience[31]. When their children disobey, they are usually punished very harshly. Dictatorial parents don't trust their children to make decisions for themselves, and they often don't explain why they make such strict rules. _____, their children are often not very good at making decisions.

---

[28] **navigable:** deep and wide enough to provide passage for boats and/or ships
[29] **enforce:** to make sure that people follow the law or rules

[30] **impulsive:** doing things suddenly and without thinking carefully
[31] **obedience:** the state of doing what someone tells you to do

Authoritative parents are in the role of authority figures, but they are not dictators. They expect their children to obey their rules. _____, they are caring, flexible, and often willing to listen to their children's opinions.

| for example | furthermore | in conclusion | instead |

Emotions

According to psychologists, all humans show distinctive facial expressions for six basic emotions: disgust, sadness, happiness, fear, anger, and surprise. _____, these expressions appear to be universal. This means that people from different cultures across the world use and recognize the same expressions for the same emotions. Of course, not every person will have the same emotional responses to the same things, but we do seem to have the same way of showing these six emotions without using language.

In general, when we experience an intense feeling, we don't just feel "normal" after that feeling passes. _____, we often go beyond that middle ground[32] and experience the opposite emotion. _____, if you have just given a presentation to your classmates, one that you have dreaded[33] for weeks, you might feel wonderful when it's over instead of feeling just OK. Similarly, it is not unusual to feel a little sad or depressed after experiencing a lot of joy or excitement for a period of time. If your parents live far away and they visit you only once a year for a short time, you might feel very happy during their visit. However, once they leave, you may experience some sadness or depression in their absence.

F Y I
Some linking adverbials require several sentences or even a paragraph to build up to them. Examples include *furthermore, in conclusion, on the contrary,* and *therefore.*

QUESTIONS

1. Do you think each writer above uses too many linking adverbials or just enough? Why?
2. How many other adverbials can you find in the paragraphs above? Circle them.
3. What adverbials does each writer use to hedge some of the claims in these textbook excerpts?

---

[32] **middle ground:** halfway point; intermediate position

[33] **dread:** to be afraid of something that is going to happen

WRAP-UP Demonstrate Your Knowledge

A | TIC-TAC-TOE Follow these instructions.

1. Work with a partner. Student A is X. Student B is O.
2. Student A: Choose a square. On another piece of paper, write a sentence with an example that supports the statement in the square. Use *for example* or *for instance* in your sentence.
3. Students A and B: Check the sentence together. If the sentence has no errors, write an *X* in the square. If the sentence is not correct, do not write an *X* in the square.
4. Student B: Take your turn. Write an *O* for each correct answer.
5. The first person to get three *X*s or three *O*s in a line is the winner.

Professional athletes are paid a lot of money.	Not all languages use the Roman alphabet.	There are a number of things you can do to improve your memory.
Some cities have great public transportation.	Not all animals need to drink water every day.	You need a lot of different skills to run your own business.
People use a variety of facial expressions to show their emotions.	Some actors are also good singers.	You can learn a lot from living in a different country.

You need a lot of different skills to run your own business.
For example, you need to be good at making a budget.

B | WRITING Consider this essay test prompt and take notes on your ideas. Then write a paragraph in which you present your ideas to your classmates. Use adverbials where appropriate. (Look again at the sample essay responses in Activity 29.)

Essay Prompt: If your doctor told you that you had only a few months to live, how would you change your way of life? Discuss.

C | WEB SEARCH Choose a free online academic course and download a transcript of the first lecture. Look for examples of adverbials that the speaker frequently uses. Share what you learned with your classmates.

TYPES OF ADVERBIALS	PURPOSE	COMMON EXAMPLES			
TIME ADVERBIALS	Explain *when, how often,* or *how long*	then always already usually	now still ever this morning	never today sometimes	again yesterday often
PLACE ADVERBIALS	Explain *where* or *how far*	here	there	outside	upstairs
ADVERBIALS OF MANNER	Explain *how, in what way, in what manner,* or *by what means*	fast	significantly	together	well
ADVERBIALS OF PURPOSE	Explain *why, for what purpose,* or *for what reason*	as a result of because of	due to on account of	to let everyone know *to* + base form of verb (*to-* infinitive)	
DEGREE ADVERBIALS	Explain *to what degree*	absolutely quite rather truly significantly about fairly somewhat	completely incredibly pretty perfectly much almost slightly	entirely extremely really reasonably approximately less	considerably highly so very nearly a (little) bit
FOCUSING ADVERBIALS	Focus attention on a word or a phrase	especially particularly	even	just	only
STANCE ADVERBIALS	Express an attitude about or comment on the information in a clause or sentence	hopefully fortunately of course undoubtedly perhaps actually	luckily certainly obviously clearly maybe really	surprisingly definitely very likely probably honestly in fact	thankfully no doubt without a doubt possibly seriously technically speaking to tell you the truth
LINKING ADVERBIALS	Connect ideas within and across sentences	**Result/Consequence** as a result **Contrast** however instead anyhow still **Additional information** for example in addition **List** first first of all to begin with **Summary** in sum in summary ultimately	consequently in contrast though nevertheless nonetheless for instance likewise second secondly second of all in conclusion to conclude to summarize	therefore in comparison on the contrary at any rate in any case furthermore firstly lastly finally all in all overall	thus on the other hand besides in spite of that moreover for one thing for another thing next

6 Adverb Clauses

Never look back unless you are planning to go that way.

—HENRY DAVID THOREAU,
WRITER AND PHILOSOPHER
(1817–1862)

Talk about It What does the quotation above mean? Do you agree or disagree?

WARM-UP

A | Match the beginnings and endings of the proverbs. Then choose one proverb and tell a partner what it means to you.

PROVERBS FROM AROUND THE WORLD

1. Knowledge is the most valuable treasure __d__
2. Don't count your chickens ____
3. When spider webs unite, ____
4. A snake will emit[1] poison ____
5. The eyes are of little use ____
6. Make hay ____
7. Even though the old man is strong, ____

a. they can tie up a lion. *(Ethiopian)*

b. **even though you feed it on milk.** *(Indian)*

c. **while the sun shines.** *(English)*

d. **because it can't be stolen or consumed.** *(Sanskrit)*

e. he will not live forever. *(Ghanaian)*

f. **if the mind is blind.** *(Arabic)*

g. **before they hatch[2].** *(Greek)*

B | The words in blue in the proverbs above are adverb clauses. Based on these examples, what can you say about adverb clauses? Check (✓) *True* or *False*.

	TRUE	FALSE
1. An adverb clause has a subject and verb.	☐	☐
2. Adverb clauses always come at the end of a sentence.	☐	☐
3. An adverb clause is connected to another clause.	☐	☐
4. Adverb clauses always begin with *when* or *while*.	☐	☐

C | Look back at the quotation on page 172. Identify any adverb clauses.

[1] **emit:** to send out something such as gas, heat, light, or a sound   [2] **hatch:** to come out of an egg

6.1 Overview of Adverb Clauses

We use an **adverb clause** to add information to a main clause. The adverb clause explains *why, when, where, how,* or *under what conditions* something happens. There are several important things to remember about adverb clauses:

A

	main clause	adverb clause
1	He didn't get involved in politics	**until he was in his 50s.**

	adverb clause	main clause
2	**If you need me,**	I should be in the library.

← An adverb clause needs to be connected to a main clause, as in **1 – 2**. We use a comma (,) after the adverb clause when it comes first, as in **2**.

	subject	verb			subject	verb	
3	I	learned	to drive	**when**	I	was	16.

← Both the adverb clause and the main clause must have a subject and a verb, as in **3**.

	main clause	subordinator	
4	I enjoy my job	**when** **because** **even though**	it is challenging.

← Adverb clauses begin with **subordinators** (connecting words) such as *until, if, when, because,* or *even though,* as in **4**.

B

BOTH CLAUSES REFER TO A PRESENT TIME FRAME

5 As children **grow** older, their interests **change**.
(simple present / simple present)

6 I **don't know** how to cook because no one **has** ever **taught** me.
(simple present / present perfect)

BOTH CLAUSES REFER TO A PAST TIME FRAME

7 After she **got** a BA, she **went** back to school to get an MA.
(simple past / simple past)

8 The store **wasn't doing** very well when my father **bought** it.
(past progressive / simple past)

THE TWO CLAUSES REFER TO DIFFERENT TIME FRAMES

9 This book **is** special to me because it **was** a gift from my uncle.
(simple present / simple past)

10 This book **has** always **been** special to me because it **was** a gift from my uncle. (present perfect / simple past)

It's important to pay attention to the **form of the verb** in the main clause and the adverb clause.

- When both clauses refer to a present time frame (or general/timeless), we use present verb forms in both clauses, as in **5 – 6**.

- When both clauses refer to a past time frame, we use past verb forms in both clauses, as in **7 – 8**.

- When the two clauses refer to different time frames, we can use different verb forms, as in **9 – 10**.

For information about future time frames, see Chart 6.2.

1 | Noticing Adverb Clauses Read this information and take notes in the timeline on page 175. Then answer the questions on page 175. `6.1 A`

VANESSA-MAE

Like many famous musicians, Vanessa-Mae started playing music at a very young age. She was only 3 years old **when she had her first piano lesson**, and she started playing the violin **when she was just 5**. Then, at the age of 8, she had to make a difficult decision. She had to choose between the violin and the piano. **Although she had just won a prize at an important piano competition**, Vanessa-Mae decided to focus on the violin. **Once she made her decision**, she worked hard to improve her playing, and **by the time she was 12**, she had made three recordings of classical music. **Although she loved classical music**, she wanted to play other kinds of music, too. To many people's surprise, she got an electric violin and started playing rock music. Today Vanessa-Mae is known as both a great classical violin musician and a great rock musician. That's quite a combination.

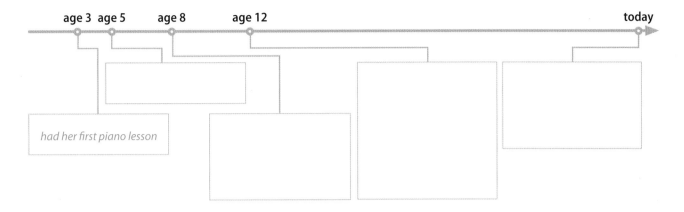

age 3   age 5   age 8   age 12   today

had her first piano lesson	

QUESTIONS

1. What are the subject and verb in each **bold** adverb clause in the Activity 1 text on page 174? Circle them.

2. What subordinator (connecting word or phrase) begins each adverb clause? Underline it.

3. Which adverb clauses come before the main clauses? What punctuation marks does the writer use in these sentences?

4. Vanessa-Mae was a child prodigy—a person who develops a special skill at a young age. Can you think of other child prodigies? What did they accomplish at a young age? Try to use adverb clauses in your answers.

2 | Identifying Verb Forms Underline the verb in each main clause and each adverb clause in the sentences below. Then identify the form of each verb. `6.1 B`

PRESENT VERB FORMS	simple present	present progressive	present perfect
PAST VERB FORMS	simple past	past progressive	past perfect

1. When I <u>have spent</u> a lot of time exercising, I <u>sleep</u> better at night. _____*present perfect / simple present*_____

2. When I was younger, I thought a lot about my future. _____

3. My parents are important to me because they have always been my best friends. _____

4. Once I start something, I don't stop until I'm done. _____

5. I try to stay completely focused while I'm studying. _____

6. My hometown has always been special to me because it's so beautiful. _____

7. Once I've made a decision, I never change my mind. _____

8. I didn't have any friends while I was growing up. _____

9. A year after I had finished high school, I started college. _____

10. Shortly after I moved here, I got a job. _____

11. Although I worked hard yesterday, I don't feel like working this morning. _____

12. I am applying to this college because my father attended the same school. _____

Talk about It Are any of the sentences above true for you? Tell a partner.

Think about It Which sentences above have actions that take place in different time frames? What verb forms are used in each clause?

6.2 Adverb Clauses of Time and Reason

A

ADVERB CLAUSES OF TIME

1 One study shows that babies can learn **before they are born.**

2 **Once the process began,** it was irreversible.

3 The lights automatically turn off **when people leave the room.**

4 **As plastic bags break down,** they release poisonous material into the water.

An **adverb clause of time** tells when one event happens in relation to another event in the main clause, as in **1 – 4**.

- We use some subordinators to show that one event happens before or after another event:

after	before	once	until
as soon as	by the time	since	when

- We use some subordinators to show that two events happen at the same time:

as	when	whenever	while

B

FUTURE ADVERB CLAUSES OF TIME

5 Nobody **will care** when you get there tomorrow.
(NOT: ~~Nobody will care when you will get there tomorrow.~~)

6 What **are** you **going to do** while we're away?
(NOT: ~~What are you going to do while we will be away?~~)

7 After you read this, you'll probably **have** some questions.

8 We **aren't going to leave** until you get back.

When we make a prediction or talk about a future plan, we usually use a future verb form in the main clause but a present (not future) verb form in the adverb clause, as in **5 – 8**.

C

ADVERB CLAUSES OF REASON

9 My watch is important to me **because it was a gift from my father.**

10 **Since we have some new people here today,** let's start with introductions.

11 The meeting was canceled **as no one could get there.**

12 **Now that prices have gone up,** we can't afford to travel.

We can also use an adverb clause to give a reason for something in the main clause. **Adverb clauses of reason** usually begin with the subordinator *because*, *since*, *as*, or *now that*, as in **9 – 12**.

D

OTHER WAYS TO GIVE REASONS

because of + noun phrase
13 Because of the increase in prices, we can't afford to travel now. (*because of* = phrasal preposition)

independent clause + *so* + independent clause
14 Prices have increased, **so** we can't afford to travel now. (*so* = conjunction)

two separate sentences
15 We can't afford to travel now. **Prices have increased too much.**

GO ONLINE

3 | Noticing Adverb Clauses of Time Read these sentences and underline the adverb clauses of time. Then check (✓) *Good Advice* or *Bad Advice*. `6.2 A`

ADVICE FOR UNIVERSITY STUDENTS	GOOD ADVICE	BAD ADVICE
1. <u>Before you turn in an assignment</u>, check it over carefully.	☐	☐
2. It's important to review your notes from class as soon as you get home.	☐	☐
3. Don't study for a test until your instructor tells you to.	☐	☐
4. Take notes while you are reading assigned texts.	☐	☐
5. Study with a large group of classmates whenever you can.	☐	☐

	GOOD ADVICE	BAD ADVICE

6. Ask to meet with your instructor whenever you are confused about the course material. ☐ ☐

7. As you read your class assignment, you should listen to loud music to help you think. ☐ ☐

8. Ask questions in class when you don't understand something. ☐ ☐

9. Always stay up late while you are studying. ☐ ☐

10. Once you have read a text, don't look at it again until you need to study for a test. ☐ ☐

Talk about It Which advice in Activity 3 was good or bad? Compare with a partner and say why.

Write about It Write new sentences using the time clauses in the sentences in Activity 3. Use your own words to write a different main clause.

Before you turn in an assignment, be sure to put your name on it.

4 | Understanding Subordinators Choose the subordinator on the right that best completes each sentence. Then answer the questions on page 178. 6.2 A–B

QUOTATIONS FROM FAMOUS PEOPLE

1. __As_____ you grow older you will discover that you have two hands: one for helping yourself, the other for helping others. *(Sam Levenson, writer and humorist)*

> as
> before
> whenever

2. _____ I crave³ junk food, I want salty things like peanuts or potato chips. *(Tyra Banks, model)*

> after
> until
> whenever

3. There's only one way to have a happy marriage and _____ I learn what it is, I'll get married again. *(Clint Eastwood, actor)*

> as soon as
> by the time
> while

4. _____ you are over 30, 35 years old, I think everyone should get down to the gym and start moving again. *(Warren Cuccurullo, musician)*

> once
> until
> whenever

5. Life is what happens _____ you are busy making other plans. *(John Lennon, musician)*

> before
> until
> while

6. I've now been in this country . . . _____ I was 17. So this is my second home. *(Hakeem Olajuwon, athlete)*

> by the time
> since
> when

³ **crave:** to need something strongly or urgently

7. I still love making hamburgers on the grill⁴. I guess _____ I eat them, childhood memories come up for me. *(Bobby Flay, chef)*

before
until
whenever

8. Champions keep playing _____ they get it right. *(Billie Jean King, athlete)*

before
until
whenever

9. _____ you do the common things in life in an uncommon way, you will command the attention of the world. *(George Washington Carver, scientist)*

after
since
when

10. _____ I hear music, something in me starts to vibrate⁵. *(Suzanne Farrell, dancer)*

as soon as
by the time
until

11. I could develop a picture _____ I was 12. *(David Bailey, photographer)*

by the time
since
whenever

12. A lie gets halfway around the world _____ the truth has a chance to get its pants on. *(Winston Churchill, statesman)*

before
until
when

QUESTIONS

1. In which sentences in Activity 4 do the two events happen at the same time?
2. What verb form does each speaker use in the main clause and the adverb clause of time?
3. In which sentences in Activity 4 is the speaker making a prediction or a plan? How do you know?

Talk about It Which quotation in Activity 4 is the most interesting to you? Tell your classmates why.

5 | Using Adverb Clauses of Time to Talk about the Future Complete these sentences with the correct form of the verbs in parentheses. Then check (✓) *Prediction* or *Plan*. 6.2 B

UNDERGRADUATES DISCUSS THE FUTURE	PREDICTION	PLAN
1. When the economy __*improves*__ (improve), more people _____ (have) jobs.	☐	☐
2. It _____ (be) years before the economy _____ (become) steady again.	☐	☐
3. I _____ (not / get) a job unless I _____ (be) very lucky.	☐	☐
4. Most students _____ (start) at low salaries when they _____ (leave) college.	☐	☐
5. When I _____ (graduate), I _____ (get) a job right away.	☐	☐
6. As soon as I _____ (finish) school, I _____ (apply) for as many jobs as possible.	☐	☐

⁴**grill:** a metal frame that you put food on to cook over a fire   ⁵**vibrate:** to move very quickly from side to side or up and down

7. I _____ for employment until I _____
    (not / look)   (graduate)
from college. ☐   ☐

8. We _____ good jobs unless we _____ new skills.
    (not / get)   (learn)   ☐   ☐

9. I _____ to get some work experience while I
    (try)
_____ in school. ☐   ☐
    (be)

10. I _____ after I _____ my final exams. ☐   ☐
    (travel)   (pass)

Talk about It Work with a partner. For each prediction in Activity 5, agree or disagree. For each plan, say true or false for you.

Write about It Rewrite each sentence in Activity 5 using a different main clause.

When the economy improves, people will start taking vacations overseas again.

6 | Noticing Adverb Clauses of Reason Underline the adverb clauses of reason. Then circle the subordinator in each clause. `6.2 C`

Tips for Staying Healthy in Hot Weather

1. Avoid very cold drinks (as) they can cause stomach pain.
2. Don't assume the heat won't make you sick just because you never had a problem before.
3. Avoid high-protein foods since they increase body heat.
4. Don't exercise in very hot, humid weather. Your body will sweat because it is hot, but the sweat won't evaporate[6] because of the high humidity.

Tips for Staying Healthy in Cold Weather

5. Since you lose most of your body heat through your head, it's important to wear a hat in cold weather.
6. Wearing layers[7] of clothing helps keep you warm because your body heat gets trapped[8] between the layers.
7. Don't wear tight shoes or boots as they increase your chances of getting frostbite[9].
8. Be especially careful on cold, windy days because the wind can carry heat away from the body.

---

[6] **evaporate:** to change from a liquid into steam or gas and disappear
[7] **layers:** things that lie on other things or between other things
[8] **trapped:** caught or kept in place
[9] **frostbite:** an injury to the body caused by extreme cold

Think about It Which sentence in Activity 6 has a comma after the adverb clause? Why?

Talk about It Think of two to three more tips to add to each list in Activity 6. Explain them to a classmate.

7 | Identifying Subordinators Underline the subordinator in each adverb clause of reason. Then add a comma where necessary. 6.2 C

MODERN LIVING

1. <u>Because</u> the cost of living has gone up, many people are working longer hours.
2. More people are working during their vacations now that they have access to the Internet.
3. Since more people are watching TV the programs are getting better.
4. It's easier to do research now because there is so much information on the Internet.
5. Now that people can do research on the Internet they don't go to the library as often.
6. People are driving less now that the price of gasoline has gone up.
7. Because there are so many cars on the road driving has become more dangerous.
8. There is no real need to go shopping in stores as one can buy almost anything online.
9. Since it's easy to travel almost anywhere in the world there are few unspoiled places left.
10. Now that smoking is illegal in many public places more people will probably quit smoking.
11. Since fewer people are smoking deaths from lung cancer should go down.
12. Because people are living longer it's even more important for them to have health insurance.

> **RESEARCH SAYS...**
>
> The subordinator *as* sounds more formal and is used less often to introduce a reason.
>
> CORPL

Talk about It Does each sentence above describe a positive result or a negative result? Why do you think so? Share ideas with your classmates.

Write about It Rewrite each sentence above using a different main clause.

1. Because the cost of living has gone up, fewer people are traveling overseas.

Write about It Write three of your own opinions about modern living. Use *because*, *since*, *as*, or *now that*.

8 | Usage Note: *Since* and *As* Read the note. Then do Activity 9.

Some subordinators have more than one meaning: they can be used to introduce different types of adverb clauses. For example, *as* and *since* can be used to begin a time clause or a reason clause.

ADVERB CLAUSES OF TIME	ADVERB CLAUSES OF REASON
1 I've known him **since I was a child***.	**3** **Since no one is using this room,** I'm going to use it.
2 She called just **as I was leaving.**	**4** **As the president couldn't be here today,** the vice president has come instead.

* When we use *since* in a time clause, the verb must always refer to an earlier time (present perfect, simple past, past perfect, etc.).

9 | Adverb Clause of Time or Reason? Underline the adverb clauses with *as* or *since*. Then identify each adverb clause as a time clause or a reason clause. Check (✓) your answers. `6.2 A–C`

Statements from Professors

	TIME CLAUSE	REASON CLAUSE
1. "If you look at the course syllabus[10], you'll notice that I've marked three items in blue. These are the things I'm going to emphasize <u>as we go through the course</u>."	✓	☐
2. "I'd like to show you some pictures of the poet T. S. Eliot since I'm going to be talking about him in today's lecture."	☐	☐
3. "As I was reading through your papers, I noticed that some of you had trouble understanding a few of the concepts we discussed last week."	☐	☐
4. "There are several things you need to remember as we move forward in our study of basic chemistry. I'm going to post these online for you to refer to."	☐	☐
5. "I'm going to read the poem to you in class since some of you weren't able to get the packet of class materials from the bookstore."	☐	☐
6. "As the semester goes on, I'll go into more detail about different styles of architecture[11]."	☐	☐
7. "There have been several new developments in the field since we last met, and I'll be discussing these over the next few weeks."	☐	☐
8. "I can't tell you exactly when the final exam will be since the department hasn't made the schedule yet. But I'll let you know soon."	☐	☐
9. "Since I published my research paper on animal extinction[12], there's been a lot of interest in the subject."	☐	☐
10. "As none of you will be here next semester, we'll end this course with a review of European economics."	☐	☐

Think about It In which sentences above can you use a different subordinator? Which subordinator would you use?

These are the things I'm going to emphasize while we go through the course.

10 | Exploring Ways to Give Reasons Rewrite sentences 1–8 using an adverb clause of reason. Then complete sentences 9–12 with your own ideas. Pay close attention to the time frame and verb forms you use. `6.2 D`

GOOD EXCUSES/BAD EXCUSES

1. We couldn't understand him because of his strong accent.

   We couldn't understand him because he had a strong accent.

2. My brother's car broke down, so he missed his flight.

3. I couldn't get to class because of the bad weather.

4. I didn't exercise because of the heat.

[10] **syllabus:** a list of all the things that you must study in a class
[11] **architecture:** the study of designing and making buildings
[12] **extinction:** the disappearance of a type of plant or animal (it no longer exists)

5. I don't have any money, so I can't go out this weekend.

6. I don't have a computer, so I can't email my family.

7. I couldn't go away for the weekend. I had to work.

8. We don't see her very often because of her job.

9. I couldn't do my homework because of _____

_____.

10. I _____,

so I couldn't do my homework.

11. I couldn't come to class last week. _____

_____

12. I _____,

so I had to stay home.

Talk about It Share some of your ideas from sentences 9–12 in Activity 10 with your classmates. Ask your classmates to say if they are good or bad excuses.

11 | Error Correction Correct any errors in these sentences. (Some sentences may not have any errors.)

1. It's hard to compare schools in the United States and Mexico. Because my country has a different educational system.

2. I did not do very well on the examination because of I did not read the instructions carefully.

3. Since you weren't here yesterday you didn't get the assignment.

4. I couldn't sleep last night because I worry about the test.

5. Now that I have some money I'm going to take a vacation.

6. When I arrived here, I was happy because my sister was here and I hadn't seen her in a long time. At the same time, I was sad because I left my friends behind and I knew I will miss them.

7. I'm proud of myself because now I could communicate with people in English, I have a good job, and I'm going to start college soon.

8. My parents always encouraged me to make my own decisions. This was very important to me. Because made me trust myself.

9. I thought my parents would come here until the day my father call me.

10. After I left my country, I moved to Germany. While I living there, I studied at a university.

11. I want to go back home as long as I can.

12. When I will get older I will look back at this time and laugh.

13. After finished eating, they went to the bride's house.

14. At noon all my friends arrived, as soon as they arrived, they started to decorate my apartment, they finished at 5:00.

15. Because my country, Cambodia, has a very different educational system.

6.3 Adverb Clauses of Contrast

An **adverb clause of contrast** adds unexpected, surprising, or contrasting information to a main clause, as in **1 – 2**.

A

main clause	adverb clause

1 | My grandfather still works | even though he's in his eighties. | (= unexpected or surprising information)

adverb clause	main clause

2 | Though cell phones have solved some problems, | they have created many others. | (= contrasting information)

B

SHOWING CONTRAST

3 **Although she's been teaching for ten years**, she still feels nervous at the beginning of the school year.
(= She's been teaching for ten years, but she still feels . . .)

4 **Though she said she wanted to help**, she didn't do anything. (= She said she wanted to help, but she . . .)

5 He wouldn't eat anything **even though he was hungry**.
(= He was hungry but he wouldn't eat anything.)

Adverb clauses of contrast often begin with the subordinator *although*, *though*, or *even though*, as in **3 – 5**. These subordinators usually include a meaning of concession or "but . . ."

Although, *though*, and *even though* are similar in meaning. However:
- *although* is more formal
- *even though* expresses a stronger contrast or emphasis

C

CONTRASTING ASPECTS OF THE SAME THING

6 **While smokeless tobacco may be safer than cigarettes**, it is not safe enough. (= Smokeless tobacco may be safer than cigarettes, but it is not safe enough.)

7 **While a college education is useful**, it doesn't guarantee a job after graduation. (= A college education is useful but it doesn't guarantee a job.)

CONTRASTING TWO DIFFERENT THINGS

8 Hawaii is warm **while Alaska is cold**.

9 My mother was an artist and very high-strung **while my father was quite calm**.

We can also use *while* to introduce an adverb clause of contrast.

- When we use *while* to contrast two aspects of the same thing, it usually includes a meaning of concession or "but . . ." as in **6 – 7**. With this use of *while*, the adverb clause usually comes before the main clause.

- We can also use *while* to make a direct contrast between two different things, as in **8 – 9**. With this use of *while*, the adverb clause usually comes after the main clause.

D

COMPARE: OTHER WAYS TO SHOW CONTRAST

independent clause + *but* + independent clause

10 My grandfather is in his eighties, but he still works. (*but* = conjunction)

11 Cell phones have solved some problems, but they have created many others.

despite + noun phrase

12 Despite **his age**, he has never had a job. (*despite* = preposition)

13 Despite **being hungry**, he wouldn't eat anything.

in spite of + noun phrase

14 In spite of **his age**, he has never worked. (*in spite of* = preposition)

12 | Noticing Adverb Clauses of Contrast Match the questions with the answers. Then underline each adverb clause of contrast and circle the subordinator. `6.3 A–B`

FACTS ABOUT HISTORICAL PEOPLE

Questions   Answers

1. What university did George Washington attend? _d_   a. No, he didn't. Even though wigs were
                                                            fashionable, Washington didn't wear one.
2. How many children did Washington have? ____   Instead, he powdered his hair.

3. Did George Washington wear a wig¹³? ____   b. None. George Washington had no children of
                                                            his own although he helped raise two of his
4. Is he buried¹⁴ under the U.S. Capitol? ____   wife's children from her first marriage.

                                                         c. No, he isn't. Although Congress built a room
                                                            under the Capitol Building for this purpose,
                                                            Washington is not buried in it.

                                     d. He did not attend college. Although
                                                            Washington believed strongly in formal
George Washington,   education, the death of his father ended his
first president of the U.S.   formal schooling.

1. Did Christopher Columbus discover America? ____   a. Yes, he was. Although no one writes about
                                                            her often, Columbus had a wife named Filipa
2. Where was Columbus trying to go in 1502? ____   Perestrelo, a Portuguese lady. Their wedding
                                                            was on the Portuguese island of Porto Santo
3. Did Columbus sail in very large ships? ____   in 1479.

4. Was Christopher Columbus married? ____   b. No, he didn't. Columbus's biggest ship, the
                                                            Santa Maria, sailed across the Atlantic Ocean
                                                            even though it was only 70 feet long and not
                                                            designed for exploration.

                                                         c. In 1502, Columbus sailed to America for the
                                        fourth time and explored Central America
                                                            though he was still hoping to land in China!
Christopher Columbus,
Italian explorer   d. Although people have said Columbus
                                                            discovered America, this isn't in fact true.
                                                            There were many people living there already,
                                                            but of course, Columbus didn't know that.

1. What did Mozart call himself? ____   a. Even though it's hard to believe, Mozart was
                                                            only eight years old when he composed his
2. Was Mozart very rich? ____   first symphony.

3. What sort of music did Mozart compose¹⁵? ____   b. No, he wasn't. Although he was very famous,
                                                            Mozart was extremely poor when he died in
4. How old was he when he began to compose? ____   1791. His grave¹⁶ didn't even have a stone on it.

                                                         c. Though Mozart is often remembered for
                                                            writing cheerful music and funny operas, not
                                                            all his music was happy. He also wrote serious
                                                            music and even funeral music.

                                     d. Mozart's official name was Joannes
                                                            Chrysostomus Wolfgangus Theophilus
Wolfgang Amadeus Mozart,   although he called himself Gottlieb until 1769.
Austrian composer   Then he began to call himself Amadeo.

---

¹³**wig:** a covering for your head made of hair that is not your own   ¹⁵**compose:** to write something, especially music
¹⁴**bury:** to put a dead body in the ground   ¹⁶**grave:** a hole in the ground where a dead person's body
                                                                                   is buried

Think about It Look at the sentences with adverb clauses of contrast in Activity 12. What verb forms does the writer use in the main clause and the adverb clause of each?

Talk about It What was the most surprising thing you learned about each person? Tell a partner.

13 | Using Adverb Clauses of Contrast Add unexpected or surprising information to these sentences. (Many different answers are possible.) `6.3 A–B`

1. I got up early this morning even though _____.
2. Although _____,
   I drank several cups of it.
3. Although _____,
   I usually take the bus.
4. Although _____,
   I still got to work on time.
5. I worked all day even though _____.
6. I didn't eat lunch even though _____.
7. Although _____, I stayed up late watching TV.
8. Though it seemed like a bad idea, I _____.
9. I never learned to drive a car even though _____.
10. _____ though I had plenty of time.

> **F Y I**
>
> In a sentence with an adverb clause of contrast, we sometimes use the word *still* in the main clause to add emphasis.
>
> Even though she's 24, she **still** acts like a child.

Talk about It Share one of the sentences you completed above with your classmates. Think of different ways to complete the sentence.

"I got up early this morning even though it was a holiday."

14 | Using *While* in Contrast Clauses Complete these sentences to make a contrast between the adverb clause and the main clause. (Many different answers are possible.) `6.3 C`

Opinions about Television

1. While the number of programs on TV is increasing, _____
   _____.

2. While many parents don't want their children to watch a lot of TV,
   _____.

3. Some of the news programs on TV are OK while others _____
   _____.

4. Some people prefer news programs while others _____.

5. While many people admit that they watch too much TV, _____.

6. While TV is still a popular source of news, _____.

7. While TV _____, it can also be harmful for children.

8. While many TV channels show only sports programs, _____.

Think about It Which of the sentences you completed in Activity 14 use *while* to contrast two aspects of the same thing? Which make a direct contrast between two different things?

Talk about It Read your opinions from Activity 14 to a classmate. Ask your classmate to agree or disagree.

15 | Usage Note: *While* Read the note. Then do Activity 16.

We can use *while* to introduce a contrast clause or a time clause. In a contrast clause, *while* is similar in meaning to *although*. In a time clause, *while* is similar in meaning to *during the time that*.

   1 Why are some people afraid of snakes **while others aren't**? (contrast clause)
   2 A fire broke out **while people were still in the building**. (time clause)

Sometimes the word *while* could have either meaning.

   3 While I do the dishes, he does the laundry. (contrast clause or time clause?)

16 | Understanding Clauses with *While* Underline the adverb clauses in these sentences. Then decide if the subordinator *while* introduces a contrast clause or a time clause. Check (✓) your answers. **6.3 C**

	CONTRAST CLAUSE	TIME CLAUSE
1. <u>While this disease can be deadly in humans and animals</u>, it is treatable.	✓	☐
2. While people are being treated for the disease, they need constant care.	☐	☐
3. While animals can get this disease, people cannot.	☐	☐
4. While the river is being cleaned up, swimming will not be allowed.	☐	☐
5. While the river is being cleaned up, the surrounding area is not.	☐	☐
6. While it would be wonderful to clean up the river, it is unlikely to happen.	☐	☐
7. We couldn't see or hear anything while we were swimming across the river.	☐	☐
8. While it can be challenging to swim across the river, it can be done.	☐	☐
9. Several protestors had to be taken from the room while the president was giving her speech.	☐	☐
10. While the president's speech was informative, she didn't address several important issues.	☐	☐
11. While it would be nice to think that we don't need this law, we do.	☐	☐
12. The crime rate went down while the law was in effect.	☐	☐
13. While the law was effective, it was very unpopular.	☐	☐

17 | Pronunciation Note: Contrasting Information Listen to the note. Then do Activity 18.

In sentences with adverb clauses of contrast, we may sometimes stress the information (or words) that we are contrasting.

   1 He went to WORK even though he had been SICK all night.
   2 Even though most people here speak SPANISH, I want to practice speaking ENGLISH.
   3 While this book was written for CHILDREN, ANYONE can enjoy it.

18 | Noticing Contrasting Words Listen and underline the contrasting words. Then listen again and repeat the sentences. `6.3 A–C`

1. Even though she's <u>older</u>, she's not really any <u>wiser</u>.
2. While it may help to take vitamins, it's not absolutely necessary.
3. Someday I may want to move although I doubt it.
4. Even though I can understand Spanish, I can't speak it.
5. He was kind to me even though I didn't deserve it.
6. I live a quiet life although I'm really a city person.
7. I respect your decision even though I don't like it.
8. Although I disagree with many of the changes, I'm willing to try them out.
9. Even though I dislike politics, I think it's important to vote.
10. While solar panels[17] are a good source of energy, they're very ugly.
11. Although I don't like loud music, I love listening to modern jazz.
12. I rarely get any exercise even though I know I should.

> **RESEARCH SAYS...**
>
> Clauses with *although* and *(even) though* come more often at the beginning of a sentence.
>
> CORPUS

Talk about It Look back at Activities 13 and 14. Practice reading some of your sentences to a partner using stress to show the contrasting information.

19 | Exploring Different Ways to Contrast Ideas Rewrite each sentence using the **bold** subordinator. `6.3 D`

1. Bamboo looks like a tree, but it is actually a grass.

   Despite _____ *looking like a tree, bamboo is actually a grass* _____ .

2. Most people think water always boils at 212 degrees Fahrenheit, but this only happens at sea level.

   While _____

   _____ .

3. Some bacteria are harmful, but the vast majority of bacteria are harmless.

   Although _____ .

4. Some deserts are hot, dry places; others are cold and ice-covered.

   While _____ .

5. Despite the earth's being slightly flat at the poles, we say it is round.

   Even though _____ .

6. Despite looking like a tree, the banana plant is actually a very large herb.

   Although _____ .

7. In spite of the distractions, the researchers were able to focus on their work.

   Even though _____ .

8. Despite being extremely small, ants are very strong insects.

   While _____ .

Think about It How else could you rewrite each sentence above? Compare ideas with your classmates.

---

[17] **solar panels:** groups of solar cells that collect radiation from the sun, used to produce electricity

20 | Error Correction Correct any errors in these sentences. (Some sentences may not have any errors.)

1. Although she is a good wife, we are a happy family.
2. I don't know much about U.S. history. Although I took several courses.
3. Even they look very different, they have similar personalities.
4. Even though I was a good student, but I couldn't get a scholarship.
5. Although I had heard that word many times, so it sounded strange to me.
6. Although it was an old car, it didn't run very well.
7. He is very generous even though he doesn't have much money he gives everything to his friends.
8. My family lives in a small house near Seattle, Washington. Despite the only three rooms that the house has, we never feel crowded.

6.4 Adverb Clauses of Manner

A

1 She called me last night **as she always does.**

2 I prefer to leave things **as they are.**

3 **As I said at the last meeting,** I expect to finish this task by the end of next month.

MANNER VS. TIME VS. REASON CLAUSES WITH *AS*

4 Please carry the box **as I showed you.** (manner)

5 **As we were driving home,** there was a huge storm. (time)

6 We stopped at a gas station **as we were running out of fuel.** (reason)

An **adverb clause of manner** answers the question *how* or *in what way.* Adverb clauses of manner begin with the subordinator *as.* In these clauses, *as* means "in the same way that," as in **1 – 3.**

WARNING! We can use the subordinator *as* to begin an adverb clause of manner, time, or reason, as in **4 – 6.**

B

USING *AS THOUGH* AND *AS IF*

7 He **looks** as though he needs to sit down.
(Based on looking at him, I think this.)

8 It **doesn't sound** as if Jim is going to get the job.
(Based on the things I've heard, I believe this.)

9 She **feels** as though she is being punished.
(Based on her experience, this is her feeling.)

We can use adverb clauses beginning with *as though* or *as if* after a linking verb like *look, sound,* or *feel,* as in **7 – 9.**

We use these adverb clauses to say how we imagine something or how someone seems to be.

GO ONLINE

---

21 | Distinguishing Types of Adverb Clauses Underline the adverb clauses. Then decide how each adverb clause is used. Check (✓) *Manner, Reason,* or *Time.* 6.4 A

	MANNER HOW?	REASON WHY?	TIME WHEN?
1. My mother runs her house <u>as you would run a hotel</u>.	✓	☐	☐
2. My sister always gets up just as the coffee is ready.	☐	☐	☐
3. My father has a good pension as he worked many years for the government.	☐	☐	☐
4. He recited the poem perfectly as he always does.	☐	☐	☐
5. She raised herself on her elbows as she stared into the night.	☐	☐	☐
6. As I have said before, I'll be leaving early tonight.	☐	☐	☐
7. She dragged her feet as she made her way out of the house.	☐	☐	☐
8. He is in great demand as he is a good speaker.	☐	☐	☐

	MANNER HOW?	REASON WHY?	TIME WHEN?
9. The event was a failure as only 20 people came.	☐	☐	☐
10. The hotel was not a depressing place as I had imagined it.	☐	☐	☐
11. People stood and applauded as the parade went by.	☐	☐	☐
12. She looked down as her mother kissed her goodbye.	☐	☐	☐
13. As the musicians were late, there was no entertainment for the first hour.	☐	☐	☐
14. He's taking a nap as he always does in the afternoon.	☐	☐	☐
15. That's a picture of me as I used to look.	☐	☐	☐
16. As she opened the door, she heard a sharp crack.	☐	☐	☐

22 | Using Adverb Clauses of Manner Write a sentence about the people in each picture below. Use *as though/as if* and ideas from the box. (More than one answer may be possible.) Then compare with a partner. 6.4 B

In picture 1, the woman looks as though she is in a hurry.

confused about something	going to have a good time	has a lot to do	really surprised
feel pretty cold	happy to be there	in a hurry	very relaxed

Talk about It Think of another sentence for each picture above using *as though/as if*. Share your ideas with classmates.

6.5 Adverb Clauses of Purpose and Result

A

ADVERB CLAUSES OF PURPOSE

1 Cover it with glass **so that the contents are visible.**

2 It's important to keep the cables vertical **so you know where they are.**

3 We took a map **so we wouldn't get lost.**

An **adverb clause of purpose** answers the question *for what purpose* or *why*. Purpose clauses often begin with *so that*, as in **1**. The word *that* is often omitted, as in **2 – 3**.

We often use the modals *can*, *may*, and *will / would* in purpose clauses, as in **3**.

B

ADVERB CLAUSES OF RESULT

4 He talked **so fast** that I couldn't understand him.

5 I met **so many people** that I'll never remember all their names.

6 I ate **so much food** that it made me sick.

7 She is such a **generous person** that she always agrees to everything we ask for.
(NOT: ~~a such generous person~~)

8 The birds flew in such **large numbers** that the sky became dark.

9 That's such **good advice** that I should pay you for it.

10 I'm **so happy** I could cry.

An **adverb clause of result** shows the result of something in the main clause, as in **4 – 10**. The main clause usually includes *so* or *such*; the result clause usually begins with the connecting word *that*. Clauses of result almost always come after the main clause.

There are a number of ways to signal in the main clause that an adverb clause of result follows:

so	+	adjective or adverb	+	
so many / few	+	plural noun	+	**that**
so much / little	+	noncount noun	+	
such	+	(*a / an*) + adjective + noun	+	

The word *that* is often omitted when the meaning of the sentence is clear, as in **10**.

GO ONLINE

23 | Using Adverb Clauses of Purpose Choose an adverb clause from this box to complete each sentence below. **6.5 A**

so that you don't spread germs	so that you don't have health problems later	so that you lose weight
so that you feel less stressed	so you catch any health problems early	so you don't get a sunburn
so you don't get dehydrated	so you don't have too much to do at once	so you don't get cavities
so it doesn't become infected	so you feel rested when you wake up	so you raise your heart rate

Health Advice

1. You should always wash a cut _____ *so it doesn't become infected* _____.

2. It's a good idea to wash your hands frequently _____.

3. Drink plenty of water _____.

4. You should exercise energetically _____.

5. You should cover your skin when you are in direct sunlight _____.

6. Quit smoking _____.

7. Brush your teeth twice a day _____.

8. Get an annual checkup _____.

9. Eat more fruit and vegetables _____.

10. Do small tasks immediately _____.

11. Try yoga or meditation _____.

12. Aim for seven hours of sleep _____.

24 | Understanding Adverb Clauses of Result Match each main clause with an adverb clause of result. (More than one answer may be possible, but only one is correct.) `6.5 B`

DESCRIPTIONS FROM FICTION

Main clause

1. She was **so beautiful** _d_
2. He was **so funny** ____
3. He'd been **so busy** ____
4. The pain was **so strong** ____
5. He had gained **so much weight** ____
6. She sounded like **such a fascinating person** ____
7. Joe let him go, pushing him back **so hard** ____
8. He looked at me with **such sad eyes** ____

Adverb clause of result

a. **that** no one recognized him.
b. **that** I wanted to cry.
c. **that** I couldn't stop laughing.
d. **that** he couldn't find the words to describe her.
e. **that** he'd completely forgotten to call her.
f. **that** he almost fell.
g. **that** I wanted to meet her.
h. **that** she nearly fainted.

Think about It Write the **bold** words above in this list.

1. *So* + adjective + *that*: _so beautiful that_ _____
2. *So* + adverb + *that*: _____
3. *So much* + noncount noun + *that*: _____
4. *Such* + adjective + plural noun + *that*: _____
5. *Such* + *a/an* + adjective + singular noun + *that*: _____

Think about It Circle the word that best completes each sentence.

1. We **can** / **can't** use *so* before a singular noun.
2. We **can** / **can't** use *such* before an adjective or adverb alone.
3. We **can** / **can't** use *such* before *a/an* + an adjective + a singular noun.

Write about It Think of a different adverb clause of result for each main clause above.

She was so beautiful that people often stared at her.

25 | Using Adverb Clauses of Result Rewrite these sentences with *so* or *such*. `6.5 B`

1. I'm studying very hard. I'm sure to do well in this course.

   I'm studying so hard that I'm sure to do well in this course.

2. She has a strong accent. I can hardly understand her.
3. I have very little money. I can't afford to buy a car.
4. He was feeling quite ill. He went home.
5. She takes good care of her car. It looks new.
6. He was very grateful. He couldn't stop thanking me.
7. The flowers in the garden were pretty. I wanted to pick them.
8. It happened a long time ago. She can't remember the details.
9. I was late for class. I took a taxi.
10. It was a beautiful day. I didn't want to think about my problems.

Good Design

When digital audio players (DAPs) first appeared in the 1990s, they weren't very popular. In 2000, Apple realized that customers were not interested in DAPs because the players weren't designed well. Apple soon developed a new product: the iPod. It was attractive and had a fast computer connection so that songs could quickly transfer from a computer to the player. Since Apple released the first iPod in 2001, it has released many different versions. Most iPods now have touch screens to play videos. Others are so small that they can fit in your hand. Apple has also developed similar products, such as the iPhone and the iPad. Because of their excellent design, these products are some of the most popular devices for mobile communication and entertainment.

1. How many adverb clauses did you find in the paragraph above?
2. How many of these adverb clauses show the result of something in the main clause?
3. How many of these adverb clauses show the purpose for something?
4. What other expression in the paragraph shows the purpose for something? Circle it.
5. How is the Apple iPod different from earlier digital music players?

6.6 Reduced Adverb Clauses of Time and Contrast

A

COMPARE FULL AND REDUCED ADVERB CLAUSES

same subjects

1a Although **the house** is small, **it** has lots of closets.
1b Although small, the house has lots of closets.

different subjects

2 Although **the house** is small, **I** still like it.
(NOT: ~~Although small, I still like it.~~)

We can sometimes shorten an adverb clause of time or contrast when the subject of the adverb clause and the subject of the main clause are the same, as in **1a**. We call this a **reduced adverb clause**, as in **1b**.

When the subjects are different, the adverb clause cannot be reduced, as in **2**.

B

REDUCED ADVERB CLAUSES WITH THE VERB BE

3a While I **was** in school, I played a lot of football.
3b While in school, I played a lot of football.

4a Although my father **was** bothered by the news, he did his best to ignore it.
4b Although bothered by the news, my father did his best to ignore it.

5a When you**'re** looking for a job, you should be sure to keep your resume up to date.
5b When looking for a job, you should be sure to keep your resume up to date.

REDUCED ADVERB CLAUSES WITH OTHER VERBS

6a The train stopped several times before it finally **arrived**.
6b The train stopped several times before finally arriving.

7a Since David **graduated** from college, he's worked in three different banks.
7b Since graduating from college, David has worked in three different banks.

The way we reduce an adverb clause depends on the verb in the clause:

- When the adverb clause has a form of the verb *be* (as a helping verb or a main verb), we drop the subject and the form of the verb *be*, as in **3 – 5**.

- When the adverb clause has a verb other than *be*, we drop the subject and any helping verb, and we use the *-ing* form of the main verb, as in **6 – 7**.

WARNING! When you use a reduced adverb clause, make sure the subject in the main clause is clear, as in **4b** and **7b**.

We use these subordinators in reduced adverb clauses:

after	when	since	although
before	while		though

27 | Analyzing Reduced Clauses of Time and Contrast Underline the subject in each main clause and each adverb clause. Then check (✓) the adverb clauses you can reduce. 6.6 A–B

1. ☑ Although <u>my sister</u> was tired, <u>she</u> refused to stop working.
2. ☐ Lots of people listen to the radio while they are driving.
3. ☐ They left the room before we announced the good news.
4. ☐ Brothers and sisters share a lot of experiences while they are growing up.
5. ☐ I always feel good after I exercise outdoors.
6. ☐ Although this method is complicated, it is highly reliable.
7. ☐ Although the directions were written simply, they were difficult to follow.
8. ☐ After the committee members discussed the issues, they made a final decision.
9. ☐ Although the engine was new, we couldn't get it started.
10. ☐ Although this issue is important, we aren't ready to make a decision.
11. ☐ Though the findings are based on only a few studies, they are very promising.
12. ☐ You should think about your career goals before you apply to a college or university.
13. ☐ Since Joe and I started to eat more healthily, we've both felt fitter[18] and better.
14. ☐ We aren't allowed to use our cell phones while we are at work.
15. ☐ When I think about the future, I see myself changing careers completely.

Write about It Rewrite the sentences you checked above using a reduced adverb clause. Change pronoun subjects to full noun subjects if necessary.

1. Although tired, my sister refused to stop working.

28 | Using Reduced Clauses Underline the subject in each main clause and adverb clause. (If the clause uses an imperative, write *you*.) Where possible, rewrite each sentence using a reduced adverb clause. 6.6 A–B

TRAVEL ADVICE

1. When <u>you</u> travel with children, <u>you</u> should carry plenty of water and snacks.

   When traveling with children, you should carry plenty of water and snacks.

2. When you pack your suitcase, you should roll your clothes instead of folding them.
3. When you carry your own luggage on an airplane, it is less likely to get lost.
4. Although checked luggage rarely gets lost, you should put extra clothes in your carry-on luggage.
5. Make sure your flight is on time before you leave for the airport.
6. When you go through airport security, take your computer out of your carry-on bag.
7. Most passengers have to take off their shoes when they go through airport security.
8. When people are on an airplane for a long time, they should do foot and leg exercises.
9. You have to have a passport when you travel to a foreign country.
10. When you visit a foreign country, follow the customs of that country.
11. Hotel rates are often cheaper when you travel with a large group of people.
12. Take a small dictionary with you when you are traveling to a foreign country.

> **F Y I**
>
> The subject of an imperative statement is always *you*. Notice how we can reduce adverb clauses when the main clause is an imperative.
>
> (**You**) Don't forget to make a hotel reservation before **you** leave home.
>
> Don't forget to make a hotel reservation **before leaving home.**

Write about It Write your own travel advice using reduced clauses.

---

[18]**fitter:** healthier or stronger

6.7 Conditional Adverb Clauses (Real Conditionals)

A

	condition	result
1	If I'm not too tired,	(then) I usually go out in the evening.

	condition	result
2	If you mix red, green, and blue light,	you get white light.

	result	condition
3	I can come over	if you need some help.

A **conditional adverb clause** shows what must happen first (the condition) so that another thing (the result) can happen, as in **1 – 3**.

A conditional clause:
- usually begins with the subordinator *if*
- can come before or after the main clause

B

PRESENT REAL CONDITIONALS

4 If eggs aren't properly cooked, they can make you sick.

5 If we want to go downtown, we usually take the bus.

6 If you don't know the meaning of a word, look it up in your dictionary.

PAST REAL CONDITIONALS

7 When I was a child, if my father wasn't working, we usually did something outdoors.

8 Our teachers were very strict. If you didn't do all your homework, you failed the course.

We often use conditional adverb clauses to talk about real situations or events. These could be:
- facts or general truths, as in **4**
- events that happen regularly, as in **5**
- commands or advice, as in **6**
- events that happened regularly in the past, as in **7 – 8**

In these clauses, it is possible to use *when* or *whenever* in place of *if*.

GRAMMAR TERM: The present and past real conditionals are sometimes called the **zero conditional**.

C

FUTURE REAL CONDITIONALS

9 If he's had a bad day, he probably **won't come** over.

10 This hypothesis **will need** to be tested to determine if it is accurate.

11 If I can get home early, I **will call** you.

12 We **might cancel** the meeting if they can't come.

13 If you need some help tomorrow, **call** me.

14 If I take two classes next summer, I**'ll** graduate early.
(NOT: ~~If I will take two classes next summer, I'll graduate early.~~)

We sometimes use a conditional adverb clause when we make a prediction or talk about future events. In these sentences, we usually use a present verb form in the *if-* clause, as in **9 – 14**.

IF- CLAUSE	RESULT (MAIN) CLAUSE
present verb form *can* + base form *must* + base form	modal + base form imperative

Notice that we use a present form in the *if-* clause even when it has a future time expression, as in **14**.

GRAMMAR TERMS: This use of the future real conditional is sometimes called the **future-possible conditional** or **first conditional**.

29 | Noticing Conditional Clauses Underline the conditional clauses in this article. Then write each conditional and result clause under the correct group in the chart on page 195. **6.7 A**

Five Warning Signs You're Headed Toward Credit Card Debt[19]

1. **You skip[20] one credit card bill to pay another.**
   Skipping payment of one credit card bill to pay another is unwise. <u>If you usually find yourself unable to make your credit card payments,</u> you are already in trouble.

---

[19] **debt:** money you must pay back to someone   [20] **skip:** to not do something that you should do

2. **You charge more than you pay.**
Imagine trying to fill a hole while someone digs[21] out more dirt than you put in. The hole would never get filled, would it? It's the same with credit card debt. If you're charging more than you're paying, your debt will always continue to increase.

3. **You don't have a plan to pay off your credit card debt.**
"Failing to plan is planning to fail." If you're not actively working to pay off your credit card bill, you could end up paying for years to come.

4. **You use credit to "afford" expensive items.**
Credit cards trick us into thinking we can afford to buy more than we really can. You are endangering your future income if you're getting into debt to have a lifestyle you really can't afford.

5. **You have reached the limit on your credit cards.**
If your credit cards are maxed out, you're not headed for credit card debt; you're already in it. What can you do? Make a decision to pay off your credit card debt and to make wiser choices when you use your credit cards in the future.

Condition	Result
you usually find yourself unable to make your credit card payments	*you are already in trouble*

30 | Using Conditionals to Talk about Real Situations Match each clause on the left with a clause on the right. `6.7 B`

LANGUAGES

1. Any language is in trouble __d__
2. If you can speak two languages fluently, ____
3. If my grandparents came to visit, ____
4. It's difficult to travel in a foreign country ____
5. If no one speaks a language anymore, ____
6. You have a better chance of getting a job ____
7. I can understand Chinese ____
8. In the past, children were punished ____
9. In Spanish, if you know how a word is spelled, ____
10. If you travel extensively, ____

a. if you can't speak the language.
b. the language has become extinct.
c. if you know more than one language.
d. if it is spoken by only a few people.
e. if they didn't speak the official language at school.
f. you are bilingual.
g. we spoke with them in Italian.
h. if people speak it slowly.
i. you probably know some basic words in many languages.
j. you almost always know how it is pronounced.

Think about It Which sentences above describe a fact or general truth? An event that happened regularly in the past?

[21] **dig:** to move earth by making a hole in the ground

31 | Using *If*- Clauses in Predictions Complete these predictions with the correct present or future form of the verbs in parentheses. Then check (✓) *Fact* or *Myth*. `6.7 C`

HOW MUCH DO YOU KNOW ABOUT HEALTH?

	FACT	MYTH
1. If you _____*cross*_____ your eyes, they _____*will stay*_____ that way. (cross) (stay)	☐	✓
2. If both parents _____ poor eyesight, their children will, too. (have)	☐	☐
3. If you _____ a lot of carrots, you _____ good eyesight. (eat) (have)	☐	☐
4. If both parents _____ blue eyes, they usually _____ (have) (not have) a child with brown eyes.	☐	☐
5. You _____ longer if you _____ frequently. (live) (exercise)	☐	☐
6. You _____ a cold if you _____ outside in cold weather (catch) (go) with a wet head.	☐	☐
7. You _____ smarter if you _____ a lot of fish. (get) (eat)	☐	☐
8. You _____ if you _____ swimming after a big meal. (drown²²) (go)	☐	☐
9. Your heart rate _____ if you _____ smoking. (decrease) (quit)	☐	☐
10. If you _____ deeply, you _____ calmer. (breathe) (feel)	☐	☐

Talk about It Discuss your answers above with a partner. Do you know other health myths or facts?

32 | Usage Note: *Unless* Read the note. Then do Activity 33.

> We sometimes use the subordinator **unless** to begin an adverb clause of condition. *Unless* is similar in meaning to *except if*, as in **1a – 3a**. We can sometimes replace *unless* with *if + not* in these sentences, as in **1b – 3b**.
>
> **1a** You shouldn't make personal phone calls from work **unless** it is an emergency.
>   (= You shouldn't make personal phone calls from work except if it is an emergency.)
> **1b** You shouldn't make personal phone calls from work **if** it **isn't** an emergency.
>
> **2a** She isn't happy **unless** she's working.   **3a** I won't go **unless** you go.
> **2b** She isn't happy **if** she **isn't** working.   **3b** I won't go **if** you **don't** go.

33 | *Unless* or *If*? Complete these sentences with *unless* or *if*. `6.7 B–C`

1. Generally I can sleep anytime, anywhere, anyplace, _____*unless*_____ I'm anxious about work. (*Natalie Imbruglia, singer*)

2. _____ you dream it, you can do it. (*Walt Disney, entrepreneur*)

3. Fishing is boring _____ you catch an actual fish, and then (if you do) it is disgusting. (*Dave Barry, humorist*)

4. _____ you can't explain it simply, you don't understand it well enough. (*Albert Einstein, physicist*)

5. You can't push anyone up the ladder _____ he is willing to climb. (*Dale Carnegie, writer*)

6. Mistakes are always forgivable _____ one has the courage to admit them. (*Bruce Lee, martial artist*)

7. _____ you don't practice, you don't deserve to win. (*Andre Agassi, tennis player*)

²² **drown:** to die underwater because you cannot breathe

8. _____ we remember, we cannot understand. *(E. M. Forster, writer)*

9. You may be deceived _____ you trust too much. *(Frank Crane, writer)*

10. Nothing will work _____ you do. *(Maya Angelou, writer)*

Write about It Look at the sentences in Activity 33 that use *unless*. Rewrite them using *if + not*.

Generally I can sleep anytime, anywhere, anyplace, if I'm not anxious about work.

6.8 Conditional Adverb Clauses (Unreal Conditionals)

A

1 It's too bad that my brothers are away. **If they were here,** I know they would help me. (They aren't here.)

2 You'd feel better **if you exercised.** (You don't exercise.)

3 I wouldn't have met my wife **if I had moved to London.** (I didn't move to London.)

4 If you had studied harder, you would have passed the test. (You didn't study hard enough.)

5 If there were no air, sound could not travel. (There is air.)

We can use some **conditional adverb clauses** to describe unreal, imaginary, unlikely, or impossible situations, as in **1 – 5.** We might use an unreal conditional:

- when we wish the situation were true, as in **1**
- to give advice, as in **2**
- to express cause and effect, as in **3**
- to criticize, as in **4**
- to give surprising information, as in **5**

GRAMMAR TERM: This use of the unreal conditional is sometimes called the **third conditional.**

B

PRESENT UNREAL CONDITIONALS

6 If it **weren't raining, I'd go** for a walk. (= It is raining.)

7 If my sister **were** here now, she **would know** what to do. (= She's not here now.)

8 If I **didn't have to work** today, I **could go** hiking. (= I do have to work today.)

9 If I **could do** anything I wanted, I'd **move** to Japan.

FUTURE UNREAL CONDITIONALS

10 If I **had** time next month, I'd **go** to Hawaii. (= I don't have time next month.)

11 If I **had to work** next week, I **wouldn't be able to go** with you. (= I don't have to work next week.)

To show that we are talking about an unreal or imaginary situation, we use special verb forms.

When both the condition and the result refer to a present or future time frame, as in **6 – 11,** we use:

UNREAL CONDITION IN PRESENT OR FUTURE	UNREAL RESULT IN PRESENT OR FUTURE
if + a past verb form	*would* + base form
	could + base form

WARNING! When we use the verb *be* in the *if-* clause, we usually use *were* instead of *was,* as in **6 – 7.**

PAST UNREAL CONDITIONALS

12 If I **hadn't eaten** earlier, I **would have gone** to lunch with you. (= I did eat earlier.)

13 If I **had had** any vacation days last month, I **could have gone** to Hawaii. (= I didn't have any vacation days last month.)

When both the condition and the result refer to past time, as in **12 – 13,** we use:

UNREAL CONDITION IN PAST	UNREAL RESULT IN PAST
if + a past perfect verb	*would have* + past participle
	could have + past participle

C

THE TWO CLAUSES REFER TO DIFFERENT TIME FRAMES

14 If we **had left** earlier, I **would be** home by now. (unreal past condition + present result)

15 If he **hadn't been helping** me, I **would** still **be living** an hour away from school. (unreal past condition + present result)

As with other adverb clauses, the time in an *if-* clause may be different from the time in a result clause, as in **14 – 15.**

34 | Identifying Uses of Unreal Conditionals Why did each speaker or writer below use an unreal conditional? Read the reasons in the box. Then write *a, b, c, d,* or *e.* (More than one answer may be possible.) `6.8 A`

> a. because the person wishes the situation were true
> b. to give advice
> c. to express cause and effect
> d. to criticize
> e. to give surprising information

1. If I had known you were coming, I would have cooked something special. _c/d_
2. If the ice at both the North and South Poles melted, the seas would rise by over 70 meters. ____
3. It would help if you wrote the instructions down. ____
4. If something happened to her, her parents would be devastated. ____
5. If there were no gravity, things would spin off the earth. ____
6. I'd laugh if I weren't so tired. ____
7. If you hadn't wasted so much time, you'd be finished by now. ____
8. If he had the skills to work, he would be able to find a job. ____
9. If you had listened to me, we wouldn't have gotten lost. ____
10. If she had known the ice was thin, she wouldn't have gone out on the lake. ____
11. If I had told you the truth, you wouldn't have believed me. ____
12. You would have been disappointed if I hadn't come. ____
13. If you got up earlier, you wouldn't be late. ____
14. I would go to the doctor more often if I had health insurance. ____
15. Your essay would be better if it had a more interesting introduction. ____

Think about It In each sentence above, what didn't happen or isn't true?

1. I didn't know you were coming.

35 | Talking about Unreal Situations Match each clause on the left with a clause on the right. (More than one answer is possible.) Then circle the verbs in the main clause and the *if-* clause of each sentence. `6.8 B`

1. If I (won) a lot of money, _e_
2. If I were the leader of my country, ____
3. If everyone could speak the same language, ____
4. If there were fewer people in the world, ____
5. If I could choose my dream job, ____
6. If we were at the beach, ____
7. If you didn't have any water to drink, ____
8. If I had more free time, ____
9. If I could take tomorrow off, ____
10. If I had a good boss, ____

a. I would be the president of a company.
b. you probably wouldn't live for more than a few days.
c. we could go surfing.
d. my job would be great.
e. I (would share) it with my friends.
f. our cities wouldn't be so crowded.
g. we wouldn't need translators anymore.
h. I would learn a new sport.
i. I would change the tax system.
j. I would go for a long hike.

Think about It What verb forms are used in the *if-* clause and main clause of each sentence in Activity 35? What time frame is each sentence in?

Write about It Write new sentences using each *if-* clause in Activity 35. Use your own words to write a different main clause.

36 | Identifying the Time Frame
Underline the verb forms in the *if-* clause and main clause for each sentence. Then decide if each **bold** result clause describes an imaginary result in the *past*, *present*, or *future*. `6.8 B–C`

1. a. If we <u>hadn't learned</u> how to use electricity, **we <u>might still be using</u> candles at night.** ___*present*___

   b. If we hadn't learned how to use electricity, **computers couldn't have been invented.** _____

2. a. If I hadn't lost my job, **I would be able to afford a new car.** _____

   b. If I hadn't lost my job, **I wouldn't be able to travel with my family next week.** _____

3. a. If he hadn't been wearing his seat belt, **he wouldn't have survived the crash.** _____

   b. If he hadn't been wearing his seat belt, **he wouldn't be alive today.** _____

4. a. If she hadn't spent so much money, **she could have afforded a new car.** _____

   b. If she hadn't spent so much money, **she would still have some money in the bank.** _____

5. a. If the earth didn't rotate, **there would always be daylight on one side of it.** _____

   b. If the earth didn't rotate, **there would be very little life.** _____

6. a. If I didn't have to work, **I would have gone shopping this morning.** _____

   b. If I didn't have to work, **I'd feel a lot more relaxed.** _____

7. a. If my brother had become a lawyer, **he'd probably be working at a law firm.** _____

   b. If my brother had become a lawyer, **he wouldn't have been very happy.** _____

8. a. If our city wasn't so expensive, **I'd buy a bigger house next year.** _____

   b. If our city wasn't so expensive, **I would have moved into a bigger apartment.** _____

Write about It Write another main clause for each *if-* clause above. Which time frame did you use in each sentence?

1. If we hadn't learned how to use electricity, life would be much more difficult.

37 | Usage Note: Contrasting Real and Unreal Conditionals
Read the note. Then do Activity 38.

Future real and unreal conditionals may be used in similar contexts. However, with the real conditional, the speaker believes the situation is more likely to happen.

Future Real: If I **get** a new car, I'**ll drive** across the country. (= I think there is a good chance that I will get a new car.)
Future Unreal: If I **got** a new car, I'**d drive** across the country. (= I am just imagining what getting a new car is like.)

We sometimes use *would* to describe a regular event in the past. Be careful not to confuse a past real conditional with *would* and a present/future unreal conditional.

Past Real: I really liked my fifth-grade teacher. If we all did our homework, he **would give** us a treat.
(describes something that happened regularly in the past)
Present/Future Unreal: If we all did our homework, our teacher **would give** us a treat. Why don't we do it?
(describes something that is not true now; the speaker expresses something he or she wishes would happen)

38 | Identifying Real and Unreal Conditionals Does each *if-* clause describe a real condition (something likely) or an unreal condition (something less likely or impossible)? Check (✓) your answers.

6.8 A–C

	REAL	UNREAL
1. She'll be worried if you're late.	✓	☐
2. I'd be happier if I lived near the ocean.	☐	☐
3. If you tell me the truth, I won't get mad.	☐	☐
4. If my brother remembers my birthday, I'll be very surprised.	☐	☐
5. We would finish this work faster if we could talk on the phone.	☐	☐
6. This will taste great if you add a little salt.	☐	☐
7. If you take a vacation, you'll feel a lot better.	☐	☐
8. If you took the train, you'd save some time.	☐	☐
9. I'd love it if you came to dinner.	☐	☐
10. If you book the hotel, I'll pay you back.	☐	☐
11. If he fixes my laptop, I'll be amazed.	☐	☐
12. If I'd gone to the meeting, I'd know the decision.	☐	☐
13. I'd feel better if I were more organized.	☐	☐
14. When I was young and got sick, I would always feel better if my mother brought me a cup of tea.	☐	☐
15. When we were younger, my sister would always help me if she could.	☐	☐
16. My sister doesn't have much money, but I know she would help me if she could.	☐	☐
17. My mom doesn't like to criticize anyone. If I did something wrong, I don't think she would say anything.	☐	☐
18. When I was a child, if I did something wrong, my mom would always say the same thing.	☐	☐
19. If I hadn't eaten so much last night, I'd feel much better than I do now.	☐	☐
20. If I hadn't had bad teeth as a kid, I wouldn't have needed to go to the dentist so often.	☐	☐

Think about It Work with a partner. For 1–12 above, change the real conditions to unreal ones and the unreal conditions to real ones.

1. She would be worried if you were late.

Talk about It Work with a partner. Choose one of the sentences from 13–20 above, and use it to create a short conversation. Present your conversation to the class.

A: Were you close to your sister as kids?
B: Very close. When we were younger, my sister would always help me if she could.

39 | Usage Note: *As If* and *As Though* Read the note. Then do Activity 40.

We can use *as if* and *as though* to compare a real situation (in the present or past) to something unreal or imaginary. These subordinators express a sense of both manner (*how*) and condition. Notice that the main clause may use a present or past verb form. The adverb clause uses a past verb form to show that the situation is distant from reality.

PRESENT REAL SITUATION COMPARED TO SOMETHING UNREAL

1 He feels **as though he were a character in a book.**
(He is not a character in a book.)

2 She speaks Mandarin **as if she were born in China.**
(She wasn't born in China.)

PAST REAL SITUATION COMPARED TO SOMETHING UNREAL

3 She acted **as though nothing had happened.**
(Something did happen.)

4 He acted **as if he were the president of the company.**
(He was not the president of the company.)

40 | Using *As If* and *As Though* Match each clause on the left with a clause on the right. (More than one answer may be possible.) `6.8 A–C`

1. I asked her to stop, but she went ahead __g__
2. There is a photograph on his desk; it looks ____
3. He looked around and leaned toward me ____
4. She was so thin. She looked ____
5. He was walking ____
6. Her eyes were very wide, and she looked ____
7. He looked very red, ____
8. I remember my graduation day ____
9. This isn't a big problem but she feels ____
10. They spoke in low voices ____
11. He bent down suddenly ____

a. as though he wanted to tell me a secret.
b. as if they were in the library.
c. as though he'd hurt himself.
d. as if he'd been out in the sun for hours.
e. as if it were taken in the 1950s.
f. as though she hadn't eaten for weeks.
g. as though she hadn't heard me.
h. as if it were enormous.
i. as if he were going to pick up something.
j. as if it were yesterday.
k. as though she'd had a terrible scare.

Write about It Think of a different way to complete each sentence above. Then think of a different way to begin each sentence.

1. She kept talking as though she hadn't heard me.

41 | Error Correction Correct any errors in these sentences. (Some sentences may not have any errors.)

1. As if she had all that she needs.
2. If I know more about grammar, I wouldn't make so many mistakes.
3. If this happened in my country, he would have gone to jail.
4. If nobody would tell me to get glasses, I would not be successful in my classes.
5. If you ever go to California, you should go to Los Angeles.
6. You didn't wear a uniform, you can't go to this school.
7. If you want to buy something, you can probably order it on the Internet.
8. I knew I would have a better life if I study hard.
9. It is safer if you would travel with another person.
10. If you don't have self-confidence, you can't lead other people.
11. If my parents was here, I wouldn't have learned the language so quickly.
12. Her business wouldn't have been successful. If I hadn't supported her.

6.9 Using Adverb Clauses in Speaking

<table>
<tr>
<td rowspan="1">A</td>
<td>
1 A: When can I go there by myself?
   B: When you're 16.

2 A: I don't think I got the job.
   B: Because they didn't call back?

3 I have an idea. (pause) If you're interested.
</td>
<td>
In conversation, we sometimes use an adverb clause alone (without a main clause), as in 1 – 3. Sometimes the adverb clause completes another person's idea or question, as in 2. Sometimes the adverb clause is an afterthought, as in 3.
</td>
</tr>
<tr>
<td>B</td>
<td>
4 If that's Elvis, then I'm John Lennon!
5 If you need anything else, just holler.
6 If I've said anything I shouldn't have, I'm truly sorry.
7 If you really want my advice, don't bother with making a reservation. Just go there.
8 If you'll cook dinner, I'll wash the dishes.
9 If you won't open it, I will.
</td>
<td>
We often use real conditional sentences to:
<ul>
<li>speak humorously or sarcastically, as in 4</li>
<li>make an offer, as in 5</li>
<li>make an apology, as in 6</li>
<li>give advice, as in 7</li>
<li>make a deal with someone, as in 8 – 9. Notice that we use a future form in both the main clause and the if- clause for this special situation.</li>
</ul>
</td>
</tr>
<tr>
<td>C</td>
<td>
10 If everyone could look this way, please.
11 If I might have your attention . . .
12 If you'll excuse me, . . .

13 I'd like to go to sleep now if that's OK with you.
14 If you don't mind, I'd like to eat soon.
</td>
<td>
In conversation, we sometimes use conditionals to:
<ul>
<li>make a polite request, as in 10 – 12. (Here the if- clause is often used without a result clause.) Notice that we sometimes use a future form in the if- clause for this special situation.</li>
<li>show formality or request permission, as in 13 – 14</li>
</ul>
The conditional clause softens the request or statement by offering the listener a choice.
</td>
</tr>
<tr>
<td>D</td>
<td>
15 A: What if I run into any problems?
    (= What should I do if I run into any problems?)
   B: Just call me.

16 A: Is fencing dangerous?
   B: Not if you're wearing the right clothes.
    (= It's not dangerous if you're wearing the right clothes.)
</td>
<td>
In conversation, we sometimes ask a question with <i>what if</i>, as in 15. In these questions, the result clause is implied.

We sometimes answer a question with <i>not if</i>, as in 16.
</td>
</tr>
</table>

42 | Using Real Conditionals in Conversation Choose an adverb clause from the box to complete each conversation. Listen and check your answers. Then practice with a partner. `6.9 A`

1. A: Why do we have to spend so much money?

   B: We can talk about it. (*pause*) _____*If you want.*_____

   A: I don't think there's anything to talk about. (*pause*)

   _____

2. A: How long have you lived here?

   B: _____

3. A: How are you doing?

   B: _____

   (*pause*) I don't know. Could be better.

4. A: How did you know Amanda was lying?

   B: _____

> Because she wouldn't look at me.
> Because we can't really afford it.
> Because you're crazy?
> If you insist.
> If you think I should.
> If you want.
> If you're interested.
> Since I was 13.
> Since the last time we talked?
> Whenever you're ready.

5. A: Do you think I should drive or take the train?

   B: Take the train. Definitely take the train.

   A: OK. _____

   B: I do. I really do.

6. A: This is a great place for a vacation.

   B: I told you it was.

   A: I know but I was hoping I wouldn't enjoy it. You know why?

   B: _____

7. A: I'm getting bored! When can we go?

   B: _____

8. A: I have something to tell you about James. (*pause*) _____

   B: Of course I am! What is it?

9. A: Can we have pizza for dinner again tonight?

   B: I suppose so. _____

RESEARCH SAYS...

Clauses of condition, reason, and time are especially common in conversation.

CORPUS

43 | Using Real Conditionals in Conversation Why does each speaker below use a real conditional sentence? Choose *a*, *b*, *c*, *d*, or *e* from the box. Then practice with a partner. 6.9 B

```
a. to speak humorously or sarcastically
b. to make an offer
c. to make an apology
d. to give advice
e. to make a deal
```

1. A: I just can't do this math problem.

   B: Come on. If you stick with it, you'll figure it out. _*d*_

2. A: That's not a nice thing to say!

   B: If I offended you, I'm sorry. I didn't mean to. ____

3. A: I'll drive you to Chicago if you pay for the gas. ____

   B: That seems reasonable. You're on!

4. A: If you could just listen for a minute, I'll explain.

   B: Sure. I'm sorry. Go ahead. ____

5. A: Well, goodbye. It was nice working with you.

   B: Yeah. I'm sorry if things didn't work out so well. ____

   A: Me too.

6. A: If you want to chat later, I'll be up till midnight. ____

   B: Thanks a lot. I might do that.

7. A: If you think I'm smart, then you're a genius. ____

   B: Oh, come on. You're a lot smarter than me.

8. A: Look, if you hate this job, you should quit. ____

   B: I guess you're right.

9. A: If that's art, my two-year-old son is Picasso. ____

   B: I know what you mean. It's not very good, is it?

10. A: If I can be honest, I think that tie is terrible. ____

    B: Really? It doesn't go with the shirt?

    A: It doesn't go with anything.

11. A: OK, I'll try a raw oyster if you will. ____

    B: Let's do it!

12. A: If you have any questions, just call me. ____

    B: Great. Thanks so much.

44 | Softening a Request or Statement Listen and write the missing words. Then practice the conversations with a partner. `6.9 C`

1. A: Do you mind _____*if I turn down the music*_____?

   B: No, please, go ahead.

2. A: Anna seems really distracted and I don't know why.

   B: _____, I can talk to her.

3. A: I'm leaving for the bank.

   B: OK _____?

4. A: I'm going to study here _____.

   B: No, please.

5. A: _____, I have to make a phone call.

   B: Talk to you later, then.

6. A: I don't think I want to work tonight.

   B: Look, _____, that's OK.

7. A: This is delicious.

   B: Thanks. You could have a little more, _____.

8. A: _____, Mr. Jones . . .

   B: Please, Tom, come in, come in.

9. A: Hey! Let's go see a movie.

   B: Hmm. _____, could we get some food instead? I haven't eaten.

10. A: _____, I'd like to talk to you.

    B: Sure. How can I help?

45 | Using *What If* and *Not If* Choose a sentence from the box to complete each conversation. Listen and check your answers. Then practice with a partner. `6.9 D`

1. A: Are you going to work at home today?

   B: _*Not if I don't have to.*_____

2. A: I don't feel like cooking tonight.

   B: _____

   A: Sounds good to me.

3. A: What happened to your car?

   B: A car ran into it.

   A: Wow! _____

   B: Yeah, I know. It would have been bad.

4. A: Is there any cake left?

   B: Yeah, one piece—but it's mine.

   A: _____

5. A: Stop! There's a car coming!

   B: Yikes! He's going fast.

   A: That's crazy. _____

   B: I would have hit him for sure.

> Not if I don't have to.
> Not if I get there first.
> Not if you stay relaxed.
> Not if you want to get there on time.
> What if I hadn't seen him?
> What if I pick you up at 8?
> What if I refuse?
> What if we go out instead?
> What if you hadn't had your seat belt on?

6. A: Do I have time for a shower before we leave?

   B: _____

7. A: Will you lend me some money?

   B: _____

   A: Then I'll tell Dad about the scratch[23] on the car.

8. A: What's the matter?

   B: I'm just nervous. I'm afraid I'm going to forget everything.

   A: _____

9. A: What time do you want to leave?

   B: _____

   A: Sounds good to me.

Will you lend me some money?

6.10 Using Adverb Clauses in Academic Writing

A

We often use **adverb clauses** to connect two or more ideas. We can do this in a single sentence or across two or more sentences, as in **1a – 1b**. This makes our writing cohesive; it helps each sentence flow smoothly into the next.

COMPARE

1a The area of China is only slightly larger than that of the U.S. However, the population of China is more than four times greater.

1b Although the area of China is only slightly larger than that of the U.S., its population is more than four times greater.

A **subordinator** shows the relationship between the ideas, as in **2 – 8**.

2 Now I'm not so shy **when** meeting new people. (time)
3 **Because** we live in an increasingly multicultural society, it is important to study other languages. (reason)
4 **Even though** I was 26, I had never been outside of my city. (contrast)
5 The company collects and cleans used clothes **so that** they can be used again. (purpose)
6 Cell phones have become **such** an important part of our lifestyle **that** it would be difficult to live without them. (result)
7 **If** you maintain a healthy lifestyle, then you are less likely to get sick. (condition)
8 Please complete the test exactly **as** I showed you. (manner)

B

An adverb clause can come at the beginning or end of a sentence. We often choose to put an adverb clause at the beginning of a sentence to set the scene for the following ideas, as in **9 – 11**.

9 **When you sleep**, you dream about 20 percent of the time. For example, if you sleep one night for eight hours, you dream for about 96 minutes of those eight hours.
10 A baby has 270 to 300 bones—more than an adult's 213. **As you grow up**, some of your bones grow together.
11 **When you cut yourself**, you may lose some blood, but the body can replace blood and other cells[24].

We may also use an adverb clause at the beginning of a sentence to make a connection back to information in a previous sentence, as in **12 – 14**. The adverb clause acts as a bridge between the previous sentence and the new information in the main clause.

12 | I got up quickly and went down to the kitchen. | As I entered the room, | my uncle jumped up from his chair. |

previous sentence   adverb clause   new information in main clause

13 Ching-He Huang studied economics in college, but her passion was cooking. **After she graduated**, she started a food and drink company.
14 In Turkey, high school students take a national achievement exam in March. **If they pass that exam**, they take another exam in June.

GO ONLINE

[23] **scratch:** a cut or mark from something sharp   [24] **cells:** the smallest parts of any living thing

46 | Identifying the Connection between Ideas Underline the adverb clauses in these sentences and circle the subordinators. Then identify the connection between the adverb clause and the main clause. Write *time, reason, contrast, purpose, result, condition,* or *manner.* **6.10 A**

HOW TO FALL ASLEEP FAST

1. Turn the television off and step away from the computer at least one hour (before) you go to bed because — *time* they stimulate²⁵ your brain rather than relax it.

2. Before you get in bed, lie flat on the floor and stretch²⁶.

3. Although it's sometimes difficult to find a comfortable position when falling asleep, it's a good idea to lie on your back and relax until you feel comfortable. If that doesn't work, lie on your side.

4. Some people use visualization²⁷ to relax. You imagine yourself in a beautiful place such as the beach. If you are successful, you feel as if you are really there.

5. Deep breathing can help you sleep better. Slowly breathe in so that your chest fully expands. Hold your breath for three seconds. Then breathe out. Repeat five to ten times. You should feel your body relax as you breathe.

6. You may want to fall asleep so much that you become too tense to let it happen. If this is the case, get out of bed and take a walk. Try stretching again before getting back into bed.

Write about It Write two to three more sentences giving advice on how to fall asleep. Use adverb clauses. Then share your sentences with a partner. Ask your partner to identify the types of adverb clauses you used.

---

47 | Combining Ideas Combine each pair of ideas into one sentence, and make any other necessary changes to the sentence. (More than one answer may be possible.) **6.10 A**

1. I don't drink coffee in the evening.
   Drinking coffee interferes with my sleep.

   I don't drink coffee in the evening because it interferes with my sleep.
   Because coffee interferes with my sleep, I don't drink it in the evening.

2. Hassan came to the U.S.
   Hassan began studying automotive engineering.

3. People don't have to spend so much time preparing food.
   People are better off now than they used to be.

4. Clara Jbour's parents sent her to the U.S. to attend college.
   Clara Jbour graduated from high school.

5. Parents are not teaching their children correct behavior.
   Parents may need coaching in parenting skills.

6. You maintain a healthy lifestyle.
   You are less likely to get sick.

7. Cody Huelskamp works as a wildlife photographer.
   Cody Huelskamp has traveled to 70 countries.

8. I missed most of the movie.
   I was worrying about my job.

Clara Jbour

Cody Huelskamp

---

²⁵ **stimulate:** to make something active or more active
²⁶ **stretch:** to push your arms and legs out as far as you can
²⁷ **visualization:** having a picture in your mind about someone or something

9. I love sweets.

   I try not to eat candy.

10. Many mothers work outside of the home.

   Fathers must share the responsibilities of running a house.

11. He continued to play football.

   His knee got worse.

12. Roughly 36 percent of New Yorkers were born outside of the U.S.

   It's very common to hear people speaking different languages.

Think about It How many different ways can you combine each pair of ideas in Activity 47? Which one do you think is the most effective?

48 | Using Subordinators Read the science article. Choose the subordinator that best completes each sentence. `6.10 A–B`

Protecting Your Skin

_____When_____ summer comes, I get sun crazy. I like to eat on the patio and lie on the beach. I walk and
(1. because / when)

bike everywhere. _____ I was younger, I played in the sun without worry. _____
          (2. although / when)   (3. now that / when)

I'm 30, I realize how important it is to protect myself. That's _____ the ultraviolet (UV) rays[28]
                                                            (4. because / when)

from the sun harm the cells in our skin. You can't see the damage _____ you're young, but its
                                                                (5. although / when)

effects often show up much later. _____ crowds of young people go to beaches and tanning
                                        (6. as / when)

salons[29], skin cancer is becoming more common, says Mandeep Kaur. She's a dermatologist, or skin doctor,

at Wake Forest University School of Medicine.

_____ our skin works hard to protect us, few people work to protect it. The sun's UV rays
(7. although / because)

are the biggest threat _____ they damage the cells of your skin. The tricky thing is that this
                      (8. because / while)

process can take 30 or more years to become evident. "It's surprising how long it takes," says Meenhard

Herlyn, a biologist at the Wistar Institute in Philadelphia. "Even _____ kids have big,
                                                                (9. because / if)

blistering[30] sunburns every summer, they're fine _____ they're kids."
                                                  (10. although / while)

Think about It Circle the sentences above that begin with an adverb clause. Why do you think the writer put the adverb clause at the beginning of the sentence?

• to set the scene for the following ideas

• to make a connection back to information in a previous sentence

Talk about It What is something new you learned from the article above? Tell a partner.

[28] **ultraviolet rays:** light from the sun that cannot be seen
[29] **tanning salons:** places where you can expose your skin to ultraviolet light to darken your skin

[30] **blistering:** having small, painful places on your skin that are full of liquid

49 | Using Adverb Clauses Read this story and underline the adverb clauses. Then answer the questions below. 6.10 A–B

THE LEMON STORY

Alberto Alvaro Ríos

When the writer's parents buy a new house, his mother gets to choose the color for each room.

When I was about four, or maybe five, my parents bought a new house in what would later become a small suburb of Nogales, Arizona, on the border of Mexico, some four miles outside town. As we kept driving out to watch the house being built, my mother got to make a number of choices regarding details, among which was the color of various rooms.

My mother, when asked what color she wanted the kitchen, said to the workers, who were all Mexican and who spoke very little English, *limón*. She said it both because she wanted the kitchen to be yellow and because she wanted to start learning Spanish. The workers nodded yes. But when she came back the next day, the kitchen was painted bright green, like a small jungle[31]. Mexican *limónes*, my mother found out, are small and green, that color exactly, no mistake.

So that's the color that wall stayed for the next 14 years, until I left home for college. She said it was a reminder to us all that there was a great deal to learn in the world. You might laugh at first, but after 14 years you start to think about it.

QUESTIONS

1. In which sentences does the writer use an adverb clause to make his writing more cohesive?
2. In which sentences does the adverb clause set the scene for the following ideas?
3. In paragraph 1, in the sentence beginning *As we kept driving*, what does the subordinator *as* mean?
4. In your own words, retell the story to a partner.

50 | Making Your Writing Cohesive Combine the two ideas on the right to form the next sentence on the left. Decide if you think the adverb clause or the main clause should come at the beginning to make the sentence cohesive. 6.10 B

1. Americans should be required to learn another language. *Because we live in an increasingly multicultural society, this will benefit them in the future.*
   - this will benefit them in the future
   - because we live in an increasingly multicultural society

2. Many people around the world are learning to speak English as a second language.
   - communication would be even better
   - if more Americans learned to speak foreign languages

3. Yoga improves your flexibility[32]. Also, . . .
   - it is a great way to meet people
   - if you do classes

4. My favorite pastime is rock climbing.
   - I enjoy it
   - because it is something I can do inside or outside

5. In the U.S., children must be vaccinated[33] against certain diseases.
   - they must receive vaccinations
   - before they can start school

6. Competition can be very good for children.
   - it is only a problem
   - when too much emphasis is placed on it

---

[31] **jungle:** a thick forest in a hot part of the world
[32] **flexibility:** the ability to bend easily without breaking

[33] **vaccinate:** to put a substance in a person's blood using a needle, to stop them from getting a disease

7. In many families, both parents have full-time jobs. This can create problems at home.

8. Brothers and sisters spend a lot of time together. They help each other and take care of each other.

9. People like to read essays that are well organized and interesting.

10. Having children is very stressful and time-consuming, but . . .

11. Every home should have a pair of small, foldable scissors.

12. The writer Chinua Achebe was born in Nigeria.

13. Plastic bags in the ocean are dangerous for sea turtles.

14. A report concluded that 100,000 ocean mammals die each year by eating or getting caught in plastic.

15. In the 1970s, there was just one Pinta tortoise in the Galapagos Islands.

16. In the past, people brought goats to the Galapagos to raise for food. Unfortunately, the goats liked to eat the same food that the tortoises ate.

- children have to spend all day at school or daycare
- when neither parent can be at home
- they understand each other very well
- because they share so many experiences while growing up
- readers will be able to follow your ideas easily
- if you organize your essay well
- the job can be easier
- if parents are patient with their children
- they fit easily in a purse or pocket
- because they fold up and are very small
- he chose to write in English
- even though he was African
- because the bags look like jellyfish[34]
- the sea turtles try to eat the bags
- when they get caught in plastic
- they may drown or become exhausted and die of starvation
- because it was the last remaining Pinta tortoise that scientists knew of
- the *Guinness Book of World Records* called it the "rarest living creature"
- the food supply for tortoises disappeared
- as the number of goats on the island increased

51 | Making Your Writing Cohesive Rewrite each paragraph. Connect the ideas in different ways to make the writing cohesive. You will probably want to move ideas around and change words. `6.10 B`

A	B
I spend a lot of time on the road. That's why I've seen a lot of stupid behavior. I could list at least 15 driving pet peeves. I'll limit myself to two. One thing really bothers me. It's when people forget to turn off their turn signal. It's very distracting. I hate to drive for miles behind someone with a flashing turn signal. Second, people sometimes flash their headlights. I don't understand why people get so impatient. It's really irritating.	One of my biggest pet peeves is irritating cell phone users. Many people talk very loudly on their phone. You can hear everything they say. This is very annoying. Sometimes you are trying to read and you can't. Sometimes you are trying to talk to someone else and you can't. It also bothers me when people always answer their phone. You can be having a conversation with them, and they stop and answer the phone. This is extremely rude.

Talk about It Compare the paragraphs you rewrote above with your classmates. What are some of the different ways people combined the ideas into a new paragraph?

Write about It Write about one of your pet peeves. Try to use two adverb clauses in your writing.

[34] **jellyfish:** an animal with a soft, pale body that lives in the ocean

A | WRITING Study these pictures from movies. Choose one picture, and write a paragraph to explain what might be happening. Use time clauses, reason clauses, manner clauses, and *if-* clauses.

I chose the third picture. When the main character goes out into the ocean, a big storm begins. If the boy can't reach the shore before night, he'll be in a lot of danger. As soon as he realizes that his life is in danger, he starts to panic.

B | TIC-TAC-TOE Follow these instructions:

1. Work with a partner. Student A is X. Student B is O.

2. Student A: Choose a square and complete the sentence.

3. Students A and B: Check the sentence together. If the sentence has no errors, write an X in the square. If the sentence is not correct, do not write an X in the square.

4. Student B: Take your turn. Choose a square and complete the sentence.

5. Students A and B: Check the sentence together. If the sentence has no errors, write an O in the square. If the sentence is not correct, do not write an O in the square.

6. Continue to take turns. The first person to get three Xs or three Os in a line is the winner.

Before I came to this school, I _____ _____ .	If I'm good-looking, _____ _____ .	Even though it wasn't a good idea, I _____ _____ .
If it's OK with you, _____ _____ .	As soon as I get home, _____ _____ .	Once you've tried _____ , you _____ _____ .
My brother is so _____ that he _____ _____ .	I won't _____ unless _____ _____ .	You look as though _____ _____ .

C | PERSONAL REFLECTION Read this advice. Choose one piece of advice that you strongly agree or disagree with. Make notes to support your opinion. Then explain to your classmates why you agree or disagree with the advice. Use adverb clauses in your writing.

1. You should follow your dreams no matter how crazy they seem.
2. It's better to be cautious than to make mistakes.
3. Never have regrets. Leave the past in the past.
4. Live for today!
5. Always look after No. 1: that's you.
6. Don't make promises.

I completely disagree with the first piece of advice. If you have crazy dreams, you're probably not going to achieve them. Although it may seem like a good idea to have dreams, it can be hard to make them come true. Instead, you should set yourself easier goals so that you succeed. Even if you think that's unambitious, it's a good idea to think about it. For example, if you wanted to become a famous detective, you'd still have to learn the job. You can't become famous until you've proved you're good.

D | WEB SEARCH Look online for information about an interesting city to visit. Copy the information and underline the adverb clauses you see. Then write an advertisement to describe the city.

As soon as you get off the plane in Belgium, you'll start feeling hungry! Before you start visiting the main tourist sites, be sure to get a good lunch in the town square. If you like mussels, you're sure to love Brussels!

6.11 Summary of Adverb Clauses

TYPE OF ADVERB CLAUSE	COMMON SUBORDINATORS	EXAMPLES
Time When?	*after, as, as soon as, before, by the time, once, since, until, when, whenever, while*	**As soon as he graduates,** he'll get a job. **Whenever I see her,** I feel happy. **Once you travel the world,** you're never the same again.
Reason Why?	*as, because, now that, since*	**Since none of the students were ready,** the test was postponed. **Now that all the results are in,** I'll announce the winners.
Contrast	*as though, even though, though, while*	**Even though it was very cold,** we decided to go ahead with the hike. I was determined to become a doctor **although my parents didn't want me to.**
Manner How? In what way?	*as, like*	Please check your spelling **as directed in the instructions.**
	as if, as though	He looks **as though he has a bad cold.**
Result	*so* + adjective or adverb + *that* *so many/few* + plural noun + *that* *so much/little* + noncount noun + *that* *such* + (*a/an*) + adjective + noun	She was **so beautiful that people stared at her.** There were **so many** people in the audience **that we could hardly see the stage.** It was **such** a funny movie **that I couldn't stop laughing.**
Purpose For what purpose? Why?	*so that*	I closed the blinds **so that I wouldn't wake up too early.**
Real Conditional	*if, unless, when, whenever*	**If it rains,** we'll change our plans. Don't go to Arizona **unless you love hot climates.** **Whenever I exercise,** I feel great.
Unreal Conditional	*if*	**If I weren't working next week,** I'd go to the beach.
	as if, as though	She felt **as if she had been running a marathon.**

Resources

I. Non-Action Verbs

agree	consist of	fear	include	mind	recognize	think
appear	contain	feel	involve	need	remember	understand
appreciate	cost	fit	know	owe	see	want
be	dislike	hate	like	own	seem	weigh
believe	doubt	have	look	possess	smell	wish
belong	envy	hear	love	prefer	suppose	
conclude	equal	imagine	mean	realize	taste	

Remember:

- A non-action verb describes a state (an unchanging condition).
- Non-action verbs are also called **stative verbs**.
- Some verbs have more than one meaning. They can function as a non-action verb in one context and an action verb in another.

II. Linking Verbs

appear	become	get*	look	seem	sound	turn*
be	feel	grow*	remain	smell	taste	

* with a meaning of *become*

Remember: A linking verb can have an adjective as a complement.

III. Irregular Verbs

BASE FORM	SIMPLE PAST	PAST PARTICIPLE
arise	arose	arisen
beat	beat	beaten
become	became	become
begin	began	begun
bend	bent	bent
bet	bet	bet
bite	bit	bitten
bleed	bled	bled
break	broke	broken
bring	brought	brought
build	built	built
buy	bought	bought
catch	caught	caught
choose	chose	chosen
come	came	come
cost	cost	cost
cut	cut	cut
deal	dealt	dealt
dig	dug	dug
draw	drew	drawn
drink	drank	drunk
drive	drove	driven
eat	ate	eaten
fall	fell	fallen
feed	fed	fed
feel	felt	felt
fight	fought	fought
find	found	found
fly	flew	flown
forbid	forbade	forbidden
forget	forgot	forgotten
forgive	forgave	forgiven
freeze	froze	frozen
get	got	gotten
give	gave	given
go	went	gone
grow	grew	grown
hear	heard	heard
hide	hid	hidden
hit	hit	hit
hold	held	held
hurt	hurt	hurt
keep	kept	kept
know	knew	known
lay	laid	laid
lead	led	led
leave	left	left
lend	lent	lent
let	let	let
light	lit/lighted	lit/lighted
lose	lost	lost
make	made	made
mean	meant	meant
meet	met	met

BASE FORM	SIMPLE PAST	PAST PARTICIPLE
pay	paid	paid
put	put	put
quit	quit	quit
read	read	read
ride	rode	ridden
ring	rang	rung
rise	rose	risen
run	ran	run
say	said	said
see	saw	seen
seek	sought	sought
sell	sold	sold
send	sent	sent
set	set	set
sew	sewed	sewn
shake	shook	shaken
shoot	shot	shot
show	showed	shown
shrink	shrank	shrunk
shut	shut	shut
sing	sang	sung
sink	sank	sunk
sit	sat	sat
sleep	slept	slept
slide	slid	slid
speak	spoke	spoken
speed	sped	sped
spend	spent	spent
spin	spun	spun
spread	spread	spread
spring	sprang	sprung
stand	stood	stood
steal	stole	stolen
sting	stung	stung
stink	stank	stunk
strike	struck	struck
strive	strove	striven
swear	swore	sworn
sweep	swept	swept
swim	swam	swum
swing	swung	swung
take	took	taken
teach	taught	taught
tear	tore	torn
tell	told	told
think	thought	thought
throw	threw	thrown
understand	understood	understood
wake	woke	woken
wear	wore	worn
weep	wept	wept
win	won	won
wind	wound	wound
write	wrote	written

IV. Spelling Rules for the -s/-es Form of Verbs

To form the third-person singular (*he/she/it*) for the simple present:

1 Add *-es* to verbs that end in *-sh*, *-ch*, *-ss*, *-s*, *-x*, or *-z*.

| finish | finishes | touch | touches | pass | passes | relax | relaxes |

2 For verbs ending in a consonant + *-y*, change the *-y* to *-i* and add *-es*.

| study | studies | worry | worries | deny | denies | fly | flies |

3 Three verbs have a special spelling:

| go | goes | do | does | have | has |

4 For all other verbs, add *-s*.

| like | likes | buy | buys | see | sees | speak | speaks |

V. Spelling Rules for the -ing Form of Verbs

1 The base form of the verb ends in a vowel + consonant sound + *-e*:	Drop the *-e* and add *-ing*. live–living **caus**e–causing be**com**e–becoming ta**k**e–taking
2 The base form is one syllable, and it ends in one vowel + one consonant (except *-w*, *-x*, or *-y*):	Double the final consonant and add *-ing*. **put**–putting **win**–winning **drop**–dropping
3 The base form has more than one syllable, it ends in one vowel + one consonant (except *-w*, *-x*, or *-y*), and the last syllable is stressed:	Double the final consonant and add *-ing*. for•**get**–forgetting be•**gin**–beginning com•**mit**–committing
4 The base form ends in *-ie*:	Change the *-ie* to *-y* and add *-ing*. die–dying tie–tying lie–lying
5 For other verbs:	Add *-ing*. play–playing show–showing help–helping

VI. Spelling Rules for the -ed Form of Verbs

SPELLING RULES	base form	simple past
When the base form of a regular verb ends in -e, **add -d**.	clos**e** refus**e**	closed refused
When the base form ends in a consonant + **-y, change the -y to -i and add -ed**.	study worry identify	studied worried identified
When the base form has one syllable and ends in a **c**onsonant + **v**owel + **c**onsonant (CVC), **double the final consonant and add -ed**. (Warning! Do not double a final w, x, or y: play / played, wax / waxed, row / rowed).	p**lan** **jog** d**rop**	planned jogged dropped
When the base form of a two-syllable verb ends in a **c**onsonant + **v**owel + **c**onsonant (CVC) and the last syllable is stressed, **double the final consonant and add -ed**.	re•**fer** re•**gret**	referred regretted
For all other regular verbs, **add -ed**.	open destroy	opened destroyed

VII. Common Transitive Verbs

VERB + DIRECT OBJECT

Examples: *develop a theory; include your name and address; consider several possibilities*

allow	complete	enjoy	introduce	meet*	refuse	take
ask*	consider	expect	invent	move*	remember*	teach
attempt	create	feel*	involve	need	save	tell
begin*	cut*	find	keep*	pass*	say	think*
believe*	describe	follow*	know*	pay*	see*	throw
bring	design	forgive	leave*	produce	send	use
build	destroy	hear*	lend	provide	serve	visit*
buy	develop*	help*	like	put	show	want
call*	discover	hold*	lose*	raise	speak*	wash*
carry	divide*	identify	love	read*	start*	watch*
cause	do	include	make	receive	study*	win*
close*	end*	intend	mean	recognize	surround	write*

* verbs that we can also use intransitively (without a direct object)

Remember: Transitive verbs need an object (a noun phrase or pronoun) to complete their meaning.

VERB + INDIRECT OBJECT + DIRECT OBJECT

Examples: *ask your professor a question; show her the answer*

ask	forgive	lend*	pay	save	teach*
bring	give*	make	promise*	send*	tell*
buy	hand*	offer*	read*	serve*	throw*
find	leave*	owe*	refuse	show*	wish*

* The indirect object can come before or after the direct object.

VIII. Common Intransitive Verbs

Examples: *The movie begins at 8. She doesn't hear very well.*

agree	come	follow*	leave*	rain	sneeze	wait
appear	cough	freeze*	lie	read*	snow	walk*
arrive	cut*	go	live	remember*	speak*	wash*
begin*	decrease*	happen	look	ring*	stare	watch*
belong	die	hear*	lose*	rise	start*	win*
bleed	disappear	help*	matter	see*	stop*	work
break*	dream*	hide*	meet*	shake*	study*	write*
burn*	drown	hurt*	move*	sit	swim	
call*	end*	increase*	occur	sleep	think*	
close*	fall	laugh	pass*	smile	visit*	

* verbs that we can also use transitively (with a direct object)

Remember: Intransitive verbs make sense without an object.

IX. Common Verbs Followed by Gerunds

VERB + GERUND

Examples: *appreciate having; avoid getting; denied knowing*

admit	continue*	enjoy	love*	prefer*	risk
advise	defend	finish	mean**	quit	start*
appreciate	delay	forget**	mention	recall	stop**
avoid	deny	hate*	mind	recommend	suggest
begin*	detest	imagine	miss	regret**	tolerate
can't help	discuss	involve	need**	remember**	try**
can't stand*	dislike	keep	postpone	resist	
consider	dread*	like*	practice	resume	

* can also be followed by a *to-* infinitive   ** can be followed by a *to-* infinitive but with a change in meaning

VERB + OBJECT + GERUND

Examples: *hear him talking; saw my friends leaving; found them sitting*

discover	feel	find	hear	notice	see	watch

X. Common Verbs + Prepositions Followed by Gerunds

Examples: *argue about going; apologize for being; cope with losing; dream of becoming*

VERB + *ABOUT*	VERB + *AT*	VERB + *FOR*	VERB + *IN*	VERB + *INTO*
argue about care about complain about forget about talk about think about worry about	aim at work at	apologize for blame for care for forgive for thank for use for	believe in result in specialize in succeed in	look into

VERB + *LIKE*	VERB + *OF*	VERB + *ON*	VERB + *TO*	VERB + *WITH*
feel like	accuse of approve of dream of hear of think of	concentrate on depend on go on insist on keep on plan on work on	admit to confess to object to	cope with deal with

XI. Common Adjectives + Prepositions Followed by Gerunds

Examples: *afraid of being; bad at making; excited about going*

ADJECTIVE + *OF* + GERUND	ADJECTIVE + *AT* + GERUND	ADJECTIVE + *ABOUT* + GERUND
afraid of aware of capable of fond of incapable of proud of tired of	bad at better at effective at good at great at successful at upset at	bad about concerned about enthusiastic about excited about happy about nervous about serious about sorry about worried about

ADJECTIVE + *FROM* + GERUND	ADJECTIVE + *IN* + GERUND	ADJECTIVE + *FOR* + GERUND
different from evident from exempt from free from obvious from safe from tired from	crucial in effective in important in interested in involved in useful in	available for crucial for famous for important for necessary for responsible for sorry for suitable for useful for

XII. Common Nouns + *Of* That Can Be Followed by Gerunds

Examples: *chance of getting; possibility of using*

advantage of*	effect of*	idea of*	point of	prospect of	task of*
chance of*	experience of*	importance of	possibility of*	purpose of*	thought of
charge of	form of*	intention of	practice of*	result of*	way of*
cost of*	habit of	means of*	problem of*	risk of*	
danger of	hope of	method of*	process of*	system of*	

* common in academic writing

XIII. Common Verbs Followed by *To-* Infinitives

VERB + *TO*- INFINITIVE

Examples: *agree to go; asked to leave; decide to stay*

afford	can't stand*	desire	hope	plan	remember**	threaten
agree	claim	dread*	intend	prefer*	request	try**
aim	consent	fall	learn	prepare	say	volunteer
appear	continue*	forbid	like*	pretend	seek	vow
ask	dare	forget**	love*	proceed	seem	wait
attempt	decide	get	manage	promise	start*	want
beg	decline	hate*	mean**	prove	stop**	wish
begin*	demand	help	need**	refuse	struggle	
bother	deserve	hesitate	offer	regret**	tend	

* can also be followed by a gerund   ** can be followed by a gerund but with a change in meaning

VERB + OBJECT + *TO*- INFINITIVE

Examples: *advised me to go; reminded me to call; helped them to move*

advise**	beg*	encourage**	hate*	know**	permit**	teach**
allow**	believe**	expect*	help*	like*	persuade**	tell**
appoint**	challenge**	forbid**	imagine**	love*	prefer*	urge**
assume**	choose*	force**	instruct**	need*	promise*	want*
ask*	consider**	get*	judge**	order**	remind**	warn**

* object is optional   ** object is required

XIV. Common Noncount Nouns

advice	cooperation	food*	glass*	news	rain	traffic
air	courage	fruit*	heat	noise*	research	transportation
baggage	creativity	fun	jewelry	organization*	respect	truth*
beauty	economics	furniture	knowledge	oxygen	rice	violence
behavior*	education*	gasoline	literature	paint*	safety	water
blood	electricity	grammar	luck	participation	salt	weather
bread	entertainment	hair*	luggage	patience	sand	work*
cash	equipment	happiness	mathematics	peace	smoke	
chemistry	evidence	health	medicine*	physics	snow	
clothing	excitement	help	milk	pollution	soap	
coffee*	experience*	homework	money	privacy	spaghetti	
confidence	flour	information	music	progress	sugar	

* often has a count meaning or a noncount meaning

XV. Common Prepositions

ONE-WORD PREPOSITIONS

about	at	beyond	in	on	than	unlike
above	before	by	including	onto	through	until
across	behind	despite	inside	opposite	throughout	up
after	below	down	into	outside	to	upon
against	beneath	during	like	over	toward	with
among	beside	except	near	past	towards	within
around	besides	for	of	per	under	without
as	between	from	off	since	underneath	

GROUPS OF WORDS THAT FUNCTION LIKE ONE-WORD PREPOSITIONS

according to	because of	in exchange for	instead of	owing to
ahead of	but for	in front of	near to	prior to
apart from	by means of	in place of	on account of	rather than
as for	due to	in spite of	on top of	such as
as of	except for	in terms of	out of	thanks to
as well as	in addition to	inside of	outside of	up to
away from				

COMMON ERRORS CORRECTIONS

1.2 The Simple Present (page 6)

CORRECTION	EXPLANATION
13 ✗ Everyone **have** the duty to vote. ✓ Everyone **has** the duty to vote.	We use a singular verb (**has**) with an indefinite pronoun.
14 ✗ My brother always **get** what he wants. ✓ My brother always **gets** what he wants.	I / you / we / they — get . . . he / she / it — gets . . .
15 ✗ I very proud to be a part of this group. ✓ I **am** very proud to be a part of this group.	Every sentence needs a verb. We can use the verb *be* before an adjective (**am proud**).
16 ✗ People in a big city **has** more trouble sleeping at night. ✓ People in a big city **have** more trouble sleeping at night.	The noun subject of this sentence is **people** (not *city*). *People* is a plural noun so we use a plural verb (*have*).

1.5 The Simple Past (page 16)

CORRECTION	EXPLANATION
12 ✗ Later I **remember** that I was not well prepared to take the test. ✓ Later I **remembered** that I was not well prepared to take the test.	Pay attention to all of the verb forms in a sentence. It's important to use similar verb forms when they refer to the same time frame. remembered–was didn't want–wanted don't want–want looked–wore–didn't feel got–sat–thought
13 ✗ We **didn't** want to leave home because we **want** to take care of our grandparents. ✓ We **didn't** want to leave home because we **wanted** to take care of our grandparents. ✓ We **don't** want to leave home because we want to take care of our grandparents.	
14 ✗ Although she looked nice when she **wear** that suit, she didn't feel comfortable in it. ✓ Although she looked nice when she **wore** that suit, she didn't feel comfortable in it.	
15 ✗ When I got there, I sat and **think** for a while. ✓ When I got there, I sat and **thought** for a while.	

2.2 The Simple Past vs. the Present Perfect (page 45)

C

CORRECTION	EXPLANATION
10 ✗ I have seen many things when I was a child. ✓ I saw many things when I was a child.	The time expression *when I was a child* indicates a finished time period. We use the simple past (not the present perfect) with these time expressions.
11 ✗ I have been here since three weeks. ✓ I have been here for three weeks.	since + a specific time (*January 2014*) for + an amount of time (*for three weeks / for a year*)
12 ✗ I lived in Toronto for three years. I really love it here. ✓ I have lived in Toronto for three years. I really love it here.	We usually use the present perfect (not the simple past) when we are talking about something that started in the past and is connected to *now*.
13 ✗ He is the most optimistic person I ever know. ✓ He is the most optimistic person I have ever known.	We usually use the present perfect with the time expression *ever*. We form the present perfect with *have / has* + the past participle of the main verb (**known**).

4.3 Transitive and Intransitive Verbs (page 117)

D

CORRECTION	EXPLANATION
13 ✗ They thought she was died. ✓ They thought she was dead. ✓ They thought she had died. 14 ✗ These things were happened on Friday evening. ✓ These things happened on Friday evening.	The verbs *die* and *happen* are intransitive. Intransitive verbs don't have a passive form.
15 ✗ The paintings appeared several people. ✓ The paintings showed several people. ✓ Several people appeared in the paintings.	*Appear* is an intransitive verb. We don't use an object (*several people*) with an intransitive verb.
16 ✗ Three people injured in the accident. ✓ Three people were injured in the accident.	When the subject (*three people*) is the **receiver** of the action, we use a passive verb (*were injured*).

Index

Class Audio Track List

GO ONLINE For these audio tracks and the audio scripts, go to the Online Practice.

Unit	Activity	Track File Name
Unit 1	Activity 33, p. 27	ELM3_U01_Track01_Activity33.mp3
	Activity 34, p. 28	ELM3_U01_Track02_Activity34.mp3
	Chart 1.9, p. 30	ELM3_U01_Track03_Chart1.9.mp3
	Activity 38, p.31	ELM3_U01_Track04_Activity38.mp3
Unit 2	Activity 6, p. 46	ELM3_U02_Track01_Activity06.mp3
	Activity 7, p. 46	ELM3_U02_Track02_Activity07.mp3
	Chart 2.6, p. 62	ELM3_U02_Track03_Chart2.6.mp3
	Activity 27, p. 63	ELM3_U02_Track04_Activity27.mp3
	Activity 28, p. 63	ELM3_U02_Track05_Activity28.mp3
Unit 3	Activity 33, p. 89	ELM3_U03_Track01_Activity33.mp3
	Activity 34, p. 89	ELM3_U03_Track02_Activity34.mp3
	Chart 3.11, p. 100	ELM3_U03_Track03_Chart3.11.mp3
Unit 4	Activity 6, p. 113	ELM3_U04_Track01_Activity06.mp3
	Activity 7, p. 113	ELM3_U04_Track02_Activity07.mp3
	Activity 11, p. 116	ELM3_U04_Track03_Activity11.mp3
	Activity 25, p. 128	ELM3_U04_Track04_Activity25.mp3
	Chart 4.7, p. 130	ELM3_U04_Track05_Chart4.7.mp3
	Activity 27, p. 130	ELM3_U04_Track06_Activity27.mp3
Unit 6	Activity 17, p. 186	ELM3_U06_Track01_Activity17.mp3
	Activity 18, p. 187	ELM3_U06_Track02_Activity18.mp3
	Chart 6.9, p. 202	ELM3_U06_Track03_Chart6.9.mp3
	Activity 42, p. 202	ELM3_U06_Track04_Activity42.mp3
	Activity 44, p. 204	ELM3_U06_Track05_Activity44.mp3
	Activity 45, p. 204	ELM3_U06_Track06_Activity45.mp3

OXFORD
UNIVERSITY PRESS

198 Madison Avenue
New York, NY 10016 USA

Great Clarendon Street, Oxford, OX2 6DP, United Kingdom

Oxford University Press is a department of the University of Oxford.
It furthers the University's objective of excellence in research, scholarship,
and education by publishing worldwide. Oxford is a registered trade
mark of Oxford University Press in the UK and in certain other countries.

© Oxford University Press 2014

The moral rights of the author have been asserted.

First published in 2014
2018 2017 2016 2015 2014
10 9 8 7 6 5 4 3 2 1

Director, ELT New York: Laura Pearson
Head of Adult, ELT New York: Stephanie Karras
Publisher: Sharon Sargent
Senior Development Editor: Andrew Gitzy
Senior Development Editor: Rebecca Mostov
Development Editor: Eric Zuarino
Executive Art and Design Manager: Maj-Britt Hagsted
Content Production Manager: Julie Armstrong
Image Manager: Trisha Masterson
Image Editor: Liaht Pashayan
Production Artists: Elissa Santos, Julie Sussman-Perez
Production Coordinator: Brad Tucker

Special thanks to Electra Jablons and Rima Ibrahim for assistance with
language data research.

ISBN: 978 0 19 402827 1 Student Book 3A with Online Practice Pack
ISBN: 978 0 19 402846 2 Student Book 3A as pack component
ISBN: 978 0 19 402879 0 Online Practice website

Printed in China

This book is printed on paper from certified and well-managed sources.

ACKNOWLEDGEMENTS

*Although every effort has been made to trace and contact copyright holders before publication,
this has not been possible in some cases. We apologize for any apparent infringement of
copyright and if notified, the publisher will be pleased to rectify any errors or omissions at the
earliest opportunity.*

*The authors and publisher are grateful to those who have given permission to reproduce the
following extracts and adaptations of copyright material:* p. 17 from "Leonardo da Vinci" in
The World and Its People, Western Hemisphere, Europe, and Russia, Student Edition. Copyright
© 2005. Reprinted by permission of The McGraw-Hill Companies, Inc.; p. 20 "What
Were You Doing When ...?" by Thomas Thurman, www.marnanel.org/. Reprinted by
permission of Thomas Thurman; p. 25 from "FAQ: All About Coal - A Necessary Evil"
by Michael Kanellos, December 3, 2007, http://news.cnet.com. Used with permission
of CBS Interactive, News.com. Copyright © 2013. All rights reserved; p.33 from
the abstract of "Real Men Don't Need Work Life Balance," by Tanvi Gautam,
Forbeswoman, May 23, 2012, www.apaexcellence.org. Used with permission
from the American Psychological Association; p. 67 from "Humans Have Been
Making Art for a Lot Longer Than We Thought" by Sophie Bushwick, June 21, 2012,
http://blogs.discovermagazine.com. Reprinted by permission of Sophie Bushwick;
p. 67 from "Scientists able to study atmosphere of planet outside our solar system
using infra-red" by Eddie Wrenn, Daily Mail (UK), June 27, 2012, retrieved from
http://www.dailymail.co.uk. Reprinted by permission of the Daily Mail; p. 134 from
"Lord Marmaduke Hussey; led BBC, Times Newspapers" by Mark Herlihy and Chris
Peterson, Bloomberg News, December 28, 2006. Used with permission of Bloomberg
L.P. Copyright © 2013. All rights reserved; p. 152 "just" reproduced by permission of
Oxford University Press from *Oxford American English Dictionary for Learners of English*
© Oxford University Press 2011; p. 164 from *Literacy for Life: Education for All Global
Monitoring Report 2006,* http://www.unesco.org. © UNESCO 2005. Used by permission
of UNESCO; p. 207 from "Sun Screen" by Emily Sohn, *Science News for Kids,* June 26,
2006, http://www.sciencenewsforkids.org. Reprinted with Permission of Science
News for Students; p. 208 from "The Lemon Story" by Alberto Álvaro Ríos as appeared
in *Wachale!: Poetry and Prose on Growing Up Latino in America,* edited by Ilan Stavans.
Reprinted by permission of the author; p. 218 "beauty," "food," and "television"
reproduced by permission of Oxford University Press from *Oxford American English

Dictionary for Learners of English* © Oxford University Press 2011; p. 222 "Carl Sagan:
1934-1996." Reprinted by permission of Carus Publishing Company, 30 Grove Street,
Suite C, Peterborough, NH 03458 from MUSE magazine, December 1997, Vol. 1, No. 6,
text © 1997 by Carus Publishing Company. All rights reserved. www.cricketmag.com;
p. 264 from "Stonehenge" in *The World and Its People, Western Hemisphere, Europe, and
Russia, Student Edition.* Copyright © 2005. Reprinted by permission of The McGraw-Hill
Companies, Inc.; p. 320 "Great Barrier Reef" (brief description), http://whc.unesco.
org/en/list/154, © UNESCO 1992-2013. Used by permission of UNESCO; p. 353 from
"Alexander the Great," http://en.wikipedia.org/wiki/Alexander_the_great. Permission
granted under Creative Commons Attribution-ShareAlike 3.0 Unported (cc by-sa 3.0),
http://creativecommons.org/licenses/by-sa/3.0/.

Illustrations by: 5W Infographics: p. 39, 60, 91, 264, 269, 286, 377. John Kaufmann:
p. 141. Jerome Mireault: p. 32. Tablet Infographics: p. 19, 237. Joe Taylor: p. 104.

We would also like to thank the following for permission to reproduce the following photographs:
Cover: blinkblink/shutterstock; back cover: lvcandy/Getty Images; global: Rodin
Anton/shutterstock; p. 2 Alistair Berg/Getty Images; p. 17 AP Photo/Idaho Press-
Tribune, Charlie Litchfield, DeAgostini/Getty Images; p. 21 Steve Smith/SuperStock,
LOOK Die Bildagentur der Fotografen GmbH/Alamy, Mario Tama/Getty Images, Yellow
Dog Productions/Getty Images, Barry Lewis/In Pictures/Corbis, Tetra Images/Getty
Images, Oote Boe 3/Alamy, Rubberball/Mike Kemp/Getty Images; p. 25 Dmitriy Sechin/
istockphoto; p. 38 KidStock/Blend Images/Corbis; p. 43 Caro/Alamy; p. 44 Jacques
Alexandre/age fotostock; p. 48 Studio Ghibli/The Kobal Collection; p. 49 Beowulf
Sheehan/Writer Pictures; p. 50 Jupiterimages/Getty Images; p. 52 imagebroker/
Alamy; p. 55 Yasuyoshi Chiba/AFP/Getty Images; p. 57 GAB Archive/Redferns/Getty
Images; p. 61 2xSamara.com/shutterstock; p. 70 Yannick Tylle/Corbis; p. 72 Jorge
Salcedo/shutterstock; p. 75 Huntstock/Getty Images; p. 78 Pawel Libera/Loop Images/
SuperStock; p. 79 robynmac/istockphoto; p. 85 Rubberball/Mike Kemp/Getty Images;
p. 87 Creative Travel Projects/shutterstock; p. 88 jackscoldsweat/istockphoto;
p. 93 Troy House/Corbis; p. 94 Maksud/shutterstock; p. 98 F1 ONLINE/SuperStock,
stockstudioX/Getty Images; p. 99 Eric Audras/Onoky/Corbis; p. 101 OJO_Images/
istockphoto, Monalyn Gracia/Corbis, keith morris/Alamy, John Fedele/Blend Images/
Corbis; p. 102 Johner Images/Alamy; p. 106 andresrimaging/istockphoto; p. 107
ClassicStock/Alamy, Library of Congress - digital ve/Science Faction/Corbis, akg-
images/Newscom, Bettmann/Corbis, Hulton-Deutsch Collection/Corbis, AP Photo/
Wally Fong; p. 108 Stocksnapper/shutterstock; p. 110 All Canada Photos/Alamy; p. 111
Glow Images, Inc./Getty Images, James Steidl/shutterstock; p. 112 Dudarev Mikhail/
shutterstock, majeczka/shutterstock; p. 118 HANDOUT/KRT/Newscom, Peggy Peattie/
San Diego Union-Tribune/ZUMA Press, copyright San Diego Union-Tribune Publishing
Co./Alamy; p. 119 Corbis, Ralph Gatti/AFP/Getty Images; p. 127 Lebrecht Music &
Arts/Corbis; p. 136 Courtesy of Barb Schwarz at www.Stagedhomes.com; p. 138
Marnie Burkhart/Masterfile; p. 140 OUP/Photodisc; p. 144 Doug Lemke/shutterstock;
p. 146 Scanpix Creative/Masterfile; p. 147 Nagel Photography/shutterstock; p. 148
Cultura RM/Alamy; p.149,150 OUP/Photodisc; p. 154 Brian Snyder/Reuters/Corbis,
Rungroj Yongrit/epa/Corbis; p. 157 Erickson Photography/istockphoto; p. 158
Feng Yu/shutterstock; p. 159 OUP/Photodisc, Eric Audras/PhotoAlto/Corbis; p. 162
Wilfred Y. Wong/Getty Images; p. 167 OUP/Frank Krahmer, prudkov/shutterstock,
VeronikaMaskova/shutterstock; p. 168 ONOKY - Fabrice LEROUGE/Getty Images;
p. 169 OUP/Image Source; p. 172 Raimund Linke/Getty Images; p. 175 ITAR-TASS
Photo Agency/Alamy; p. 179 Dave & Les Jacobs/Getty Images, Giorgio Fochesato/Getty
Images; p. 181 Sean De Burca/Corbis; p. 184 Corbis, PoodlesRock/PoodlesRock/Corbis,
Ken Welsh/Design Pics/Corbis; p. 185 monkeybusinessimages/istockphoto; p. 187
BIHAIB/istockphoto; p. 189 Barry Rosenthal/Getty Images, OJO Images/Getty Images,
Radius Images/Alamy, Southern Stock/Blend Images/Corbis, Asia Images/Getty Images,
Glovatskiy/shutterstock, Vadim Ratnikov/shutterstock, Graham Oliver/Juice Images/
Corbis; p. 192 Ocean/Corbis, D. Hurst/Alamy; p. 195 Brigitte MERLE/Getty Images;
p. 205 JGI/Jamie Grill/Blend Images/Corbis; p. 206 Hero Images/Corbis, Ocean/Corbis;
p. 210 Universal/The Kobal Collection/Jasin Boland, Universal/DNA/Working Title/The
Kobal Collection/Peter Mountain, FOX 2000 Pictures/Dune Entertainment/Ingenious
Media/Haishang Films/The Kobal Collection; p. 212 Taxi/Court Mast/Getty Images;
p. 214 Bettmann/Corbis; p. 217 Stuart Jenner/istockphoto; p. 222 Tony Korody/Sygma/
Corbis; p. 225 Edward Koren/The New Yorker Collection/www.cartoonbank.com, Leo
Cullum/The New Yorker Collection/www.cartoonbank.com, Mike Twohy/The New
Yorker Collection/www.cartoonbank.com, Jack Ziegler/The New Yorker Collection/
www.cartoonbank.com; p. 228 Robert Fried/Alamy; p. 236 Gerry Pearce/Alamy; p. 237
NASA/JPL-Caltech/Harvard-Smithsonian CfA; p. 245 Hill Street Studios/Getty Images;
p. 249 OUP/Mike Stone; p. 254 nobleIMAGES/Alamy; p. 257 Stanley Brown/Getty
Images; p. 260 Jtafalla/istockphoto; p. 261 Sylvain Sonnet/Corbis; p. 266 WWD/Condé
Nast/Corbis; p. 268 Michelle D. Milliman/shutterstock; p. 278 North Wind Picture
Archives/Alamy; p. 281 a witch/Getty Images; p. 288 Ariel Skelley/Blend Images/Corbis;
p. 293 Arcaid Images/Alamy; p. 299 ecostecera2/Alamy; p. 301 Sigi Tischler/epa/Corbis;
p. 302 Songquan Deng/shutterstock, Africa Studio/shutterstock; p. 306 Seth Resnick/
Getty Images; p. 308 Visuals Unlimited/Masterfile; p. 316 Atlantide Phototravel/Corbis;
p. 320 Jupiterimages/Getty Images, Handout/Reuters/Corbis; p. 322 Mijang Ka/Getty
Images; p. 324 Eadweard Muybridge/Time Life Pictures/Getty Images; p. 326 Jose
Jacome/epa/Corbis; p. 330 Novastock/Getty Images; p. 331 Odua Images/shutterstock,
Creativa/shutterstock; p. 333 Hero Images/Corbis; p. 335 Scisetti Alfio/shutterstock,
Dani Vincek/shutterstock; p. 336 Inomoto/shutterstock; p. 339 AP Photo/Patti
Longmire; p. 340 GL Archive/Alamy, Time Life Pictures/Getty Images; p. 342 Stocktrek
Images/Getty Images; p. 345 Roy Bartels/shutterstock; p. 346 Ritterbach/age fotostock,
alantobey/istockphoto; p. 350 lrafael/shutterstock, Chikei Yung/Getty Images, Africa
Studio/shutterstock, Hulton-Deutsch Collection/Corbis; p. 353 Hoberman Collection/
Corbis; p. 354 Rick Friedman/Corbis; p. 359 OUP/Chris Ryan; p. 361 ColorBlind
Images/Corbis; p. 362 Ariel Skelley/Corbis; p. 363 Sergio Pitamitz/Masterfile; p. 364
Jade/Blend Images/Corbis; p. 366 Karen Kasmauski/Science Faction/Corbis; p. 369
UpperCut Images/Masterfile; p. 371 Hero Images/Corbis; p. 376 Oleksiy Maksymenko
Photography/Alamy; p. 379 Africa Studio/shutterstock; p. 380 photosync/shutterstock;
p. 381 Djomas/shutterstock; p. 382 Roy Morsch/age fotostock/SuperStock; p. 386
StockLite/shutterstock; p. 394 LluÃs Real/Getty Images; p. 397 Corbis; p. 399 David
Nunuk/Getty Images, Luciano Mortula/Shutterstock.com; p. 401 Petegar/istockphoto;
p. 403 Keren Su/Corbis; p. 404 Don Kates/Alamy; p. 405 Kritchanut/shutterstock; p. 408
Robert Trevis-Smith/Getty Images; p. 414 Andreas von Einsiedel/Corbis; p. 416 Corbis;
p. 421 4x6/Getty Images; p. 424 Radius Images/Corbis; p. 427 Weinstein Company/
courtesy Everett Collection, Daniel Smith/Warner Bros./courtesy Everett Collection,
Warner Bros/The Kobal Collection.

ELEMENTS *of* SUCCESS
Online Practice

How to Register for Elements of Success Online Practice

Follow these steps to register for *Elements of Success Online Practice*:

1. Go to www.elementsofsuccessonline.com and click **Register**

2. Read and agree to the terms of use. **I Agree.**

3. Enter the Access Code that came with your Student Book. Your code is written on the inside back cover of your book.

       Enter

4. Enter your personal information (first and last name, email address, and password).

5. Click the Elements of Success 3 Student Book.

   It is very important to select the Elements of Success 3 book. Please click the **BLUE** Elements of Success 3 cover.

   If you don't know which book to select, **STOP**. Continue when you know the book cover to click.

6. Enter your class ID to join your class, and click NEXT. Your class ID is on the line below, or your teacher will give it to you on a different piece of paper.

   _____ **Next**

   You don't need a class ID code. If you do not have a class ID code, click Skip. To enter this code later, choose Join a Class from your Home page.

7. Once you're done, click Activities to begin using *Elements of Success Online Practice*.

Next time you want to use *Elements of Success Online Practice*, just go to www.elementsofsuccessonline.com and log in with your email address and password.